Pr
STRANG

'A tender and thought-provoking exploration of cultural and national identity, and a bewitching love letter to Australia, recounting the pain of what's been, the complications of the present, and offering hope for what is to come. Tan's curiosity and deep reverence for the land and its first inhabitants makes her the perfect travel buddy on this journey into the heart of Australia.'

Michelle Law, author of *Single Asian Female*

'With 85 per cent of Australia's population scattered along the coast, too often we look out and across the sea for meaning and adventure. Monica Tan's *Stranger Country* is a call for us to look within: at our rich and varied geography, our long and buried history of diversity, and the 60,000-year-old culture on our doorstep. The cliché that Australia has no history or culture is false—we just don't often take the time to tell it. *Stranger Country* does. A necessary Australian story.'

Rachel Hills, author of *The Sex Myth*

'Self-aware and provocative, Monica gets to the heart of what it means to call Australia home as a non-Indigenous person. Never self-indulgent, Monica looks outwards and examines herself critically as she learns about the culture of the country she grew up in. I loved it, and came away with a new lens through which to see myself.'

Bridie Jabour, journalist and author of *The Way Things Should Be*

'*Stranger Country* is a marvellously engaging, beautifully described record of a quest into the meaning of belonging, that documents both the gritty reality of a 30,000-kilometre solo road trip around Australia by one young woman, and her profoundly intelligent journey of mind.'

Isobelle Carmody, author of *The Obernewtyn Chronicles*

STRANGER COUNTRY

MONICA TAN

*Happy reading and
thanks for the
support ♡ Monica*

ALLEN&UNWIN

SYDNEY · MELBOURNE · AUCKLAND · LONDON

First published in 2019

Copyright © Monica Tan 2019

Allen & Unwin
83 Alexander Street
Crows Nest NSW 2065
Australia
Phone: (61 2) 8425 0100
Email: info@allenandunwin.com
Web: www.allenandunwin.com

A catalogue record for this book is available from the National Library of Australia

ISBN 978 1 76063 221 2

Internal design by Bookhouse, Sydney
Internal images from the author's collection
Map by Julia Eim
Set in 12.5/16 pt Arno Pro by Bookhouse, Sydney
Printed and bound in Australia by Griffin Press

10 9 8 7 6 5 4 3 2 1

MIX
Paper from
responsible sources
FSC® C009448

The paper in this book is FSC® certified. FSC® promotes environmentally responsible, socially beneficial and economically viable management of the world's forests.

To my Australian Studies students, past, present and future.

I acknowledge and pay my respects to the elders—past, present and emerging—of every nation through which I travelled on my road trip. I acknowledge that I live, work and study on Darug, Eora and Guringai Country.

I would like to extend the protection and care of my ancestors to any Indigenous Australians in China, just as their ancestors have taken care of me.

Contents

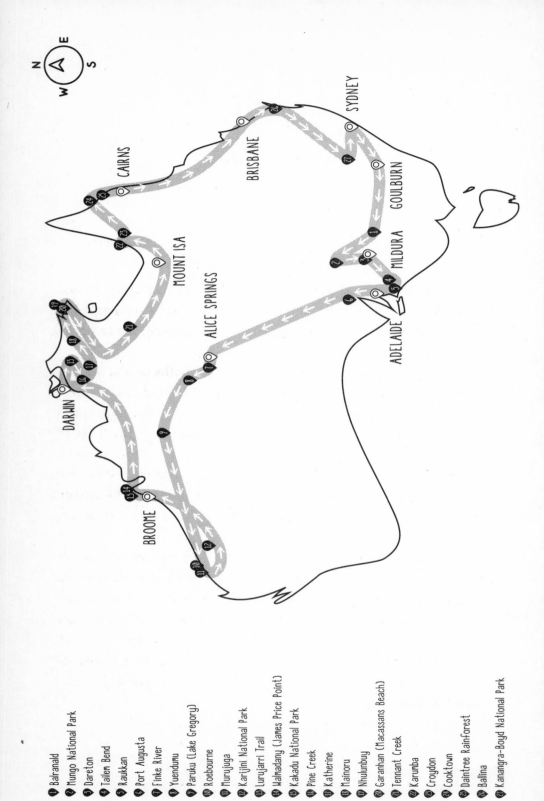

E N W S

CAIRNS
BRISBANE
SYDNEY
GOULBURN
MOUNT ISA
MILDURA
ALICE SPRINGS
ADELAIDE
DARWIN
BROOME

1 Balranald
2 Mungo National Park
3 Dareton
4 Tailen Bend
5 Raukkan
6 Port Augusta
7 Finke River
8 Yuendunu
9 Paruku (Lake Gregory)
10 Roebourne
11 Murujuga
12 Karijini National Park
13 Lurujarri Trail
14 Walmadany (James Price Point)
15 Kakadu National Park
16 Pine Creek
17 Katherine
18 Mainoru
19 Nhulunbuy
20 Garanhan (Macassans Beach)
21 Tennant Creek
22 Karumba
23 Croydon
24 Cooktown
25 Daintree Rainforest
26 Ballina
27 Kanangra-Boyd National Park

Author's note

This book documents a 30,000-kilometre solo road trip I took around Australia in 2016. To write this book I relied on eighteen journals I penned over the course of those six months, along with hundreds of photos, additional research and my memories.

Although I spent the majority of my six months on the road in central and northern Australia, this should not be read as any reflection or validation of the commonly held belief that the Indigenous Australian cultures located there are 'more authentic' than those in other parts of Australia. Rather, I chose to spend more time in those areas because they were less familiar to me than southern and eastern Australia. I considered this trip a rare opportunity for me to explore parts of Australia that are physically distant and difficult to access for a Sydney-sider.

Almost every person in this book was given the opportunity to review the passage in which they featured and suggest changes. In a small number of cases, I wasn't able to make contact. My decision to include them wasn't made lightly and was based on a strong sense that their contribution is vital to the telling of this story.

Many but not all people featured in this book are under a pseudonym. Due to word constraints, many locations, people and events were omitted.

This is a true story and, I hope, a truthful one.

Introduction

When I look back on growing up in Sydney, I don't recall meeting any Aboriginal or Torres Strait Islander people. This is despite the fact the city is home to the largest population of Indigenous Australians in the country. As far as I'm aware, none of my neighbours, schoolmates, teachers or local shopkeepers were Indigenous people. They weren't among the actors and pop singers on posters stuck to my bedroom walls. They weren't the politicians I saw on television or the authors of books on my shelves. Throughout my childhood, adolescence and even my twenties, 'Indigenous Australia' was just a concept to me, one that rarely had a presence in my life.

I was born in Australia to Chinese Malaysian parents. As teenagers in the early 1970s, they had separately migrated here from rural north Malaysia to study at university. They met and married in Sydney a decade later and raised their four children in the city's leafy and well-to-do north-west. My parents' social circle rarely overlapped with Indigenous Australian social circles. In fact, from what I can recall barely any of my parents' friends weren't of Chinese heritage.

Like many non-Indigenous Australians, I was introduced to Indigenous Australia at school. My Year 8 history teacher would stand in front of the classroom with a thick textbook open in her hands like a hymnbook, intonating in a low drone. She would lick her forefinger to turn each page, and that was the cue for all us students—although most had zoned out—to do the same. Our textbook depicted the 'Aborigines' in colonial sketches as fit, dark-skinned men holding spears. In the most prosaic of terms, the book stated that as the new settler society swept across the continent, some of these 'primitive' people were shot but the majority died from introduced diseases, and almost all of those who remained were absorbed into white society. Indigenous Australians were apparently cleared away from the land in one fell swoop, leaving a clean slate upon which Australia could be founded.

What a shame, I thought, but I wasn't ashamed. Those history lessons left me with the impression that what had happened to Indigenous Australia was awful but inevitable. It was less an advanced human civilisation and more a quaint relic, an insubstantial society that had lived lightly on this continent—no wonder it had been so quickly and easily smudged out by colonial forces.

My conscience was clear. At the time of colonisation, my ancestors were living in a China preoccupied with internal political instability and aggressive military action against the British. If you were going to blame anyone for what happened to Indigenous Australia, I decided, you should blame white Australians. And even then, could you? The colonisers were dead. What's done is done.

Thanks to these experiences in the Australian education system, I considered myself permanently immune to the charms of historical study. So I was somewhat surprised more than a decade later to see that prove untrue when I spent four years living in China in my late twenties. I loved hearing stories of emperors and empresses, while learning to draw direct parallels between the palace intrigues of the past and the machinations of the contemporary Chinese Communist Party. I loved reading ancient tales of drunken poets, immortal beings and star-crossed lovers, and suicidal martyrs to the motherland. I became intoxicated by culture, language and history.

History, I learned, can also be a people's cross to bear. Throughout his reign in the mid-twentieth century, Chairman Mao Zedong framed the past as having a stranglehold on the present, preventing China from achieving modernisation. One of the precepts of the Cultural Revolution was doing away with the Four Olds: old customs, old culture, old habits and old ideas. This triggered an orgiastic period of madness in which a great deal of renowned architecture, literature, art and sites of religious significance were destroyed or desecrated. But despite the colossal traumas and political upheavals endured by the Chinese people, some things just don't change there: everyone is still a foodie and a romantic, as well as hardworking, brash, energetic, patriotic to a fault, and preoccupied with 'face' and social status; old people still dance in the parks or increasingly in public squares adjacent to shopping malls; the lyricism of the mountainous countryside remains strong, having inspired hermits for thousands of years as it hopefully will for thousands more; and the weighty sense of the country's 3000-year history is still carried proudly by many people as though it is an ornate silk bridal sedan chair. It isn't difficult to find an uneducated farmer who can recite a seventh-century poem. National festivals honour beloved historical figures who died thousands of years ago. Primetime television is peppered with popular period dramas.

Chinese people also know the diverse regions of their country well—they know that northerners eat noodles, while southerners eat rice, and that in Shanghai women wear the pants in the relationship. Chinese tourists routinely visit different parts of their country in order to learn local stories and customs, eat local dishes, and even pick up a few new words. But if you ask your average Sydneysider what food people eat in Western Australia or what women are like in Adelaide, they will likely shrug. In this age of digital communication, mass media and rapid transportation, modern communities throughout Australia, even the most far-flung, will never experience the centuries of isolation required for the development of unique regional cultures. In the Australia of popular imagination, or at least in mainstream Australian society, we have no equivalent to Fujian, the Chinese province of my ancestry, where it's possible to drive an hour from one village to another and find mutually unintelligible local languages.

I don't remember where or when this occurred to me—perhaps I was eating a steaming bowl of famous Guo Qiao Mi Xian noodles in Yunnan province, or watching Tibetan Buddhist nuns prostrate themselves in Sichuan province—only that I thought, very clearly, *Damn, I wish I came from a country with hundreds of local languages and cultures.* My inner-leftie piped up with an objection: *I do live in such a country.*

Non-Indigenous Australians tend to view our continent as a giant biscuit with one bite taken out at the top and another at the bottom, the mainland divided into five states and two major territories, the crumb of Tasmania tethered on. But the continent is also a mosaic of over 500 Indigenous nations, each with its own distinct language, cultural practices, history and experience of colonialism. At the time of my epiphany, my knowledge of Indigenous Australia was virtually nil. Guiltily, I realised I couldn't name a single Indigenous Australian nation—yet I could name dozens of Chinese minority groups. Australia had been home to rich cultural diversity for tens of thousands of years, but I had failed to go looking for it.

When I moved back to Sydney in 2013, I promised myself that I would approach my country with the same fresh eyes I had brought overseas.

Three years went by before I embarked on my road trip around Australia. I worked at *The Guardian* as a reporter and culture editor, and I interviewed Indigenous Australian musicians, dancers, visual artists, actors, writers and cultural authorities. They mostly lived in capital cities, although occasionally I travelled further out. I headed to Broken Hill in Barkindji Country to cover the largest native title case in the history of the state, and I wrote about the ancient Ngunnhu fish traps of Brewarrina. One week in 2015, I hopped on the Fiftieth Anniversary Freedom Ride through regional New South Wales; I even swam at Moree's local pool where back in 1965 Charlie Perkins—the first Indigenous student to graduate from University of Sydney—and some local Aboriginal children had bravely defied local segregation rules to the jeers and fury of the townspeople.

Indigenous Australia stopped being just a concept to me and became one part of my life. I was getting to know Indigenous people living in Sydney and the nations from which they came—names such as Yolŋu, Wiradjuri, Barkindji and Noongar no longer stumbled awkwardly off my tongue. The false narrative I had absorbed from high school history class was replaced by lived experience: Indigenous Australia is made up of living, breathing, morphing cultures that have stories of resilience and survival as well as tragedy and oppression. These cultures, far from primitive, are simultaneously ancient and adapting to a postcolonial reality, and they hold the keys to connecting to the land upon which we all live.

For a long time I not only attributed my patchy understanding of Australian and Indigenous Australian history to those uninspiring history classes, but also to my immigrant background. As a Chinese Australian, I regarded myself a minority person surrounded by so-called 'real Australians'. Most of my schoolmates were white, and from that I assumed their family histories on this continent must go back much longer than mine. Surely they had been raised with a better baseline understanding of Australia than I had. Only later did I learn that many of these friends were, like me, descendents of recent immigrants—from Hungary, Poland, Italy, Iran, Bosnia, Germany, the UK and New Zealand. Eventually it dawned on me that in Australia skin colour is not a good indicator of indigeneity. Half of all Australians today were either born overseas or have at least one parent born abroad. Millions of Australians, white or not, grew up with some other country's songs in their ears, skies in their eyes, history in their hearts. We are a nation dominated by immigrants, their children and grandchildren, and as such our collective memory of the Australian story is short.

Why does that matter? So much is good about our country: it's one of the most prosperous, egalitarian, free and peaceful nations on Earth. It is tempting to write off the disadvantage experienced by Indigenous Australians—who are forced to carry the burden of our colonial history—as collateral damage to an otherwise successful experiment in modern multicultural democracy. But only a cruel and unjust society asks three per cent of its population to foot the bill eternally for the other ninety-seven per cent.

There is also something hollow and sad about living as permanent guests—or worse, despised intruders—on someone else's land. 'Wonderful place, but they have no culture,' I once overheard a German man glibly say of Australia to some other tourists; at first I bristled, then I wondered if he was right. I've met some Indigenous Australians who, in a similar vein, take pity on us unmoored, half-made non-Indigenous Australians. We are strange, stateless people, without a distinct language through which to identify ourselves, without shared long-standing traditions to create stability, without history to provide a framework, and without culture to draw strength from. We occupy lands whose caretakers form the oldest continuous civilisation on Earth with an unparalleled connection to Country. It's no wonder that our two groups struggle to understand each other.

Will I ever really belong to this country? As a Chinese Australian? As a non-Indigenous Australian? On my road trip, I didn't set out to definitively answer such questions. My goal was far more modest: I just wanted to know Australia. What did the Australia lying beyond the fringes of my home town look like, sound like, feel like? What stories, secrets and unexpected wisdom did it contain? How would I feel moving through these unfamiliar lands that I ostensibly called home? I was particularly keen to get out to remote areas where I had never been. Since moving back from China I had holidayed in regional New South Wales, gone trekking in Tasmania and flown to Perth, Brisbane and Melbourne for work, but the vast expanse of central and northern Australia was still a mystery to me.

I was thirty-two years old—three decades gone—and barely knew the country of my birth. It was time to change that.

PART ONE
Going West

6 JUNE
Day 1

I left Sydney feeling afraid. I was afraid of breaking down in the middle of nowhere. Afraid of getting bitten by a snake. Afraid of getting raped. Afraid of dying. And then, I was almost as afraid that nothing would happen on this trip. Afraid I had given up my apartment and chucked in my job for months on a boring, dusty road.

I wanted to learn about Indigenous Australia as I travelled, having acknowledged that like most Australians I knew not nearly enough. But I was afraid that wherever I went, I would be here and Indigenous people over there, the gulf between us unbridgeable.

Days before my departure, my colleagues and I celebrated the end of my two years at *The Guardian*. I was leaving on a somewhat sour note after falling out with my boss and mentor. For months I'd quarantined a lot of poisonous feelings. But in the final few days, whatever seal containing them had broken. High emotion was coursing through my body, leaving me pale and trembling. My eyes watered at any hint of kindness; the smallest sign of a slight left me breathless as a sharp elbow in the guts. *But it's okay—this is the bad bit*, I told myself, *it will get better from here.*

'Buy a doorstop,' advised one of my colleagues at farewell drinks. She had done a lot of solo travel and said she always put a doorstop under her hotel-room door as added protection.

'I'll be staying in a tent,' I said glumly.

I'd been watching the TV series *Wolf Creek*, which features a young woman playing a cat-and-mouse game with a serial killer in the remote Outback. Every Australian man she encounters wants to kill, rape or marry her. It seemed like foolish viewing for a woman about to embark on a trip through the Outback, but I found it morbidly empowering to watch the protagonist shoot, fight and connive her way in and out of trouble.

My colleagues gave me a farewell gift: a genuine, leather Akubra. It was my boss's idea, and she had spent two hours picking it out for me. She said that according to the saleswoman, Akubras last twenty years through rain, hail or shine. I looked down at my perfect present—it had a stylish thin headband and was cradled with paper in a white hatbox—and burst into tears.

That weekend I moved all my stuff out of my rented inner-west townhouse, where I'd been living with one of my best friends, and drove it to my two-storey brick childhood home.

I started packing. It was the middle of winter, and I planned to camp most of the way, so I had to bring all my cold-weather gear— down jackets, woollen socks, thermal underwear—stuffed into two duffel bags. I'd purchased three cubic black storage boxes: I filled the first with cooking utensils and a briefcase-sized portable gas stove; the second with foodstuffs like noodles, cereal, herbs, cooking oil; and the third with bits and bobs like toilet paper, a camping lamp, cans of gas, washing detergent and a packet of sponges. But the list of things to bring felt never-ending: sleeping bags, a pillow, hiking boots, empty jerry cans, water tanks, a medical pack, toiletries, presents for people I planned to visit, diaries and books, and a case of CDs that I had to brush the dust off, for those sections of the Outback where I'd have no phone reception to stream music. What I'd expected to take only a couple of hours to pack required half the night, and I was amazed at how my Toyota RAV4—a large five-seater car with a spacious boot—strained to fit everything.

I had a terrible night of sleep tinged with an uneasy feeling, as if a foul smell was in the air. I awoke in the dead of night with the sensation that all the cells of my body were coated in a cold, metallic sweat. For the first time I was confronted by the gravity of not what I was leaving behind but what I was getting myself into. Being *out there*. I tried to calm myself down by thinking, *This is my land and I shouldn't be afraid of it. Fear of the land, fear of a great inland expanse of nothingness, is a colonial mentality. If I do right by the land, it will take care of me.* After all, part of what had pushed me to plan this trip was a desire to experience 'Country'. In this context, Country means so much more than just a group of people living on a piece of land ruled by a government. It is an Aboriginal term that embodies a holistic view of one's homelands, incorporating every living creature, every element and feature; the land is laced with story, history and spirits, and imbued with a deep sense of home and belonging.

I wanted to view land the way that Yawuru man and Western Australian Senator Patrick Dodson once described it in 1976:

> We heard the other day land being described as 'piece of dirt'. That would be the same as someone who considered St Peter's just a barnyard to Catholics. For the Aboriginal people land is a dynamic notion. It is something that is creative. Land isn't just bound up with geographical limitations that are placed on it by a surveyor, who marks out a plot and says, 'This is your plot.' Land is the generative point of existence; it's the maintenance of existence; it's the spirit from which Aboriginal existence comes. It's a living thing made up of sky, of clouds, of rivers, of trees, of the wind, of the sand, and of the Spirit that has created all those things, the Spirit that has planted my own spirit there, my own Country . . . It's a living entity. It belongs to me—I belong to the land. I rest in it, I come from there. Land is a notion that is most difficult to categorise in [non-Indigenous] law. It is something that is very clear in Aboriginal Law.

I wasn't sure if it was possible for me, a non-Aboriginal Australian, to experience Country. Was it cultural appropriation to even try? I was certain this wouldn't be the last time I asked myself that question.

My understanding of colonial history had been that in any given country town, Chinese people often ran the market gardens and would hire Aboriginal workers—by many accounts treating them well. Some Chinese men even married into Aboriginal families. I regarded my trip as an extension of that historical friendship. I wanted to focus on what I, as a Chinese Australian, shared with Aboriginal Australians. After all, weren't our two ancient cultures both steeped in spirituality, rich in languages, traditions and customs, and took pleasure from words, songs, ceremonies and art?

On the other hand I was acutely aware that this road trip and any attempt to write a book about Australia might sound like an innocent enough proposition, but history has left race relations in a delicate state. Was I destined to repeat a pattern of exploitation, fetishisation and appropriation of Aboriginal Australian culture by non-Aboriginal Australian storytellers? Even now I remained plagued by doubt.

The next morning I woke to a sombre grey sky. I felt slightly nauseated from lack of sleep. *Everything is about to change. Fuck me dead.* I ate breakfast slowly and wordlessly, like a prisoner on death row, and took a few remaining items to my car: two maps rolled up in a cardboard tube—one a conventional map of Australia, and another showing the continent broken up in Aboriginal and Torres Strait Islander language regions—and a daypack. I told myself that despite my carload of stuff there were only three essentials: my phone, credit card and car keys. Everything else was easily replaceable.

Before I climbed into the car I hugged my mum, lightly, and promised to call her soon. I was grateful she seemed composed because I was anything but.

My family have become accustomed to my penchant for solo travel and general life instability—I tend to quit enviable jobs, moving from place to place. They worry, but they also trust me. I have proven capable and resilient. They respect my need for independence and to live a meaningful life.

As I reversed out of the driveway, taking one final glance at the lowering garage door and behind it my long-suffering mother, standing there silently, my brain struggled to comprehend I wasn't just running an errand or taking a short holiday. Or the fact that when I returned in December, it wouldn't be to the life I was now leaving behind.

A light rain began to fall. For two hours I drove south through western Sydney, jostling with raging semitrailers, past rows of fast-food joints, budget furniture stores and car dealerships.

By the time I reached Sydney's city limits, two hours had passed and my eyelids felt made of lead. Boy, an accident on the very first day of my six months away would be plain embarrassing. Near Goulburn I pulled off the highway at a roadside McDonald's to take a quick nap in the half-empty car park. I cranked my seat back, wrapped a scarf around my face to keep the stark winter sun out, and almost instantly fell asleep.

My phone alarm detonated with harsh, insistent bleeping half an hour later. I cursed, feeling groggy and still panicky. My anxiety had the coldness of a doctor's needle sliding into my arm, except it pierced my entire body. What a melancholic June day. I found the fresh silence in my car unnerving. Remind me again why I had abandoned my familiar Sydney life? I was a *somebody* there—not somebody important, but a daughter, sister, friend, colleague and journalist. Now who was I? Just a single, thirty-something nobody on the road with a car full of camping gear and a box of blank journals.

Thanks to my habit of setting my life on fire, this panicky feeling wasn't new to me. And upon dropping the match on a fortunate life I had vigorously doused with fuel, I was often paralysed by the thought that perhaps I'd made a gigantic mistake.

Parked in that ubiquitous roadside McDonald's, I lay tipped backwards in my car seat staring at my side-view mirror. It showed a square of hard blue Australian sky stamped with white clouds. I was gripped by a dizzying sensation that perhaps I could just fall through that square and emerge into some floating parallel universe.

I took a deep breath—mistake or not, I had to see through what I'd set in motion. I brought my seat upright and slid the key into the ignition. As I headed back onto the main road I felt, yet again, my former life going up in flames.

＊

Lake Mungo is a thousand kilometres dead on west of Sydney, at which point you're still in New South Wales but not too far from both the South Australian and Victorian borders. If you gunned it all the way, you could reach Lake Mungo from Sydney in a day. But I wasn't in any hurry and took a week, with a stop at the Aboriginal Tent Embassy in Canberra and stayed with friends in towns along the rivers that trickle from the mountains to the interior. The curling Murrumbidgee River converges with the Lachlan, running into the mighty Murray River. Rainwater funnels off the Great Dividing Range into these all-important waterways and is carried to the long, flat western plains.

Among Australia's many cultural faultlines—rural versus urban, northern Australia versus southern Australia, Indigenous versus non-Indigenous—the Great Dividing Range, a 3700-kilometre-long chain of plateaus and low mountain ranges, stands out as a physical demarcation of a divided country. This natural wall splits three states—Queensland, New South Wales and Victoria—into east and west. To its east is a thin strip of verdant land where one finds the country's three largest cities—Sydney, Melbourne and Brisbane— overlooking a powerful blue ocean, while to its west is an expanse of land that quickly flattens out, becoming drier until it turns into the red heart of the country.

'There's something psychological about that barrier that discourages people from coming over,' my friend Tim said to me when I stayed with him and his young family in Wagga Wagga, a town just west of the Great Dividing Range. 'West of the divide is the "real" Australia, and all those millions of people on the east coast might as well live in a different country. Australia is vast, Australia is arid; forests and sandstone belong somewhere else.' And it's true that while the physical barrier was long ago breached, most people in the three major eastern cities never developed the habit of heading west for their holidays; they prefer sliding up and down the coast, swapping one pretty white, sandy beach for another. When eight out of ten Australians live 'on the rim of a soup-plate', as it was once described by a visiting American academic, whatever lies in between coastlines is anybody's guess: some sheep, some cows, a few blackfellas and a bunch of nothing, probably.

Balranald was the last town on the Sturt Highway before I'd have to turn north and drive a few hours for Mungo National Park. On my approach to the town, where I planned to stock up on supplies, I stopped on the side of the highway during a prolonged spell of featureless plain. I snapped a photo of myself wearing my ash-brown Akubra with a duck feather in its band, and span around in a circle. Nothing interrupted the horizon line, the precise fold used to make an origami figurine, halving the green shrub-covered land from blue sky. Locals claim their plains are the flattest in the southern hemisphere. Distances felt impossible to judge: how far was that line of trees—one kilometre, ten kilometres? You could probably cycle for hours here without breaking a sweat.

There are geological reasons why flyblown Australia is so low, flat and dry. Having drifted far away from active plate boundaries, in ancient times our continent retired into relative geological stability. Much of our continent is deeply weathered: millions upon millions of years of wind and water have scoured its surface, with some of our rocks dating back more than three thousand million years. The Ikara-Flinders Ranges in South Australia once rivalled the current Himalayas; now the ranges' tallest peak, St Mary, is one eighth the height of Mt Everest. Because the continent's average elevation is only 325 metres, many of our major rivers flow slowly inland, ending with ephemeral salt lakes.

In its peaceful old age, the continent has indulged in a hobby of collecting all manner of mementos from the passing years in its layers of earth. It is not uncommon to find mind-bogglingly old objects preserved in near-perfect perpetuity, and Lake Mungo in western New South Wales is the archaeological equivalent of Treasure Island.

I drove through the tree-lined streets of Balranald, which did not appear too different to the suburbs I'd grown up in except there were fewer cars about; parking is rarely a problem in Australian country towns. On a street corner I located the Balranald Discovery Centre: modern buildings painted in the understated cool blue-green of a gumleaf and encased by well-maintained gardens.

Inside I found a middle-aged man sitting on a low stool behind the counter. He looked up at me. I looked back. When I opened my mouth to speak, he turned to the back door and shouted a name. A woman emerged, dabbing the remains of lunch from the corner of her lip with a tissue. 'How can I help you?'

'I was wondering if you could tell me anything about the Aboriginal culture of this area.'

'No,' she said.

I waited for more, but no more was to come. 'Well,' I coughed, when the silence felt too unbearable, 'I also want to know how to get to Mungo National Park.'

She appeared to relax and plucked a pamphlet from a stack, then on a mud map briskly marked the distances between points. This section of the trip would be my first taste of remote driving and sleeping outdoors in the middle of winter. I planned to put my back seats down so I could sleep in the car instead of my tent—surely it would be at least a few degrees warmer? After camping two nights at Mungo, I would head south to the town of Mildura. A frisson of nervous anticipation raced through me as the woman told me that between here and my next fuel stop lay at least 250 kilometres of dirt-road driving, with no mobile reception at the national park.

After thanking her for the instructions, I wandered through an adjacent building of the centre. A display stated that at one point in Balranald's colonial past, its population of just four hundred supported six drinking holes. In 1858 the *Sydney Morning Herald* wrote of Balranald as 'this obscure and miserable township, situated on the Lower Murrumbidgee', which was 'attracting a considerable share of attention as being one of those rowdy places for which the Australian bush in the interior has become famous'. The article then outlined a bizarre chain of unlucky deaths: the town's publican, 'poor Graham', was killed and the murderer hanged not long after at Goulburn; the doctor who attended the trial drowned on his way home; his widow, 'having gone to Deniliquin to get married', was absent when her child burnt to death in an accident; and the messenger sent to inform her drowned while crossing the Murrumbidgee. The reporter gloomily reasoned: 'it would seem that there are certain phases through which these townships have to pass. Formed by neither nature nor art, many of them drag on a miserable existence.' I wasn't sure if Balranald was still in a state of misery, but I suspected that most of these towns on the river had shaken off their bad-boy colonial pasts and were now known more for their fishing spots, senior-friendly bushwalks and heritage woolsheds. Part of me wished I could have seen these places when they were a little more raucous—although no doubt they would have been precarious places for a Chinese woman on her own.

I was eager to get into the Outback; so far my trip had been too comfortable. From here on, the drives between fuel stops would get longer and the patches without mobile reception larger. For me there was no line defining the beginning and end of the Outback, rather it was any place I was forced continuously to contemplate what was necessary for my survival. *Where am I sleeping? What will I eat? How can I stay warm? Where is my next fuel stop? Do I know how to get where*

I'm going? How do I find out the road conditions? Even though I estimated my fuel tank could hold more than enough to last me to the next petrol station, I had geed myself up with so much impending doom I filled an extra twenty-litre jerry can. At the supermarket I bought two plastic tanks of water, and a packet of dry Chinese noodles, veggies, some cheese and sandwich bread for lunch.

Everything I needed was inside my car; I could go anywhere, any time. Euphoric with the sense that I was the bright centre of my own universe, I hit the road.

✹

As I drove, the view reminded me of a Dreamtime story told by Wamba Wamba man Ron Murray in a recording I'd listened to at the Balranald Discovery Centre: 'the world was as flat as a saucer and the sky hung so low over the earth that everything was small and living creatures were small as ants'. Eventually Baiami the Creator drank from a magical pool of water that was sweet and clear, and he grew so strong he used a digging stick to push up the sky to its present position, providing room for all the animals to enlarge. I felt as if I was experiencing the story in reverse: the land was paring back all forms and features, reducing itself to nothing as the blue ceiling dropped and flattened the ground.

The Dreamtime or the Dreaming isn't a concept well understood by non-Aboriginal people. I certainly struggled with it and had long accepted much of it would remain elusive to me. What I knew was that every Aboriginal Australian nation had their own distinct set of Dreaming stories and were sometimes compared to the Bible's Genesis: an ancient collection of creation stories, spiritual in nature, describing in detail how the land was formed, the purpose of all things, and the principles by which all must live to maintain balance and order throughout the universe. I suspected the comparison was an awkward fit—any attempt to shoehorn one culture into the framework of another inevitably is.

Is this beautiful? I asked myself after an hour of uninterrupted sameness, of primal, lifeless earth. Land with shape provides a path for the eye to follow: along a snaking river or through a gap between hills. When high mountains turn into low valleys, it's natural fodder for drama. The sublimity of the French Alps, Grand Canyon or Himalayas is symphonic and plain to see. But this? Certainly it is provocative, and its fascination more psychological than aesthetic—more Yves Klein and Mondrian than Turner and Monet. Depending on who you are, a thousand kilometres of nothing can seem oppressive and distressing or liberating and calming. It is a landscape-sized sensory deprivation tank.

In another remote part of New South Wales is the Yetta Dhinnakkal Correctional Centre for Aboriginal men that is minimum security in the most literal sense: it has no high walls, bars, armed guards or razor wire, and lies smack bang in the middle of a former cattle station—nothing but 10,500 hectares of mulga and gidgee scrub. With its open spaces and bush environment, it aims to put its clients on the right track and eventually out of prison for good.

I knew a local art teacher who took university students on photography expeditions through the part of the country I was driving through. One year her charges included a student from New York City who had grown up on the seventeenth floor of a skyscraper. The teacher told me, 'After we left town and the view emptied out, the poor thing began to have a panic attack.' How do you comfort a native of that frenetic, vertically built, glass-and-concrete habitat thrust into such a tremendous stretch of nothingness? Perhaps tell her to close her eyes and put her head in her lap, and then whisper into her ear recollections of gleaming skyscrapers, yellow cabs, honking buses and dirty, crowded subways.

Australia's unrelenting desolation poses no questions to its travellers and inhabitants, nor does it invite curiosity from them. Instead, it demands total submission. In failing, you risk going stir-crazy.

The horizon was so even you could balance a marble on it. I sent my Toyota RAV4 racing up a road that disappeared into a rudimentary vanishing point. There was no sign of life other than a thin layer of ankle-high scrub. Such commitment to austerity has an element of fanaticism about it; a cleanliness usually found in the abstract world of pure mathematics.

Thank god for this road! Even devoid of other cars, it was evidence of mankind's presence, announcing that others had been here before and would pass through again. Out here a road is the only lifeline to places beyond the horizon with buildings, food, electricity and water, where other humans gather and have shored up our own safety. There was no faster way for me to die than to veer off this road and fling myself into the terrifying nihilism of the flat scrub. I was reminded of the tagline to the 1979 classic film *Alien*: 'In space, no one can hear you scream.'

After two hours the land began to undulate, and I arrived at a large sign decorated with a setting yellow sun on a strip of red land against a black sky, evoking the Australian Aboriginal flag. The flag was designed by the Luritja and Wombai artist Harold Thomas, who still holds the copyright, and flown for the first time in 1971; the yellow represents the sun, red the earth and black the Aboriginal people.

I parked the car to stretch my legs and read the sign's Mutthi Mutthi words 'Telki thangurra. Pirnmatha', translated as 'Our Country is beautiful. Please come.' I noticed the land was dipping into shallow bowls—these were the relict lakes, I guessed—the edges of which masked what lay beyond the horizon. There were few trees, mainly greyish-green saltbush with tiny, hardy, succulent buds. I found it difficult to imagine how Mutthi Mutthi people ever sustained life out here. I plucked one of the buds and tentatively licked it, detecting the faint taste of salt.

As daylight slipped away and the temperature dropped, I arrived at a campsite crowded with a dozen other campers in four-wheel drives: some young families along with grey nomads, as travelling retirees have been affectionately nicknamed. Grey nomads often dominate remote-area campsites, being the main cohort of Australians with the luxury of time and money to cover the Outback's tremendous distances. I picked a spot on the edge of the clearing that looked out at some thin bush. It didn't seem to matter how often I went solo camping, I always felt a touch self-conscious; it was just so bloody rare to see a solo camper, let alone an Asian solo camper. Looking different made me feel vulnerable, and so I preferred to camp away from everyone else.

I'd forgotten to bring firewood, and the trees around the campsite weren't the lovely, thick eucalypts from my days along the Murrumbidgee River, continually dropping heavy branches perfect for burning. The compact red dirt only supported some gnarled pine trees and a thinner type of tree with needle-like leaves. The few dropped branches were no thicker than my leg. In any case it was a national park, where you aren't supposed to collect wood—a rule I appreciated was necessary for environmental preservation but always gave me a wistful pang as it robbed me of one of the pleasures of camping.

On the positive side, something about being in open country, freshened with cool, clean air, made me feel as if my trip had finally begun.

I reorganised my belongings so I could set up bedding in my car, moving everything into the front two seats. Beside my car I erected a small cooking and wash station: just a water tank propped up on a stool and a box of utensils next to my fold-out table. For dinner I threw chopped-up carrot and garlic, along with a biscuit of dry noodles, into my pot bubbling with chicken-stock soup.

Back when my parents were still together they never took our family camping—not atypical of immigrant Chinese. My dad didn't have much money growing up in rural Malaysia, and after moving to Australia as a nineteen-year-old, long-haired university student, he studied medicine in the day and drove a taxi at night. Later, as a doctor, he provided a good life for his family. His is a classic Australian immigrant tale. The recent rise of China on the world stage and its newfound wealth was also a source of pride for him as an overseas Chinese person.

My family spent several summer holidays in Malaysia. However, once we took a holiday to Tasmania, and one afternoon went on a river tour. From the heated comfort of a luxury cruiser, I watched a white family setting up their tents on the riverbank.

I thought, *Is that what Aussie families do on their holidays?*

I turned to my dad. 'How come you never take us camping?'

He had a glass of white in one hand; with the other, he cut a wedge of cheese and placed it atop a cracker with a sliver of local salmon.

'Camping?' he said, as if he'd never uttered the word before. 'Isn't this better?'

Tramping through mud, battling bugs and fishing for dinner is not my dad's idea of a holiday. If anything, it sounds exactly like the way of life a thousand generations of Tan family commoners endured, something he'd strived hard to avoid.

A friend of mine, a fellow Australian-born Chinese, has long been terrified of the Outback because she is convinced those who live there are racist towards Asian people. She's never put this thesis to the test, but my general impression of the Chinese community in Sydney is that her assumptions aren't uncommon. The bush is regarded as dirty, ugly, boring and dangerous, and its human inhabitants as redneck and boorish, perhaps the sour dregs of the former convict colony. Such spooky shadowlands are better off mined, farmed and locked in concrete, neutered and tamed—the sooner, the better.

These immigrants aren't to be blamed for this: their prejudices are an extension of colonial fears and postcolonial cultural cringe that has long viewed the Australian natural landscape as a dark and menacing place, likely to swallow up everyone from wandering virgins (as in the classic *Picnic at Hanging Rock*) to swimming prime ministers (Harold

Holt in 1967), and featuring townships that have devolved into a primal state (see the booze-soaked, violence-studded *Wake in Fright*).

Also, the food sucks out there.

Yet here I was—a wet behind the ears, idiot hipster, Asian gal townie, stumbling through the Australian wilderness for six months. Or at least, so I appeared. In truth I was no longer a total newbie when it came to going bush and knew first-hand much of my friend's prejudices against the countryside were unfounded.

Soon I was sitting in my camp chair and scooping hot noodles into my mouth. Between bites, I looked up at a night sky sprayed with white dots like those on a lizard's skin. I felt a rush of pleasure. My Sydney life already seemed like a figure shrinking on the horizon as I sailed steadily away. I was freezing, and tired, but satisfied I had survived one more day on Earth and had done all that was needed to survive at least another day more.

I went to sleep in my car, but woke only a few hours later with my nose, the only part of my body I'd left exposed, hurting like hell from the cold. I pictured grabbing it between my gloved fingers and snapping it off like an iceblock. My breath was visible as hot steam; the temperature had dropped to zero. It was amazing to think I'd essentially crawled into a giant refrigerator for the night. I tried to check my phone for the time but in the cold my battery had drained. I was almost happy to see I remained more resilient than our clever digital devices—the robots hadn't defeated us yet.

I had on nearly every item of clothing I'd packed: thermal leggings, pyjama pants and waterproof pants I usually only wore hiking; a thermal long-sleeved top, pyjama top, polyester-fleece zip jacket, polyester jumper and down-stuffed jacket; two pairs of thick socks, gloves, a scarf, neck warmer and beanie. To protect my nose I wrapped my scarf around my face. Draping an aeroplane blanket over my shoulders, I wriggled back into my down sleeping-bag feeling every bit the bandaged-up mummy. I was exhilarated to be sleeping in the kind of chill that shot through all my layers and went straight to my heart.

As I drifted back to sleep, an image of the toasty fire that Mutthi Mutthi people would have kept roaring all night—and probably still do when they're out on Country—hovered in my mind, as did the thought that a megafaunal wombat-fur cloak would feel mighty nice right about now.

*

There are certain places in Australia where, even if you aren't from there, you can detect an emanating spiritual power. The region of shallow dry lakes in Mungo National Park is such a place. One need not be a member of the park's three groups of traditional owners— the Barkindji, Ngiyampaa and Mutthi Mutthi peoples—to feel one is walking on holy, ancient ground. You could even be the first in your family to have been born on this continent, and a total dunce when it comes to Aboriginality, yet sense a presence in the park's endlessly whispering trails of sand.

I'd given myself a full day to explore the park. It forms part of nineteen dry lakes once strung together by a channel of water, and is sandwiched between mallee trees and dune fields to the west and the riverine plain I'd just driven through to the east. This area, geologically speaking, has long been quiet and stable; for thousands upon thousands of years, sediment washed out from the distant mountains and collected in this low-lying stretch of lakes like a sink strainer. The area is also where Mungo Man, some of the oldest modern human remains outside of Africa, was found.

I drove out to the edge of the main lake, after which the remains were named, and joined a dozen tourists milling about. We were booked to do a two-hour tour led by a park ranger. At 9 a.m. the sky was bright blue, but the day was still thawing out from its ice-cold slumber.

Very shortly the ranger appeared, a stocky man with a bristly moustache, wearing a green uniform and a baseball cap. We gathered close around him as he opened by speaking in Barkindji language, briefly translating for us: 'Nai means "welcome" and kira means "Country", so welcome to Country,' he said, looking to the ground but speaking meaningfully. He gave a small smile that made his moustache crinkle like a furry caterpillar. 'Now, you're probably wondering where Mungo Man, Mungo Woman been found. They been found that direction there.' He pointed up towards a horizon dusted with yellow sand. 'Where that white wall, is known as the southern end of Mungo Lake.'

It was there in 1968, he explained, that a young geologist called Jim Bowler stumbled across an intriguing mound of old bone and charcoal. The following year Bowler returned with some archaeologists who, with excitement and in the midst of a trampling flock of sheep, identified the aged bones as human. It was a discovery so fragile 'the whole thing could be swept away in a heavy downpour', as one archaeologist later described it in the documentary *Message From Mungo*. Caught off guard by such a significant find, another of the archaeologists collected the bones in a small suitcase and used his clothing to keep them steady while they were transported to a university.

Studies revealed the remains were of a woman who had lived at the lake roughly forty-two thousand years ago. She had been twice-cremated, then buried in a round hole in one of the sand dunes. The discovery single-handedly blew out the scientific community's timeline of how long Aboriginal people had inhabited Australia, and put these lonely fields of sand on the global map.

Not content to make just one incredible discovery, five years later Bowler was riding his motorbike on the same dry lake shores when he discovered a human skull. This time his team uncovered the complete skeleton of a 1.7-metre-tall male, roughly fifty years old—an impressive height and age for such an early human. Mungo Man, as he was later known, had been carefully positioned in his grave on his back with hands interlocked over his groin and body sprinkled in a brownish-red ochre.

That ochre wasn't found in the area, the ranger told us. 'So it was traded in from somewhere else. For someone to have that ochre scattered over his remains, he must have been high up. He must have been a king or a chief of the tribe at that period of time.'

I had read that at the time of Mungo Man's discovery, Western scientists presumed all these early modern humans around the world were nothing but blockheaded cavemen, scratching around in the dirt, not evolved enough to conceive of anything as sophisticated as an afterlife or a soul. Yet here was stunningly clear evidence of ritualised, spiritual care from these early humans.

'We got a lot of burial sites around this here area,' the ranger said. 'But we don't want no one to go round test or carbon date our elders or our human remains. We know how old they are.' He nodded gravely.

It was a good reminder of the fact that not everyone was happy to learn Mungo Woman's remains had been thrown into a suitcase and stolen away as if by thieves in the night. To the traditional owners, Mungo Woman and Man were their Auntie and Uncle. You could stick as many 'greats' as you wanted in front of those words, it wouldn't change the fact that the traditional owners had a sacred responsibility to care for the people buried at the lake.

Within a short period following the discovery, the region was crawling with 'cowboy archaeologists': bearded white men bragging about the size of their Pleistocene sequence—as one woman archaeologist later described it in *Message From Mungo*—while pocketing stone tools and human remains willy-nilly under the time-honoured legal defence of 'finders keepers'. To the Aboriginal community, these archaeologists were digging up their past without consent and appropriating it for their own professional advancement. Some traditional owners began to speak out, led by the 'four Aunties': Mutthi Mutthi woman Alice Kelly, and Barkindji women Alice Bugmy, Tibby Briar and Elsie Jones.

'The best thing the archaeologists can do is study these old fireplaces and that will tell you an accurate date,' said the ranger. 'It also tells us about the weather and the climate at that period of time. The evidence shows we been round here for over sixty thousand years. Maybe longer.'

'A long time,' said a long, lean woman who stood next to her husband and daughters.

'Yeah,' said the ranger.

'A very long time,' the woman repeated.

The ranger chuckled. He capped off each section of his lecture with a distinct laugh that was wheezy like a squeeze toy. I admired his charitable approach to the tensions between his people and the scientific community, a quality I recognised in many Aboriginal Australians I knew.

'Anyway, we're grateful that Jim Bowler did find Mungo Woman,' he said. 'If it weren't for him, Mungo wouldn't be on the map today. But people always been told that the old people used to live out here, that was long before Jim Bowler.'

I found that surprising. 'You already knew there were people buried here from a long time ago?'

He said his people had always spoken about the burial sites as places to be avoided. Then he held out one bare arm. 'The hairs on your hand stands up. And when that happens to us we know straight away there's something here. We always take off.' If they had to visit those burial sites, they first cleansed their bodies with the smoke of burning mallee leaves, to prevent the old spirits following them back home.

There were now plans to construct a keeping place that would store the hundreds of skeletal remains taken from Mungo.

'Who took them?' I asked.

'Probably scientists,' the ranger said.

'I suppose people thought they were doing the right thing at the time,' another tourist added politely.

The ranger led us to the lip of the sand dune, or 'lunette' as it's known by geologists. Tourists were forbidden from walking over its fragile surface unless accompanied by a ranger or tour guide. We walked down a ramp with the ranger unlocking a gate at the end so we could pass through onto the lunette. I held up my hand to block the harsh sun and cast my eyes around this strange arid place of sand and shrub. Pinnacles on the horizon looked like the stiff peaks of whipped egg white. I found 'lunette' an evocative name, apt because the clay and sand lip was crescent-shaped, its grey-dust surface reminding me of a lunar landscape. As our feet met the lunette's surface, it turned out to be surprisingly compact. The sands gently sloped upwards with the hardened silt crunching underfoot. Here and there I saw pools of fresh, soft golden sand where the ghostly wind had left a rippled imprint.

A lunette lines the downwind side of each relict lake. Over forty-five thousand years of occupation, people's hearths, middens (ancient 'trash heaps' where they discarded shellfish remains, and fish and animal bones), stone tools and burials, along with the bones of megafauna and other animals were captured in the lunettes' orderly layers—a goldmine for scientists wanting to establish accurate timelines.

In a revered place, you instinctively know not to whoop and holler. As we followed the ranger up and across the twenty-metre-high lunette, the usual bubbling chatter of a tour group failed to froth up. Most of us walked in thoughtful silence or talked in hushed tones as if we were inside a library—and not a local library, but one of those grand state libraries where you can almost hear voices from the past murmuring restlessly from the pages of all those musty old books.

We marched past human-sized sand monuments rippled with buttresses like the many folds of a draped sheet. A fierce wind howled from the west, blowing grey sand from the pinnacle peaks. Occasionally the ranger made comments as we walked, and at some point he mentioned that the region is too large for archaeologists to dig at random. Instead, the spirited westerly winds—here and there, now and then—lift the lake's sand shroud to reveal treasures and long-dead things. Of course, the westerlies are just as likely to cover a relic up again, so some sprinkling of good fortune is required for discoveries.

'Our ancestors? They lived through the Ice Age,' continued the ranger. 'Even with the megafauna animals. A lot of people asked if we killed the megafauna animals; I think it might have been the climate change that killed them.'

The day prior, when I'd just arrived at Mungo National Park, inside the visitor centre I'd seen a model of a wombat-like creature with a piggish upturned snout, the size of a mini car, called a *Zygomaturus*. Among several other megafaunal fossils found in the park were a short-faced, giant kangaroo called a *Procoptodon*, and a stout flightless bird called a *Genyornis* that was larger than today's emu.

I was blown away by the climatic and environmental changes the ranger's ancestors had survived. They had outlived the megafauna, while over tens of thousands of years the lake had filled and dried up several times, and then remained mostly dry for at least the past ten thousand years. Through it all, the land's human caretakers had adapted to the changes and maintained their intimate connection to this place.

But it's no wonder that in the 1970s, Western scientists and archaeologists didn't regard contemporary Aboriginal people as the direct descendants of the Mungo pair and were baffled by the anger from the traditional owners to their work. The idea of an unbroken ancestral chain many thousands of generations long seemed fantastical, when for thousands upon thousands of years mass movements of people have been common—driven by war, greed, the desire for a better life, or to escape natural disasters. Take my people, the Han Chinese of Fujian province: in the past two thousand years alone we were chased all over China, frequently spurred to conquest and colonise or to escape conquest and colonisation.

Yet, in the decades since the Mungo discoveries, science has continued to confirm the exceptionalism of Aboriginal Australia's connection to Country. A study of mitochondrial DNA from Aboriginal hair samples (collected during anthropological expeditions in the early to mid-1900s) has revealed just how little geographical movement took place after the initial occupation. According to the study, today's Aboriginal Australians are the descendants of a single founding population that arrived in Australia fifty thousand years ago and spread rapidly around the continent's east and west coasts, meeting somewhere in southern Australia a couple of thousand years later. After that, distinct Aboriginal Australian groups remained in discrete regions using local resources.

In the visitor centre I had also been amused to see a cabinet of notes posted from contrite visitors who, following divine retribution, had come to regret their thievery of rocks and sand from the park, including:

> Dear Tanya, I enclose a 5 million-year-old piece of Rock from Lake Mungo. I know you said not to—I did—and I'm sincerely apologetic. Especially as I spent a week in hospital on my return home from Mungo at Easter time after crashing my bicycle into a car! I can't say you didn't warn me. I have a fascination for rocks and collect them in my travels from time to time. We really enjoyed the tours we took with you.

These were not the only items stolen from the park that had found their way back home. Eventually the traditional owners and the scientists of Mungo reconciled, agreeing to shared research agendas, and sealing this spirit of good faith was the repatriation of Mungo Woman from the university in 1991—the culmination of overcoming countless economic and bureaucratic hurdles.

On the lunette, our tour group gathered around a slight mound of crunchy greyish sand. Some weedy-looking plants had sprouted from its surface. Beads the size of kangaroo droppings, made of grey, orange and white clay, were scattered about. The ranger picked one up and rolled it around in his palm. 'Our ancestors used to collect all this mud and roll them into balls. They'd throw them into the fireplace because two of these here worked as a heat bead, cooking the food at a steady rate, where it wouldna been burning.'

While the burial sites are off limits to scientists, these fireplaces remain accessible, and despite their underwhelming appearance contain important secrets. Baked clay hearths preserve a record of the alignment of the Earth's magnetic field, revealing a significant shift in this field some thirty thousand years ago. Known as the Lake Mungo Geomagnetic Excursion, it has been confirmed at other locations around the world.

The ranger showed us more of these lightly scorched patches of sand and said they were the remnants of cooked wombat fat mixed in with the silt. 'This fireplace here,' he pointed, 'I call it a young one— it's about nine thousand years old. So it's older than the pyramids! That fireplace there, folks, that about thirty-three thousand years old.'

Along with the other tourists I oohed and aahed on cue, albeit a little half-heartedly. Sure these hearths were older than the pyramids, but weren't they also just thin layers of ash? I tried reminding myself that what made these fireplaces compelling was how they formed a physical connection to Mungo Man. I pictured him in my mind: an Ice Age hunter-gatherer warming his sore elbow by a roaring fire on a night just as cold as the one I had experienced. Studies of Mungo Man show signs of osteoarthritis in his dominant spear-throwing right arm and two missing lower canine teeth, which some academics posit were knocked out in a ritual, consistent with initiation rites.

Around when the ranger mentioned finding what he said was a 14,000-year-old carpet snake skeleton ('which was still curled up!'), then pointed out a pile of wombat bones—22,000-year-old, 'probably'—I began to feel fatigue at all these stupendously large numbers. In the same way that Australia's wide, sunburnt plains and immense sky deflate in photographs, our brains fail to grasp figures so far beyond the scale set by our puny lifespans.

'How big were they?' asked the lean woman. 'They wouldn't have been big people?'

She had a habit of saying whatever was on her mind, while her husband hadn't spoken all morning. They had three blonde daughters, each the spitting image of their mother, and wearing matching bright pastel wind jackets and fluffy beanies.

'Yeah, they would have been very tall,' said the ranger. A biomechanical analysis of a trail of Ice Age footprints showed that several of the men approached two metres tall.

'Oh, they were tall?' the woman said.

'Yeah, they was tall.'

'Uhhhn.' She reminded me of my high school PE teacher, unhewn and salt of the earth. 'Aboriginal people aren't very tall, though, are they?'

'Look at me, I'm only short fella,' the ranger replied congenially. He said those old people were running and hunting every day. 'They reckon their burst of speed was much greater than the fastest runner we've got today.'

I thought about a photo I'd seen in the park's visitor centre, with the caption: 'This photo is of the Nanya tribe. Harry Nanya, born shortly after the Rufus River massacre, shunned European society and lived a traditional life in the mallee country with his huge family.' The photo showed five tall men with strong, thick torsos standing on a grassy patch near the bend of a river, each armed with a spear double their height. Women knelt on the ground, as bare-chested as the men, and in front sat a row of children with skinny legs stretched out. Nobody smiled showing their teeth but several wore amused looks and all appeared dazzlingly fit. They had very dark, clear skin that shone.

Nanya, I later read, was considered one of the area's last head clansmen to resist being absorbed into European life. Incursions with Europeans had killed most of his family, with at least thirty of his people dying at the hands of South Australian police in 1841 in the Rufus River Massacre. As a young man, he went into the waterless mallee country between the Great Darling Anabranch and the South

Australian border, armed with a steel axe and accompanied by two women, and lived in isolation for the next three decades. Other than reports of tracks and piles of freshly cut mallee roots, there were few sightings—at least by whitefellas; Aboriginal stockmen were said to be aware of the group's movements.

There's something beautiful about the Nanya tribe's quiet resistance. For possibly tens of thousands of years Aboriginal Australian nations had held true to their languages, cultures and kinship traditions with faithful conservatism and remarkable consistency, and maintained their equilibrium with the natural world. In their isolation this worked perfectly, but once punctured it was vulnerable to destruction. As all remote corners of the globe were absorbed into a singular reality, mainly via colonialism, for Aboriginal Australia the shock of butting heads with a radically different civilisation was something they have yet to recover from.

By the 1890s, the population of Harry's family had grown, and with more frequent sightings European settlers became uneasy. The twelve men, eight women and ten children were eventually persuaded by Aboriginal stockmen to come out from hiding, then taken to a station. Initially they refused to eat whitefella food, but according to biographer Robert Lindsay a photo that was reportedly taken two years later showed two of Nanya's daughters had 'become stout on a flour and sugar diet'. After Nanya died many of his children would follow, succumbing to introduced diseases. In 1905 his son Billy boarded a paddle-steamer to Point McLeay Mission in South Australia and was so tormented by crew members, he jumped into the steamer's engine and was cut to pieces.

I find it impossible not to feel heartbroken that with the end of Aboriginal Australian isolation came such thorough abuse of their ancient cultures. It's as though colonisers picked them up with two hands like an antique vase and threw them against a brick wall.

'Aboriginal people generally aren't tall these days, no?' the PE teacher said doubtfully, her head cocked to one side. She was standing next to her three minion daughters who all wore the same dull expression. The youngest was chewing the end of her shirtsleeve. I considered the possibility that fifty thousand years ago in some dank European cave, a child much the same chewing the end of her little caveman fur coat.

'A lot of the desert people are skinny and tall,' said the ranger, with the patience and good humour of a saint.

'Uhhhn.'

'Around the coastal areas they're solid, stocky built Aboriginals—'

'Uhhhn.'

'—so I think it might be weather and climate-related.'

We came to the end of our tour on the lunette, and the ranger led us back through the gate and up the ramp. We stopped at a piece of carved rock on the path that led back to the car park.

'We got a lot of Dreamtime stories here,' said the ranger. 'We got one about the brolga.'

'The brolga,' I said, 'is that a bird that . . . that still exists now?' I hesitated, half-worried the brolga was a non-existant creature and my question was as stupid as asking if the unicorn or dragon was extinct now.

'You see the brolgas at every lake, river or creek, and you always get a welcome by these birds. They'll dance for you. We have Dreaming stories that explain why they dance.'

The ranger reminded us that aeons ago this dry lake was full of water, possibly home to birds like brolgas and swans, and fringed with edible reeds, teeming with fish, yabbies and freshwater mussels.

'You wouldn't believe it, ay,' he said, 'but we get a lot of people still come out here with their boats.'

I *couldn't* believe that. 'Because they think it's a lake . . .'

'. . . and they can go fishing?' finished a woman. We were all laughing.

The ranger smiled. 'This one fella walked into our centre with his fishing rod: "Ay, matey, where's the water?" And we started laughing because we thought he was having us on. But he was for real.

'He said, "I've come out here to do a bit of fishing."
'I told him, "You're about seventeen thousand years late, mate!"'

✱

Most Australians live in state capital cities and have limited inter-actions with large native fauna. You're unlikely to see a koala in an inner-city tree or an emu drinking from a suburban waterway. Yet images of these animals are familiar to all Australians—from the media, school, children's books, our currency, and government and corporate branding—and so it's easy for us to forget how objectively odd some of these creatures are. There's simply no equivalent to a kangaroo or a platypus elsewhere in the world.

When Captain James Cook first encountered our famous hopping marsupial, in current-day northern Queensland, his description lumped together a number of European references. He wrote in his journal, 'the Skin is cover'd with a short hairy fur of a dark Mouse or Grey Colour — Excepting the head and ears which I thought was something like a Hare's . . . it is said to bear much resemblance to the Gerbua excepting in size the Gerbua being no larger than a common rat'. He concluded, correctly: 'it bears no sort of resemblance to any European animal I ever saw'.

When in 1798, a naturalist sent a pelt and sketch of the platypus back to the British motherland, a staff member at the British Museum used scissors to check for stitches that might explain how such a duck-like beak could wind up on such a beaver-like body.

Because the echidna resembles the porcupine and hedgehog, it has never raised as many eyebrows as the platypus. But these two animals are the world's only egg-laying mammals (or monotremes) and share a common ancestor. The spiky creature was named by the Europeans after Echidna, an ancient Greek goddess who was half-woman and half-snake. Although I didn't grow up seeing echidnas shuffle down the suburban streets of my part of Sydney, during my trips out bush in my thirties I've come to love these introverted creatures. Each roams the Earth on its own, in a slow but purposeful waddle, and when you get too close they comically curl up into frightened spindly balls.

However, I'd never seen an echidna like the one before me: half-skinned, trussed with wires and dipped by a young Barkindji man into a black tin of water boiling over a wood fire.

The day before I had left Mungo National Park and driven south until I was back on the Sturt Highway. I spent the night at a friend of a friend's place in Mildura. The town sits near the intersection of the Murray River with another critical Australian waterway, the Darling River. This part of the Murray makes for a state border so that among the huddle of towns, those that sit to the north of the Murray, such as Wentworth and Dareton, are in New South Wales while those that lie south, such as Mildura, are in Victoria. I'd seen the famous river dotted with plush houseboats that drifted, sun-soaked, under an open sky. It rains very little out there.

Now I was at the men's shed in Dareton near Mildura, run by the Barkindji Maraura Elders Environment Team, to meet with program manager Dameion Kennedy. I'd found him standing in a tight circle on the grass with a group of teenage boys. The boys all wore hoodies and baseball caps, and were slouching through that stage of adolescence in which, between a few grunts and occasional mumbles, bodies do all the talking.

Only up close, when their circle opened, did I see—to my utter amazement—what they were doing to the echidna.

They'd killed this poor bugger somewhere on the side of a road. Now spines were flying everywhere. Scalding the helmet-shaped 'porcupine', as Dameion called the echidna, made it easier for the group to get its quills out.

One gangly boy plonked the carcass, which was giving off billows of steam, on the table and continued vigorously dragging his knife across it in steady, swift strokes at the base of the remaining black spines.

'Give him a bigger knife,' said Dameion. He was forty years old with a wispy salt-and-pepper beard and warm, liquid brown eyes.

Someone passed the boy a knife—a dead ringer for Crocodile Dundee's this-is-a-knife knife—and a pair of wraparound sunnies to protect his eyes from the pointed missiles shooting into the air.

'Does it taste like chicken?' I asked, the obvious question when confronted with a half-skinned echidna. Now bloated from several dunkings, it was the size of a large chicken, and the same whitish colour but with a grey rather than pink tinge.

'Like pork but oily,' said Dameion, moving back a little when a flying spine popped him in the chest like a tiny spear trying to take down a giant. They still had to gut the thing and remove its four ant glands before it would be ready to eat, he said—otherwise the meat would taste of nothing but ants.

I wondered what ant tasted like. I assumed acrid.

'Do you mind if I take some of the quills?' I asked.

'Go ahead.'

I crouched and began to pick them from the grass, dropping them one by one into a sandwich bag I had with me. They were beautiful: needles that at their tips darkened from ivory to ebony like freshly sharpened lead pencils.

Dameion said that the Barkindji women used to make necklaces out of them and advised I solder the ends so they weren't so pointy. He leaned down to pick up one of the animal's paws. 'Take this as well,' he said, placing it carefully in my open palm. I smiled with delight. It was the size of a cat's paw but with five very thick nails. A petrified high five. I added it to the sandwich bag.

I'd heard of Dameion through an unexpectedly fortuitous series of events. On arriving in Mildura I had, as was now my custom, pulled into the town's visitor centre. Like in Balranald, the centre was in a modern building tastefully landscaped and decorated with art. Inside, sunlight poured through some skylights. I approached the counter, and a middle-aged woman looked up at me with a smile.

'Hello,' I said. 'I'm just a tourist passing through, and I was wondering if you happen to know anything about the local Aboriginal culture.'

She scrunched up her nose. 'Ooh, you might have to go to the library for that.'

When I said I was also interested in history, she passed me a pamphlet titled 'Mildura: Australia's First Irrigation Colony'.

Feeling uninspired, I headed to an adjoining cafe to sit for a bit and contemplate my next move. I ordered a hot chocolate and at a table flicked through the pamphlet and learnt it was here in Mildura that some of the earliest irrigation schemes were set up. While there were plenty of bumps and hiccups along the way, the seeds of that experiment eventually sprouted and proliferated across over a million hectares of neatly quartered fields in south-east Australia. The Murray-Darling Basin today is known as Australia's food bowl and responsible for one third of the country's agricultural output. In coming to Mildura I had driven through some of this agri-industrial complex: green fields from which grains of rice and bales of wheat are harvested, along with maize, canola, citrus and wine grapes.

This genteel agricultural town was founded on Mildura, an old cattle station whose name had unclear but likely Latje Latje etymology, meaning 'red earth'. A considerable number of Australian places have Indigenous names, but their connection to Indigenous Australia was so long ago severed and the words so thoroughly acclimatised into Aussie English that this aspect of the country is often forgotten or even unknown by locals. Foreigners and new arrivals, I've often noticed, are better at pointing out how alien words like Bondi, Coogee and Parramatta are from the English language.

I returned to my car and drove ten minutes up the highway, passing through Dareton. It's a separate town but close enough to feel like an outer-suburb of Mildura. Up a short main street, I past a Vinnies, chemist, supermarket and takeaway chicken shop, and felt a listlessness about the town. Several of the stores were boarded over with 'for lease' signs in the front windows. When I had to slow down for a trio of Aboriginal people crossing the road, on impulse I decided to park my car and take a poke around.

By chance I found myself directly opposite a door painted in ochre-coloured Aboriginal designs. I had no idea if the local Aboriginal community (whose nation name I had yet to learn) had been side-lined by the white mainstream and that making a connection would just require a bit of effort on my part, or if the community stayed out of sight by choice. I didn't want to be an imposition, nor did I want to *not try*—such an awkward situation. On my travels I'd encountered so many non-Aboriginal Australians in remote towns who hadn't once driven around the corner or up the highway to visit the Aboriginal communities in their own backyard—communities that, when I visited, proved warm and welcoming—that this no longer shocked me. It was so easy to fall into a town's pattern of segregation.

What to do? From inside my car I stared at the door. It had no visible signage, and the storefront windows were papered up. What kind of idiot just knocks on a random door? I came up with a compromise: I'd go gently, and pull back at the first sign I was sticking my nose in someone's private business.

I got out of my car and approached the door, then gingerly rapped on it. It was unlocked. I hesitantly pushed it open. 'Hello?' I asked.

An older man with a charcoal-grey goatee was busily tidying up his desk. His told me his name was Greg. He didn't seem entirely sure what I was doing in his office. I wasn't too sure either and mumbled something about being on a road trip and having an interest in Aboriginal culture.

'Good, more young people like you should be interested,' he said in a clipped tone, and began scribbling contact details for me on a piece of paper. It had been floating like flotsam on the stacks of books, folders and pamphlets that rendered his desk invisible. As he wrote I babbled self-consciously about my time at Lake Mungo.

Greg handed me the slip of paper; in block capitals he'd written the names and phone numbers of Aboriginal organisations thousands of kilometres away in south and central Australia. None appeared to be related to any of the Aboriginal groups around here.

'It might be best not to say you used to be a journalist—although writing a book is probably okay,' he told me, in a manner both brusque and encouraging. 'You might have to be a bit devious.' He frowned, sensing 'devious' wasn't the best word. 'I mean, you might need a journalist's nose.'

'Persistence?'

'Yes, precisely.'

No shit, I felt like saying. Only through persistence had I wound up in this office.

Greg was still shuffling papers, looking for phone numbers, as I cast my eyes around. Flyers advertised Aboriginal health services and local festivals. 'What is this place, anyway?' I asked. I'd guessed it was some sort of employment agency.

Greg stared at his table until he found what he was looking for. 'Here it is!'

He passed me a brochure titled 'BMEET: Barkindji Maraura Elders Environment Team'.

'I'm really sorry,' he said, looking apologetic and harried, 'but I have to be somewhere. If you're keen to learn more, you should meet our program manager, Dameion Kennedy.'

And that's how I wound up at BMEET's shed further up the main road, watching Dameion and his young charges boil and skin an echidna.

By the time the animal was spine-free, with one boy trying to burn its remaining hairs off with a lighter, Dameion suggested we take a look around BMEET's new gallery and art workshop. It hadn't yet officially opened to the public—hence the unhelpful woman at the Mildura visitor centre.

As we walked past displays of beautiful hand-carved redwood plat-
ters and painted didgeridoos made from local gum trees, Dameion
told me more about BMEET. 'We do caring-for-Country programs
and teach a lot of our young people about our cultural heritage.'

'If not for BMEET, the kids are just on the streets,' he told me.
'There's not much to do around here—it's a pretty boring little town.'
He shrugged, adding, 'Unless you go fishing and hunting. That's
good fun.'

Dameion seemed to me to be an upstanding guy: selfless, humble
and motivated. The area around Dareton was Dameion's grandmother's Country. She was of the Barkindji people of the Wiimpatya
clan group.

'Is there a Barkindji word for river?' I asked him, picking up a
platter and turning it over in my hand. It was the warm colour of
amber beer, and its sanded-down surface was riddled with a dark
mottled pattern like the cross-section of a lung.

'Yeah, barka,' he said.

'Oh.' I realised my question had probably sounded dumb.

'Barka means "river" and ndji means "belonging to",' he said, 'so
Barkindji means "we belong to the river".'

I thought back to Mildura's colonial irrigation propaganda. 'I'm
guessing there's a difference between how your people see the river
and how the whitefellas see it?'

'Huge difference! Obviously our people never irrigated.' He shook
his head. 'The whitefellas drain and drain and drain to grow their
crops and to get rich. But we're not about getting rich. We need our
Country rich. The plants and the bush tucker and the animals and
that, that's what we live on. And as you seen today we're cooking a
porcupine, that's a native food for us people.' Irrigation was why the
rivers were in such a mess, the wetlands were shrinking and the birds
had all but disappeared, he told me.

In one of the tourist brochures I'd picked up at the Mildura visitor
centre, I'd read some chipper stats on fresh produce from the region:

seventy-five per cent of Australia's table grapes, sixty-nine per cent of its almonds, forty-eight per cent of its pistachios. What the figures don't show, however, are the issues that drove the town's irrigation pioneers, the Chaffey brothers, into bankruptcy continued to plague Murray-Darling farmers over the following two centuries.

Australian soils are among the most nutrient poor and unproductive in the world. Our continent is also particularly saline because a hundred million years ago most of it was submerged under a shallow sea; the clearing of native vegetation along with invasive irrigation systems bring all that residual salt up to the surface. Thirty years ago salinity levels hit such alarming heights, they threatened the viability of the agricultural industry. The Murray-Darling Basin Authority was forced to introduce salt interception schemes: bores and pumps that take highly saline groundwater and dump it far from the river, like a colossal dialysis machine.

In order to manage unpredictable water flows, the Murray-Darling Basin was plugged up by state governments long ago with hundreds of reservoirs, lock and weirs, coastal barrages and dams. While stabilising supply, this has wreaked havoc on the natural flood-drought cycles of the river ecosystems. During the severe decade-long drought of the 2000s, growers sucked the waterways dry until a number just stopped flowing and the entire system was close to collapse.

In an effort to repair the damage, BMEET has been collaborating with scientists to conduct tree surveys and implement water-health programs. It seemed to be paying off, and Dameion was clearly happy and proud to report that areas which hadn't seen water in years were beginning to flow again.

'We all know the country needs water. It's natural—if you got a tree and it's dying, you give it a drink.'

This part of Australia, river country, boasts the most incredible gum trees I'd ever seen. Among the nearly 900 varieties of eucalypts, 'river red gums' are towering and grand. Their ribbons of bark reminded me of impressionist paintings, dripping and swirling with creamy white, tan, stormy grey and silvery sheens. This icon of the Outback lines rivers across most of the country, even dry central Australia. The tallest of them are hundreds of years old and able to grow fifteen storeys high. I had been advised by a friend never to set my tent directly underneath one. They have a habit of dropping their very heavy boughs without warning—hence their rather ominous nickname 'widow maker'.

These magnificent trees have suffered from the basin's water shortages, with record numbers of river red gums in the lower Murray stressed, dead or dying. Throughout the nineteenth and twentieth centuries they were chopped down and hacked into sleepers for the railway network that crosses the country in long, flat ladders. They continue to be massively undervalued.

'We all got to work together as *Australians*,' he emphasised. 'I tell a lot of people this is all our Dreaming now. We got to dream our river back to life because we all live here.'

✳

The next morning as I crossed into South Australia from Victoria on the Sturt Highway, the earth became sandy and red. From my speeding car all I could see were scorching bald plains, fenced off with barbed wire and splintering posts.

A quarantine inspector checked me for fresh fruit and veggies—South Australia is trying to keep the fruit flies out. He raised his eyebrow at the insides of my car, jammed tight with gear like organs in a body. 'Moving?' he asked, bemused.

'Nope, camping.'

Most of the travellers I was sharing the road with lived out of caravans or utes fitted with drawers and fold-out kitchens that kept everything hidden. But in my RAV4 I had no option but to keep my gear in boxes and bags that, along with my water tanks and jerry cans, were shuffled around in an infuriating, never-ending game of Tetris. I maintained the same rules as I would have living in a ship's cabin:

keep immaculate order, or else watch everything turn into a tangle and spend hours looking for that spare set of batteries or the bottle opener you swear you packed somewhere.

I wanted to keep following the Murray River downstream to its mouth where it meets the Southern Ocean in the sacred Coorong region. This stretch of the river, crossing through South Australia, has arguably suffered the most from the accumulated agricultural activities upstream in Victoria and New South Wales. It's also Pelican Dreaming Country, and I saw plenty of those self-possessed birds nonchalantly paddling up and down the green water like miniature black-and-white sailboats.

In the Coorong I planned to visit the home town of David Unaipon. The Ngarrindjeri polymath preacher, writer, inventor and musician— once known as Australia's Leonardo da Vinci—was born in 1872 at Point McLeay Mission. His portrait is on Australia's fifty-dollar note.

The internet didn't offer much about what I might find in Point McLeay Mission, now called Raukkan, on the secluded banks of Lake Alexandrina. I suspected that the hundred-person settlement wasn't set up for tourists—and it was a long way for me to go if it turned out to be for nothing. So I pulled into the more accessible town of Tailem Bend to discover if any trace of Unaipon remained there.

I headed to the visitor centre, where I met the elderly Ray Bolt near some glass cabinets. The centre doubled as a railway museum and felt like an old wooden box carrying a mixture of trash and treasure. Luckily, Ray knew a thing or two about Raukkan.

'I don't know why people have a problem with them,' he said to me conspiratorially. 'They're just people like you and me.'

'Do some people in town have a problem with them?' I whispered back.

'Yeah, some people.' He rested his hand on my arm in a way that felt warm and grandfatherly. 'But I don't understand why you'd have a problem with someone just because they have different coloured skin or are a different race!'

Ray opened the wooden doors of an antique railway ticket holder. Taped to the back was a photocopied image of Unaipon's church that Ray said still stood in Raukkan. Underneath was a photocopy of a plaque with a quote from Unaipon: 'In my despairing moments Providence has enabled me to take heart again and continue my advocacy of the rights of Aborigines to occupy a more worthy place in the life of the nation.'

'How wonderful,' I said.

'It is, isn't it? David Unaipon was a very clever man.' Ray turned to me with a jubilant smile. 'You know, I worked in locomotives for forty-four years!'

He was dressed in a plaid shirt and an old-fashioned black cap that said, 'OLD GHAN TRAIN LOCOMOTIVE DRIVER'. He flicked through photos in a plastic folder, including one from 1983 of a younger, but not exactly young, Ray Bolt. His jolly face beamed from the driver's section of a stout sooty-black locomotive.

'Do you feel sad now that you're retired?' I asked.

'I was at the beginning, and for two years every evening I'd dream I was still working on them,' he said, with a touch of woe.

I could relate. Every night I dreamt I was still working in the *Guardian* office. Sometimes the dreams were so detailed I awoke remembering the words I'd been typing on my laptop: 'Mr Trump, the New York billionaire businessman running for US president . . .' Although lately there had been some signs my dream self was finally catching up to reality, with colleagues interrupting me: 'Didn't we have a farewell for you?' 'You just can't keep away from us, can you?'

Having concluded I had cause to visit Raukkan, I said goodbye to Ray and hit the road.

There isn't much left of the Murray after Tailem Bend; it curves once or twice more before emptying out into Lake Alexandrina, named after Queen Victoria back when she was known as Princess Alexandrina. The undulating land was slicked here and there with silver strokes of shallow water, around which the road was forced to perpetually wind its way. The ground was covered in tussocky dark-olive grass.

By now I had well and truly settled into these long drives through landscapes that melted imperceptibly one into another, and had lost that fear from the start of my trip. My calls home had turned into brief text messages, and the time between those messages grew longer. I now took so much pleasure in a quiet country drive, I could barely recall the version of myself who, only five years before, was a real city bug and didn't have her driver's licence. I felt safe and empowered behind the wheel. I could carry all that I needed, and I had the ability to go any place and—just as importantly—leave any place. When necessary, in a hurry. I was reminded of how the bicycle became a tool, and therefore a potent symbol, of women's liberation in nine-teenth-century Western society.

As I drove I listened to the music of Ngarrindjeri singer-songwriter Ruby Hunter, who died in 2010, and her husband and music partner Archie Roach through my car stereo. The pair fell in love as homeless teenagers living on the streets of Adelaide. They were survivors of the Stolen Generation—a long and dark chapter of twentieth-century Australian history, in which mixed-descent children were removed to 'smooth the pillow of a dying race'. Officials were of the mindset that as the rest of their race died on government and church-funded missions, these children could be assimilated and interbred with white society, then employed as cheap labour for colonial settlers—thereby reducing their burden on the state. A national inquiry into the forced removals produced a 1997 report called *Bringing Them Home*, stating that when a child was forcibly removed that child's entire community lost, often permanently, its chance to perpetuate itself in that child. 'The Inquiry has concluded that this was a primary objective of forcible removals and is the reason they amount to genocide.'

I was particularly haunted by Roach's ballad 'Munjana', a tender and melancholic tale of an abused young woman whose baby boy is taken from her. The separation kickstarts a fresh cycle of violence and pain, and the song ends with a bittersweet reunion over the phone: Munjana has located her now-adult son in a prison far, far away from his homelands.

Still in my car, I took a short ferry ride over a watery gap in the land called The Narrows. The ferry was small enough to be operated by one woman sitting in a plexiglass booth. She wore a high-vis vest, her stringy blonde hair tucked under a knitted beanie. I waved to her, and she returned it with a relaxed shake of her hand before going back to gazing out at the water. What a peculiar life, wadded in silence. Days passing on that ferry going back and forth over this slender funnel of water. Lonely as a lighthouse keeper. It was so serene out here, yet solemn too, with sodden skies and gloomy moors that could inspire a *Wuthering Heights* sequel.

On the other side of The Narrows were a pretty picnic spot and a wooden jetty. At the end of the jetty sat three large pelicans in a tete-a-tete. A muted sun strained through a cloud bank and turned the waters of Lake Alexandrina into polished liquid mercury. I laughed at a group of odd-looking birds pecking in the grass on the bank; their navy and black feathers had the sheen of a freshly brushed tuxedo, and they walked with the exaggerated high-step of a flipper-wearing diver as if their webbed feet were too big for them. I wondered what they were called and took a photo so I could look it up later. They showed a keen interest in my sandwiches, and I had to shoo them away like pigeons.

A light rain was falling on Raukkan, a community of matchbox-shaped homes spread over a series of gentle hills. I drove down the single road that led to the town entrance. There I found an open gate and a low stone wall with a sign reading 'Nguldi arndu' ('Welcome') on one side. After that, the road was bordered by brick houses and then a grassy park with a playground and a couple of colonial-era buildings. All seemed quiet.

I pulled out my phone, which I'd recently used to take a photo of the church taped to the back of Ray Bolt's cupboard. I compared it to one of the buildings before me, a lovely red-and-white brick church—yes, that was it! I walked up to its wooden door, which was shut. There were three people with camera equipment shooting something nearby. I decided to ask a young man who didn't too look busy if he minded taking a photo of me in front of the church. He agreed, and just before he snapped a photo of me grinning, I pulled a fifty-dollar note out of my wallet and held it up.

'You know the church is on the note?' he said.

'No way!' I said.

'Take a look.'

I peered at the note.

It has a portrait of Unaipon, and to his left some technical drawings of his many patents. The best known is a modified handpiece for sheepshearing, which was quickly adopted by the wool industry. Over his lifetime he made patent applications for many other inventions, including a centrifugal motor, the multi-radial wheel, and a mechanical propulsion device, but those patents all lapsed.

Then I saw the church: behind Unaipon's right shoulder is a miniature sketch of a pentagonal building with a bell hanging at the top. Also on the note, standing in front of the church, is a man called Milerum 'Clarence' Long, the last initiated member of his clan, with his wife Polly Beck—a couple who were long gone from Raukkan.

'Amazing,' I said.

I felt humbled to be standing in front of a church that millions of Australians carried a portrait of in their wallets, yet had no idea it still stood, let alone where it could be found.

Unaipon is one of those fascinating figures from Australian history who confounds stereotypes and defies easy categorisation. He read widely, could play the organ, was a non-smoker and teetotaller, a savvy media personality, and a reputable orator who drew links between Ngarrindjeri and Christian spirituality and was obsessed with proper English. He 'embodied the potential—in White terms—for Aboriginal advancement', his biographer Philip Jones once wrote—or, said in another way, he flipped the white man's upper hand by proving he could do everything they could, only better.

He had a complex range of views: he once advocated for a separate Aboriginal state, pushed for Aboriginal self-determination, and appeared to support the end of Aboriginal isolation and a transition into the Australian mainstream facilitated by European-style education. In 1938 he had a disagreement with the New South Wales branch of the Australian Aborigines' League over its National Day of Mourning on Australia Day, striking at the heart of so many questions that remain relevant today. Where does the balance lie in demanding restitution and defending cultural autonomy, while still taking a pragmatic view of surviving and thriving in the white man's world? Is adaptation without assimilation possible? Back then, as now, every person draws the line in a different place.

Unaipon spent the ninth decade of his life in this settlement, having retired from so many years of travelling and preaching. Not one to kick back and relax, in his waning years he was fixated on cracking the secret of perpetual motion—the holy grail of physics that had eluded so many before him ('Oh ye seekers after perpetual motion, how many vain chimeras have you pursued? Go and take your place with the alchemists,' said Leonardo da Vinci in 1494). Unaipon died in 1967, just months before a national referendum ended the exclusion of Aboriginal people from the national census, an expression of their broader participation in Australian society.

I drove up Unaipon Street, which led from the edge of town to the top of a hill. Here the brick homes faced Lake Alexandrina, stretching so far and wide it could be mistaken for a subdued ocean.

Not far from the lake, at the Mouth, the Murray ends its 2500-kilometre journey and is united with the sea. This area is known as Tapawal to the Ngarrindjeri people, a profoundly spiritual place where the fresh water of the river mixes with the saltwater of the sea. There are several of such sites around the country and often sacred to their traditional owners. In a previous trip to north-east Arnhem

Land I had learned of how the mix of two waters has taken on an added meaning as a metaphor for reconciliation: two radically different cultures, such as Yolŋu and European, interacting in a way that's healthy and beneficial to the country as a whole.

But the seasonal processes that have dictated the life of Tapawal for thousands of generations of Ngarrindjeri people have been thrown out of kilter by whitefella ways. So much water has been siphoned away, with the Murray's natural movements halted by dams turning off and on like a tap, that water flowing through here is less than half of what flows under typical conditions. Without enough water to flush out the sand and silt, Lake Alexandrina begins slowly drying up and exposes acid sulphate soils. Several times in the past few decades, the Murray has petered out to the point that the Mouth shut down and only reconnected to the ocean with the assistance of dredge pumps and excavators. Scientists dourly predict climate change is set to cause further stress to the water system.

On this rainy day, the circumspect waters took on the grey hue of the sky. I wrapped my black sports jacket tighter and popped my hoodie up to stop the wind whipping my hair about. I sighed heavily.

As a former Greenpeace activist, I suspect I'm prone to take a doomsday view of the future. But in this case greenies and traditional owners aren't alone in speaking out about water mismanagement. So many farmers living in the Murray-Darling Basin are mourning the state of our rivers and recognising that their livelihoods are at risk. Short-term gains have been too heavily prioritised over long-term sustainability. And the signs are plain to see: rivers across the basin that decades ago gushed with clear water and teemed with native fish are sluggish and dry; on the riverbanks the roots of sickly trees show from erosion; and the reeds that were nurseries for aquatic animals and birds are dying or have already disappeared.

There's no silver bullet to save the Murray. Rather what's needed is a balance between community action and technological fixes, between environmental protection and supporting an industry that feeds our nation, between the states and territories coming together and cooperating in good faith—and, naturally, between Aboriginal and non-Aboriginal ingenuity.

I cast my eyes over the water and allowed its calming presence to fill my mind. I contemplated the distances the water travels to pour into this lake. Afterwards, seeping through a narrow channel between sandbanks, it's pushed back by the roar of the ocean. The two waters—fresh and salt—swirl, a model from nature that could inspire us to set things right.

It was lovely out here. I could feel my spirit mending, my soul growing stronger.

PART TWO
Central Australia

1 JULY
Day 26

'Mm, nice, I wanna fuck you.'

I was sitting in my car with the door open, parked in front of the Alice Springs aquatic centre. Who'd said that? I looked around. I saw plenty of parked cars but there wasn't anybody about.

Then I spied a skinny kid in a bright yellow T-shirt and shorts. Perched on a bike, he sailed past behind my car. He was looking at me, insolently.

Surely not.

'Did you say something to me?' I called to him.

He rode over. 'Hmm?' he said.

My eyes narrowed. 'Just now, did you say something to me?'

For a second, he said nothing. Then he tipped his nose into the air and sneered. 'Yeah, wanna suck my cock?'

I was dumbstruck. 'Oh my god. Are you serious?'

He looked at me without flinching, his eyes black and hollow. 'Yeah, wanna suck my cock?'

'How old are you?'

'Fourteen.'

'I'm thirty-two. More than double your age. Do your parents know what you're saying?'

He didn't reply, just kept staring at me. I felt a flicker of fear. Even though he was just a kid on a bike whose voice hadn't broken yet, I couldn't predict what was about to happen, and that made me nervous.

Mostly, though? I felt sorry for him. Anyone who behaved like that had some serious shit going on in their life.

He kept his bike steady with one foot in a pedal and the other on the ground. 'Suck my cock,' he demanded.

My face scrunched up in disgust. 'You know I'm new here. What kind of welcome is that to give someone?' How could I show this kid that this wasn't the right way to talk to a fellow human being?

'C'mon. Suck my cock.'

He reminded me of a pair of teenage boys I'd seen days ago while passing through a remote South Australian town. They'd been sniggering and throwing rocks at a lizard near some abandoned train tracks. Now, every time this kid said, 'Suck my cock', it was like a pebble hitting my face.

I decided to take a different tack. 'Where's your home?'

He frowned. 'I don't have a home.'

'Where's your,' I wondered how best to rephrase my question, 'place?'

He hesitated, then begrudgingly answered. 'South Australia.' As I contemplated what to do next, he nodded at my car. 'C'mon, how about I get in there and we can fuck?'

'Ha!' I jeered. 'You wouldn't know what to do with me.'

Ugh, was that the right thing to say? All these wrong turns. I felt shock, pity and paralysed by my inability to take control of this situation. For him, however, I suspected today was just another ordinary, rage-filled day spent treating a stranger with contempt.

'C'mon, just suck my cock a little.'

I grimaced, then pushed onwards. 'What's your name?'

He hesitated again. 'Sheridan.'

For a moment neither of us said anything. Then I saw his hand go to his crotch.

'Wanna see it?' He began to unzip.

Something inside of me snapped. I'd been walking on eggshells with this little shit, trying my best to reach him. But now I could see it was hopeless. He was determined to follow through with something truly disgusting.

I quickly got out of the car. My keys had been sitting in my lap, and they dropped to the ground. I walked over to him rigid with fury. 'No, I don't want to fucking see your cock. "Suck my cock, suck my cock. Fuck, fuck, fuck,"' I mimicked.

He quickly backed away on his bike. 'Fuck you, you fucking bitch.'

'No, fuck you!'

When he was a safe distance away, he stopped and turned to face me. He had one more pebble to throw. 'Fuck you, I'm gangster,' he said, making a gang sign.

It was so lame I should have laughed, but I was so angry that I kept shouting and swearing as he rode away.

Later I felt ashamed that I'd been unable to keep my cool.

✻

I arrived at the low-slung town of Alice Springs via the Stuart Highway. Like the thorax of a butterfly, this road splits the continent into two halves, connecting the south and north coasts. The highway begins at a crossroads town, Port Augusta, on the bottom edge of South Australia. I'd headed there almost two weeks after leaving Raukkan; I had spent a few days in Adelaide with a friend and gone camping in the Flinders Ranges.

Just outside Port Augusta's city limits, I had spotted a hitchhiker standing on a lonely, tree-less spot, where the buildings petered out and the desolation of the landscape began to hum. He was a rangy, young blond guy with a duffel bag, his thumb sticking out. He wore a thick hooded jacket and burgundy denim jeans. In the tossing wind and with so many trucks screaming past, I imagined it wasn't a comfortable spot for him.

Without thinking too hard, I screeched to a halt.

As he jogged to catch up to me, I jumped out of my car and began rearranging my things to make room for him in the front passenger seat.

'Where you headed?' I asked when he reached me.

'Woomera! You?' He had a Continental European accent and pronounced 'Woomera' with a long ooh like the hoot of an owl. That wasn't how we Australians said it, but for all I knew we were doing it wrong. The word means 'spear thrower' in the Darug language of western Sydney and is a clever nod to the village's establishment by the Australian defence forces in the mid-1940s as a long-range weapons testing facility.

'Perfect, I'll pass through there,' I said, squashing his bag on top of my boxes of cutlery and food.

I pulled back onto the highway. Soon the sky opened up and there was nothing but tussocky grass and some distant lakes. Their shorelines were so devoid of hills and trees, they looked less like lakes and more like ginormous puddles that had appeared on the flat earth after a morning of heavy rain.

My hitchhiker was called Thomas, a 21-year-old Belgian who had just finished his geology degree at a Melbourne university. While studying he had fallen in with a crew of locals he absolutely adored and had been gutted when the time came to say goodbye. 'I wasn't even that sad to say goodbye to my friends back home,' he said.

I nodded, feeling nostalgic for that intensity of friendship I'd experienced at his age.

'Also, I started to do a bit of modelling,' he added, somewhat abruptly. He told me of being scouted on the streets of Melbourne one day and pulled out a portfolio from the front pocket of his daypack. The main photo was black and white and featured him shirtless, pouting and angular. A not too shabby attempt to channel a Calvin Klein ad.

'You look nice,' I said.

We settled into the drive and, after three weeks of driving solo, I took advantage of having someone in the passenger seat:

'Could you pass me my water bottle?'

'Could you change the music?'

'Could you grab the end of my sleeve and help me take off my jacket?'

Thomas was pliant and obliging—my requests a small price to pay for a free ride.

'Could you take some photos with my phone out the window?' I asked and nodded at my phone sitting in the car cup-holder. Thomas snapped away. 'Oh, and a video,' I said, hastily adding, 'please. I want to remember what it felt like driving all these crazy long distances.'

Thomas told me he was eventually headed to Darwin where he planned to pick up some casual work. I didn't think much of his plan to hitchhike there and said so. 'Listen, hitchhiking might be fine in Europe where there's always a friendly village half a day's walk away. But mate, you're in Australia now. You can die out here. Anything worth seeing between here and Darwin can't be found on the side of the highway. You have to go up some really remote tracks, and once you get stuck out there without food or water or phone reception, you're fucked!'

I had unintentionally slipped into a broad ocker accent. It seemed to happen whenever I began to bluster and brag about the fearsome Outback.

Outside the car, the view became dry and bleak as if to illustrate my point.

I knew I was talking in clichés. Australians love to shake our heads at stories of bumbling German trekkers or young French couples in two-wheel drives, stuck in some remote patch of country, having to be rescued by emergency services. But the truth is, most of us haven't seen half of what these young backpackers have of our own country.

Never mind, Thomas had his own stereotypes of Australians. 'You're all so lazy when it comes to walking. Even short distances, Aussies always choose to drive.'

I didn't disagree. 'That's because most of the country is empty so walking feels long and boring.'

In fact, I liked walking and for this trip had contemplated a combination of hitchhiking and catching public transport, rather than driving. Eventually I'd concluded it would seriously complicate my trip and wasn't worth the hassle.

'How long were you on that corner before I picked you up?' I asked him.

'Three hours,' he admitted.

'Oh my god, see? There's no way I'd want to spend half my day waiting around for rides.'

Thomas had heard that truckies picked up hitchhikers and let them drive, which I thought sounded highly dubious. He added, 'And they run down any animal in their way. They have to, for their own safety and truck safety. When they finally stop for the night, their kangaroo bars are covered in blood and ducks come to lick it all off.'

Ick. There was something grotesque about that image.

He mused over the differences between hitchhiking on our respective continents. 'You know, when you hitchhike in Europe there are lots of young people on the road. But here it's all old people and they get too nervous to pick up a hitchhiker. And when I saw you, I thought no way she's going to stop—a Chinese girl with all this crap in her car?'

'Ha! Showed you.'

Thomas said while living in Melbourne, to his amazement, any time a flash car rolled down the street it was always a Chinese person sitting behind the wheel—often a Chinese person as young as he was. 'What the fuck?' he asked. 'How are they all so rich?'

'Chinese people are so rich now they buy apartments in Australia like you and I buy a new pair of shoes,' I said garrulously. The only thing Australians like doing more than trading tall tales of hapless European backpackers is trading tall tales of nouveau riche Chinese. *Did you hear? They all shop for real estate via helicopter and turn up to house auctions with Gucci handbags full of cold, hard cash.*

Hours passed as the road cut through stumpy grey-green scrub, and it began to feel as if we were driving on a treadmill. I had forgotten what trees looked like. Then we saw that, in fact, we had been going somewhere—for a drug-testing police unit appeared on the horizon. They were picking drivers seemingly at random. When we slowed down, an officer indicated I should pull over.

'That's your fault,' I said to Thomas, who had the long hair of a stoner. He smiled at me nervously.

As soon as I opened my doors, the sniffer dog went nuts. 'Do you have anything in there?' the officer asked sharply.

'Nope,' I said.

'Well, you have something,' he said, stern and impatient.

'Chinese tea?'

'No, something else.'

I shrugged, feeling unruffled. I had done nothing wrong and predicted, with perfect confidence, I would soon be on my way and that later I would recall this incident as a moment of mild inconvenience. Not being afraid of the police is a privilege of belonging to Australia's upper-middle class. I was an upstanding, law-abiding taxpayer. They worked for me.

Three officers pulled my gear from the car in long entrails strewn across the side of the highway. They were unzipping bags and opening lids while the dog excitedly wagged its tail and yipped, trampling over my gear.

Soon it became clear the dog was getting hopped up over one item in particular: Thomas's duffel bag.

'You definitely have something, mate,' the officer in charge said to Thomas.

The policeman was shaped square as a Lego piece. His cap covered his eyes and made him indistinguishable from every cop I'd ever seen on television. When he said 'mate' it sounded menacing, as if nothing could be further from the case.

'Did you have anything in the past?' he growled.

Thomas looked sheepish and nodded. 'A few weeks ago.'

'That stuff stays in your clothes for months,' the policeman said.

The officers took the bag to a nearby table and went through its contents while I packed up my belongings. Thomas stood nearby, looking guilty, his hands dug deep in his pockets. Presumably he was wondering what Australian prison food tasted like.

Finally satisfied that we had nothing on us, the senior police officer issued Thomas a stern warning and let us go. The dog was still barking like mad at the offending bag.

We got back in the car and I pulled away, relieved to be on the road again. Once we'd driven a short distance, Thomas apologised. I said I didn't care, and laughed when he told me how scared shitless that cop had made him feel.

We were now driving through an otherworldly landscape. In the distance were purple-blue flat-topped mesas rising like long loaves of bread from dry plains covered in green shrubs and salt lakes the colour of rust. Spurts of voluminous white cloud suspended in the blue sky made me feel as if I were driving along the cold and dark bottom of the ocean, looking up at a school of jellyfish.

I enjoyed seeing the country through Thomas's eyes, the way he was excited by the Wild-Wild Westness of it all. To the urbane European, Australia represented something vast, raw and unhinged. When a ball of dried spinifex tumbled across the road like in an old Warner Bros. cartoon, Thomas laughed hard. 'That was the most Outback thing I have ever seen!' Later, we spotted a visitor sign sprayed with bullet holes. 'What have I gotten myself into?' he said, but his voice was full of glee.

After another hour we came around a tight curve and across the scene of an old car accident. Feeling nosy, I suggested we stop to have a poke around. Thomas agreed, so I slowed down and parked on the side of the highway.

The car had flipped over, surely speeding on the bend we'd just rounded, and landed stomach-side up. It was crushed like a gold-coloured soft-drink can, and the driver's belongings scattered about the red dirt almost artistically. Having previously visited parts of the Top End, I'd known to expect plenty of bombed-out cars left to rust on the side of the road. The cost to get them towed and repaired often exceeded the value of the car.

I was reminded of one of the finest-ever openings of an essay. It's by Kim Mahood, quoting a Western Desert woman about whitefellas who work in Aboriginal communities: 'Kartiya are like Toyotas. When they break down we get another one.' Mahood continues:

> Unlike the broken Toyotas, which are abandoned where they fall, cannibalised, overturned, gutted and torched, the broken kartiya go away—albeit often feeling they have been cannibalised, over-turned, gutted and torched. They leave behind them dying gardens and unfinished projects, misunderstandings and misplaced good intentions. The best leave foundations on which their replacements can build provisional shelters while they scout the terrain, while the worst leave funds unaccounted for, relationships in ruins and communities in chaos.

Thomas and I walked several times around the flipped car whose wheels were gone. The twisted metal carcass had an unusual racing stripe with a checkerboard design. I felt as if this were the belly of a machine beast with its internal organs on display: battery, radiator, engine, alternator.

'Do you think he died?' I asked Thomas, of the driver.

'I think they might have tried to pull him out here,' he said with the grim concentration of a *CSI* detective, pointing at the driver's window.

But we had already made a fundamental error: the 'he' was, in fact, a 'she'. Scattered letters were addressed to a 'Lucy Sanders' living in Victoria. When I spotted a calculator buried in some grass nearby, I exclaimed, 'She's a scientist!' not considering the many reasons why one might require a calculator. It was unnerving to see Lucy's nine-inch, lace-up black platform boots, plastic gloves, car manual, cleaning spray and unpaid fines being gradually swallowed up by red dirt, among old animal bones and clumps of hardy desert plants.

Eventually a police car pulled up and two officers got out, directing us to bugger off. We didn't need to be told twice.

Back on the road, we found ourselves the smallest and fastest vehicle heading north, overtaking cautious grey nomads in enormous caravans and families in four-wheel drives towing trailers. Whenever we got trapped behind hefty fifty-metre road trains, pulling multiple trailers loaded with livestock, freight or fuel, I'd take the terrifying step of getting into the oncoming lane to overtake.

The sun glowed white-hot like an ember on the horizon, precisely where the road ended. It was blinding, but I had no option but to look directly at it if I wanted to see the road, which had been transformed into a river of liquid gold. Alarming visions of a head-on collision flashed through my mind.

A semitrailer approached us from the other side of the road. My entire car shook nervously as it passed and the harsh jangling from the metal trailers filled the air.

'FUCK!' I said.

A pair of neat bullet holes had appeared in my windscreen. The road train had kicked up a spray of rocks, sending two straight through the glass.

'Shit, that could have killed you!' said Thomas, although afterwards we concluded that this probably wasn't correct. I made a mental note to get my windscreen fixed in Alice Springs and hoped the holes wouldn't turn into a spider web of cracks.

Thomas changed his plans slightly and asked if he might follow me further up the highway. Now he wanted to go all the way to Coober Pedy, a tourist-ridden opal-mining town on the approach to the NT border, which I'd reach the following day. He thought aloud: he could spend a couple of nights there and then nab a ride from someone else. Despite my concerns, he remained steadfast in his resolution to hitchhike the whole way to Darwin. 'Out of principle,' he said.

When the sun dipped behind the horizon and the winter cold came rushing in like a high tide, we decided to stop for the night. We found ourselves on a vacant bit of land next to a petrol station and picked a spot beneath the slowly spinning blades of a tin windmill.

I noticed that my car's front grille was sprayed with terracotta mud, and I was glad that the next day I would enter the Territory without any trace of my city-slicker origins remaining. That bit of dirt announced to the world that a genuine country gal was behind the wheel. A real road warrior.

❋

Having dropped Thomas at Coober Pedy, I crossed the border alone. I was amazed to see the speed limit bump up to 130 kilometres per hour. Then I remembered my friend Ryan—an Arrernte man from Alice Springs who now lived in Sydney—had once told me most of the Territory had no speed limit at all.

I'd seen through Facebook that Ryan, coincidentally, would be back in his home town around the same time as my visit. Over the past few days we'd been chatting via Messenger without locking in any concrete plans to meet. When he had eventually told me his dates, I'd gunned it to Alice to have a couple of days' overlap. I really wanted to hang out—mostly because the golden rule of travel is that knowing a local is better than not, but also because I was excited to see someone from back home and felt it would give me some perspective on how far I'd come since leaving Sydney.

Stuart Highway was named after John McDouall Stuart, the first European explorer to cross the continent south to north and return alive, albeit barely. The names of stops along the highway reflect his party's prime concern: Finke River, Stuarts Well, Alice Springs, Barrow Creek. Stuart's terse regulations issued to his party in 1862 speak volumes about the conditions in which they were travelling and the inclinations of his men:

—No horses are to be abused, kicked, or struck about the head,—When leaving the camp no one is to go without arms and ammunition,—No one is to fire on natives without orders unless in self defense,—When on the march no water is to be used from the canteens without permission of the leader.

I particularly liked his restrictions on notetaking: 'No journal to be kept or notes taken (except the Naturalist)', which I assumed was the equivalent of today's 'no recording devices to be used'.

Once again, the view had changed. I was in a sparse red landscape broken up by piles of speckled-egg orange rocks and tufts of spinifex. A few desert trees dominated the view, one with needle leaves shimmering in the wind like the fringe of a hot jazz flapper dress, and another that was thin and short but sturdy, with coarse bark bleeding dark red sap.

Over the past month, I'd noted my mind was growing more attuned to the natural world. I'm part of that generation frequently derided for recognising more corporate logos than native plant and animal species. In our defence, that just illustrates what constitutes useful information for a life where parrot calls, wattle flowers and roo tracks rarely come up in conversation or are necessary for survival. But now I was paying careful attention to plants, animals and geology, reading any signage erected at tourist sites and national parks. For the rest of my life, I would remember Mungo as the place of wind and yellow sand, and the Murray River shaded by towering gum trees as it hosted paddling Zen pelicans, and now here I was in the Central Desert, where the horizon opened up and tiny slips of pale white ghost gums haunted red rock crevices.

A few hours later I reached Heavitree Gap, a small missing chunk in the MacDonnell Ranges, through which everyone entering Alice Springs from the south must pass. In these ranges oasis-like gorges and spiritually charged waterholes can be found, the only water sources for miles. During the late 1800s these rare wellsprings became the first battlegrounds between the Arrernte people and an outlandish group of pale-skinned men never before seen on their country and who brought with them heavy, horned and hooved, water-polluting animals.

The gap in the ranges is called Ntaripe by the Arrernte people. During colonisation the white men ran a long line of wooden poles through the gap, which is considered sacred to the traditional owners. I'd watched the documentary *First Australians* in which Arrernte Luritja elder Max Stuart said, 'People thought the noise that the telegraph line made was some sort of monster snaking across the country.'

Soon I was approaching Alice Springs. A flimsy service town, it's mainly populated by an itinerant tribe of tourists, hospitality workers, miners, military staff, art dealers and others working in the 'Aboriginal sector'. Even among the Aboriginal residents there are a lot of blow-ins. But the town of twenty-five thousand is the most significant human settlement for thousands of miles. Smack bang in the red heart of the country, it's roughly equidistant from Adelaide on the south coast and Darwin on the north.

When I reached Alice, I drove straight to the aquatic centre to take a shower. But six dollars seemed a little steep for something I could probably get for free soon enough—although I hadn't worked out where to sleep that night, which made me nervous.

I was still in my car, parked at the aquatic centre and recovering from my run-in with Sheridan, when my phone beeped. It was a message from Ryan.

Hey! Welcome! Or as us local Arrernte people say, 'Werte'. He suggested we meet at a bar called Monte's around 8 p.m. I breathed a sigh of relief. I felt unnerved from Sheridan's graphic introduction to Alice and needed to see a friendly face.

I pulled out of the car park, and on the way to town stopped at a petrol station. As I was pumping petrol, who should I see across a multi-lane road but Sheridan. He was still on his bike, talking to an Aboriginal man. From that distance he looked very young and small, but I noticed he still seemed just as indifferent as he had while casually uttering foul obscenities at me. No doubt I'd remember our encounter long after he'd forgotten it.

It was Territory Day, and the intermittent explosion of home-lit fireworks made Alice Springs feel, disconcertingly, like Mosul under attack. I headed towards the pedestrian mall on Todd Street, with art galleries, tourism agencies and cafes, and supermarkets and other brand stores all within a four-block radius. I found Monte's on the corner of some tidy streets. Nearby was the town council, more pubs, a KFC, Thrifty car rental, and the Central Australian radio station and music studio CAAMA. Monte's was probably the closest thing Alice had to a hipster bar, decorated in a circus theme. I wandered in, making my way through a crowd of young locals looking relaxed and happy, sipping on frosty pints of beer and snacking on thick-cut fries.

Ryan was sitting near an outdoor heater. He was a handsome guy with a footballer's physique and tawny-gold skin. Each time I'd seen him there had been a twinkle in his bright blue-green eyes as if life were nothing but a lark—although was that ever the full picture?

He flashed me a megawatt smile. 'Werte, Monica! How's your trip been?'

'Amazing!' I said.

Ryan dressed smartly in a long-sleeved denim shirt and a single diamond stud earring. Even though we were in Alice, he retained the polished sheen of a Sydney urbanite, and suddenly I wished I'd sprung for that shower or at least put on a fresh set of clothes.

'And you?' I asked. 'You happy to be back home?'

Ryan put his outstretched hand on his chest, dramatically. 'So good. I just came back from a big trip with the family out bush. There's nothing like it.'

'You must sometimes feel torn between that life in the big smoke and your life here, hey?'

'Of course. Here there's all this culture and language. My nan— she has some amazing knowledge.'

He led me to the inside section of Monte's, which had a stage for live music. We ordered beers from bar staff who all had tattoos and art-school hairdos. With our drinks, we joined two of Ryan's cousins from different sides of his family. They both looked around the same age as me and Ryan, with Chris dressed in a skate T-shirt and the taller cousin Adam in a T-shirt emblazoned with an image of Muhammad Ali's face.

Ryan introduced me and added, 'She's interested in Aboriginal culture! So I reckoned she oughta meet you fellas.'

As I slid into the leather-bound booth, I smiled weakly. Man, I wondered if that intro made me sound like one of those old-school anthropologists with a thick moustache, wearing a safari suit, trekking through the wilds of Australia to document 'the natives'.

Chris told us about his new job at the Granites Gold Mine, the same company where Adam worked, although this year he was on sabbatical. The mine was four hundred kilometres away from Alice up the remote Tanami Road, but it had its own airport that flew workers in for two-week periods, with one week off in between. They operated around the clock, so they were put on either day or night shifts. Chris worked on an above-ground drill, while Adam drove a truck through ninety kilometres of underground roadways drilled one kilometre below the surface.

'Whoa, like a mini-city,' I said.

'And it's dangerous down there,' Chris said. 'Sometimes if you come head on to a truck, you have to back up and hope to god you can find a space to squeeze into.'

A lot of their mob worked at the mines. On his first day at work, on a lunchbreak, Chris had walked into the canteen and found an entire table taken up by extended family members.

'Dunno if you mind me asking,' I said to Chris, 'but how much do you make working at the mine?'

He hesitated and looked coy, but Adam was happy to jump in. 'I make 120K.'

I whistled—it was double what I'd been making at *The Guardian* as a deputy culture editor. On the other hand, mining is repetitive, physically demanding, lonely work far away from your family: not a life I would quickly sign myself up to. Not while I had other options, anyway.

Adam said he'd already bought his own home and was paying off a second, 'so my son doesn't have to'. He was tall and powerfully built. I noticed that his Everlast shirt was emblazoned with a quote beside Muhammad Ali's face: 'I'm young, I'm handsome, I'm fast, I'm pretty, and can't possibly be beat.' But in contrast to the boxer's braggadocio, Adam seemed softly spoken and a man of simple priorities: to live peacefully and provide for his five-year-old son.

As the guys chatted away, I could tell mining was just a paycheque; their real passions were footy, motorbikes and heading out bush. Ryan grinned at me. 'Most of these boys use their first few paycheques to buy a Holden Commodore.'

I asked about the freak hail storm that had recently swept through this town. I'd seen photos and videos posted on Facebook: trees had come down over cars, and a river of ice had flowed down Todd Street Mall. Ryan's cousins told me it had been utterly bizarre—the entire city had come to a standstill.

'Desert people get super excited when it rains,' explained Ryan, who'd been in Sydney when the storm hit.

In Alice, rain is a brief and infrequent interruption to long periods of dry. As desperately thirsty plants and animals take a refreshing drink, it transforms the land.

'When it rains here everyone goes out for a drive,' said Ryan. 'Then I moved to Sydney and found when it rained, my flatmates would just get grumpy and complain. But me?' He mimed pressing his nose against the window in a marvellous impression, his eyes lit up in wonder.

After an hour we left Monte's and headed to another bar. As we walked the guys gave me a bit of background to Arrernte territory: their land covers much of Central Australia, including Alice, and can be subdivided into dialects so distinct they're arguably languages in their own right.

'Luritja riffraff,' snorted Chris derisively, as we passed half a dozen scamps loitering about on pushbikes in the street. Chris was Alyawarra Arrernte, and he was deliberately needling Ryan whose grandmother was Luritja.

Ryan took his cousin's bait with a smile. 'We're only home to some of this country's top scientists, political leaders, artists, thinkers—not to mention the nation's greatest warriors with the finest physiques.' He pointed at his buff body and pulled a duck face.

We tried a bar on Todd Street but a beefy bouncer told us there were 'too many guys' in there already. Eventually we wound up at The Rock Bar, not far from Monte's, having walked a full circuit. It was a small bar with an all-black facade and two large windows facing the street. Inside, paintings of rock luminaries Jim Morrison, Jimi Hendrix, Gene Simmons and David Bowie were hanging on the walls. The bar was plastered in beer ads, and behind the bartenders a glowing fridge stocked with beer bottles was the brightest object in the room.

It was sweaty and noisy—also a bit of a sausage fest—and the patrons, mostly in the vicinity of my age, seemed more working class than those in Monte's.

Another thing about the crowd and about Alice more generally: I'd been surprised to discover how multicultural the town was. In just half a day I'd seen Indians, Chinese, Filipinos, Sudanese, Zimbabweans, Americans, South Americans and Europeans, as well as Aboriginal and Anglo Australians. The stereotype of the Outback is that it's racially monochrome, but I was learning that since the early days of the gold rush, mining and major infrastructure projects have drawn people from all over the globe to the most remote corners of Australia.

Chris bought a round of shots, and the Baileys sloshed about as he passed the glasses back to us over the heads of three rows of patrons. The floor was sticky, and a DJ played shitty commercial music. It was already midnight, long past my usual bedtime on this trip, and everyone in the bar was halfway to hammered.

More of Ryan's family had joined us—his cousin Jennifer and her young aunt Amy (no relation of Ryan's), although Jennifer called her 'Mum' as is customary for her people. Together we clinked our shot glasses and threw back the drinks, although I only drank half of mine. It was strange—I was usually quite a good drinker. In Sydney I loved nothing better than to drain ice-cold glasses of white wine on a Friday night after a week of intense work. I'd feel my tongue loosen and let my inner extrovert take the wheel. But now I had no raging weekend mad dogs to release. After all this time in the bush, with consistently early nights and dawn rises, I seemed to have lost the appetite for alcohol.

Ryan nodded at an Aboriginal guy with a black moustache sipping his beer with some friends at another table. 'Danny Glover,' Ryan said to us. All night he and his cousins had been playing a game where they spotted strangers and associated them with a celebrity.

'Nah, nah, Richard Pryor,' replied Chris, and everyone laughed.

The women and I were chatting when Jennifer suggested we go outside for a smoke. I didn't smoke but agreed to tag along, happy to take a breather from all the sweaty, drunken bodies.

We elbowed our way through the crowd and emerged to an outdoor section at the back of the bar, where patrons sucked on cigarettes between slurping plastic pints of beer.

I asked the women what dating was like here—my usual 'in' with women I've just met.

'The NT has the highest ratio of men to women in the country,' said Jennifer. She had a wide, open, pretty face and her dark hair was dyed sandy blonde.

'Clearly I should move to the NT,' I said.

'But you don't want to date any of them.'

While Jennifer looked a few years younger than me, Amy was probably a few years older, with long brown hair and lips painted fire-engine red. I suspected the beaming smile plastered on Amy's face was a happy side effect from the drinking. 'The men here are terrible! Don't mess around with them. Although you're only passing through so it'd probably be okay. Otherwise it isn't a good idea because everyone would know.'

'Don't shit where you eat,' I said.

'Exactly,' she replied, although with her slurring it was more like 'essshhhackly'. Amy had first moved to Alice as a baby thirteen-year-old from remote Central Australia. 'I can proudly say I've never fucked anyone in Alice Springs.' She jabbed her elbow into my side and winked. 'Darwin, on the other hand!'

Back inside we joined the guys on the dancefloor. Everyone in the bar was letting loose, laughing, drinking, dancing. Jennifer seemed less inebriated than everyone else. As she danced among the madness, straight-backed and dressed in a tan turtleneck sweater that complimented her figure, she wore a cool, sardonic expression.

A young man in a chequered shirt and denim jeans sidled up to her shyly. His hair was styled into stiff peaks using cheap hair wax. 'Howyadoin?' he managed to say, his eyes glued to the ground.

'Good, thanks,' she replied politely.

He nodded and his eyes flickered up to her for just a second, before they settled back onto an evidently comforting spot on the floor. He cleared his throat. 'Howyadoin?'

She erupted into giggles and whispered to me, 'Oh my god, that guy can only say one thing! I like country guys, but I've never met anyone that country.'

I was about to respond but the words died on my lips because I noticed Amy was staring at me peculiarly. She took a step closer to me and, over the din, shouted, 'Your English is soooo good!'

I smiled wryly. 'Well, I was born here.'

She was standing so close she had me backed into a wall, and she still wore that huge, stupid grin. 'I'm so sick of foreigners who can't speak English!'

'Technically, I'm not a foreigner,' I said, but it fell on deaf ears. She was looking at me as if I were a dog reciting Shakespeare.

'Look, look, I'm Aboriginal and your English is better than mine!'

It was close to 2 a.m. and I was feeling unsure and unhappy about the prospect of driving to a campsite. Ryan and Chris, also in town temporarily, were staying together in a hotel room. To my immense gratitude, Ryan nudged Adam to come to the rescue.

'Thank you, thank you, thank you,' I said, accepting his offer to sleep on his spare mattress.

'No worries,' he said.

I turned to Ryan, who pulled me onto the dancefloor. I half-shouted over the music, 'Teach me some Arrernte!'

I repeated after him until I felt I'd remember it the next day:

Werte—'Hey, welcome.'

Unte mwerre—'How are you?'

Mwerre antherre—'Well, thanks.'

Ryan put his hand on his chest in mock appreciation. 'Ooh, Monica, you keep speaking like that and I might fall for you.'

I shook my head, smiling. *Charming bastard.*

The guys were looking at a roughneck hanging off the end of the bar, dressed in a daggy cut-off denim vest. 'Shannon Noll, but missing his little—' said Chris, pointing at where the former *Australian Idol*'s triangle goatee would be on his chin. If you squinted, perhaps the man could pass for Nollsy minus the chin muff.

Everyone exploded with laughter.

'Okay, okay, I've got it,' said Ryan between gasps. He pointed to another patron—a pale white guy in a hoodie. 'Mark Zuckerberg!'

✻

I crashed at Adam's that night and explored Alice the following day. Adam had kindly offered to let me stay a few extra nights while I figured out my next move. His son was staying with his mum over the weekend, so I slept the night on a spare mattress on the floor of the boy's bedroom, surrounded by Lego pieces and toy cars.

Central Australia is renowned for its art. The region's dot-style of art was first transferred onto canvas in the Papunya community, 250 kilometres north-west of Alice, and quickly became synonymous with Aboriginal art more generally. Some of the country's most famous painters have come from here, such as Emily Kame Kngwarreye and Clifford Possum Tjapaltjarri, with works selling for millions of dollars.

At the Araluen Arts Centre on the western edge of town, I saw paintings that blew me away, including those by the region's arguably most famous painter, Albert Namatjira. Now that I'd seen for myself the red rocks and thin white saplings that star in his keenly composed, sensitive watercolours, the works seemed to take on a deeper meaning. I noticed that many paintings were by artists who shared surnames: Kngwarreye, Tjakamarra, Mpetyane, Napaltjarri. The notion of the artistic 'lone genius' is at odds with the spirit of Central Desert communal life, so artistic dynasties aren't uncommon; stories, designs and painting traditions are passed down through the generations.

Back in the town centre, many of the commerical galleries I visited that lined Todd Street Mall covered every inch of their wall space in paintings, sometimes sloppily hung, and piled up their bargain bins with unstretched, colourfully painted canvases. Most of the art being sold in Alice originated in the tiny Aboriginal communities that dot the remote desert. The town acts as an artistic hub, and a journalist friend of mine once described the mainly non-Aboriginal gallerists as pimp, benefactor and manager rolled into one for their Aboriginal painters. That said, when I profiled some Central Desert painters while at *The Guardian*, they gave me the impression that, in contrast to the carpetbaggers rampant in the 1970s, their relationships to their art centre managers and gallery curators were mutually beneficial. I also kept in mind it was hard to get a sense of how pervasive such feelings were.

In a cafe on Todd Street, I ordered a piece of chocolate cake and used the town's free public wi-fi. I overheard a young family at the next table chatting in American accents. It reminded me that last night Ryan and his cousins had mentioned an American base called Pine Gap, half an hour's drive out of town. They said all the Americans lived in big fancy homes and celebrated Halloween, and whenever you asked them what they did out at the base, they'd say, 'I'm the janitor' or 'Just some grounds-keeping work'. Access to the base is heavily restricted, but on my phone I googled photos and saw a series of white domes hidden in the Central Australian hills, like oversized Kool Mints.

The base completes round-the-clock US control of spy satellites and plays a 'significant role' in supporting intelligence and military operations, as revealed in the 2013 Snowden leaks. That means the base has been contributing to US military operations in Afghanistan, Iraq and Syria, and drone operations in other parts of the world. The location's remoteness is no accident—it offers a place relatively absent of signal interference and can't be reached by spy ships passing in international waters.

But not everyone in Alice has appreciated the giant target sign painted in their backyard—why should they get involved in someone else's war? The Pine Gap Women's Peace Camp in 1983 not only became part of a long-running campaign against the base but birthed an unexpected feature of Alice: it has a healthy lesbian population, one of the highest outside the rainbow pockets in Australia's capital cities.

Glancing out the window I saw a group of young Aboriginal people wearing Everlast tracksuits cross the street. A woman in her early twenties had a baby in a stroller and a couple of little kids trailing behind her. It reminded me of something a grey nomad once said to me about visiting Australian country towns: 'You see babies pushing babies.' All of a sudden I was feeling my age. In the city to be thirty-two, single and childless is perhaps a little late in the day, but in the countryside you're so over the hill you are nothing but a speck in the sky.

I had mixed feelings about being single. It was one of those things I mostly didn't think about, and then I'd fall for someone who inevitably didn't like me back and suddenly I'd be tearing my hair out and cursing the universe and everyone in it for my perpetual loneliness. I'd never had a long-term relationship; the longest I'd dated someone was three months. I'd never been in love, not really. And it wasn't uncommon for me to go long periods without sex—in my early twenties I'd let five years slip away between encounters. I'd stopped analysing why, having long ago settled upon the simplest of explanations: it was bad luck, plain and simple. Having so much good fortune in most other aspects of my life, it seemed almost greedy to demand more.

I wandered into Red Kangaroo Books with the leisurely sense of being a holidaymaker, browsing titles on history, nature, the Central Desert and local languages. Eventually I settled on buying two books. The first was *Whitefella Culture* by Susanne Hagan, which is slim enough to be a stapled-together pamphlet, with a bright orange cover. Inside it's written in plain English and illustrated in the style of an aeroplane safety manual. It uses common scenarios to demonstrate how Central Desert and whitefella cultures diverge and the best ways to navigate differences. For example, from the chapter 'Being Friendly':

> The new whitefella thought Joe and the other artists would smile at him and ask him questions. He thought they might ask him about his trip and how soon he and his family would be coming. That is how white people show friendliness when they meet someone new. It's a bit different in Aboriginal culture. Aboriginal people don't like to hurry into meeting new people. They like to wait awhile and see what the new person is like. Then they know more how to act toward that person. And Aboriginal people think it is rude to ask lots of questions, especially to strangers.

I found its matter-of-fact style disarming. And by inverting the dominant gaze, it shows how through the eyes of Central Desert peoples, whitefella ways can seem bafflingly peculiar, such as their penchant for direct eye contact, separating work and family, using praise as a form of encouragement, and stinginess with their personal belongings.

The second book was Michael Morcombe's comprehensive *Field Guide to Australian Birds*. I was tired of being unable to name all the colourful birds I kept encountering. Each of the 850 species listed in the book is depicted in a beautiful illustration and a compact yet evocative description that verges on literary. I looked up the comical bird I'd seen on the drive to Raukkan. It was the 'purple swamphen' and part of its entry read: 'clumsy, leg-dangling, crash-landing flight. Great variety of sounds: harsh, abrupt "kak, kak" rising to sharp, grating "kiark, ki-aark"; also querulous, grating "qua-ark" and loud, harsh squawks of warning when with small chicks. At night often gives wild shrieks and boomings, perhaps basis of bunyip stories.'

I had been birdwatching just once in my life, with a friend of mine (who was not into birds) and his friend Daniel who was the enthusiast among us—also known as a 'twitcher'. One morning we went out bush together, and like the Yoda to my Luke Skywalker, Daniel mentored me in the ways of the twitcher: how to identify a bird, such as by observing its size, colour, markings, tail and body shape, as well as how to adjust your binoculars, and ideal times and conditions. I found his unbridled passion for these feathered creatures to be contagious. Daniel spoke of the 'black-faced cuckoo shrike', 'Australian ringneck', 'singing honeyeater' and 'rufous whistler' like they were old friends whose personalities and habits he was deeply intimate with. At times he need not even see the bird or hear its call; rather, hearing the flap of its wings was enough for him to identify the 'budgerigar' or 'crested pigeon' in question.

I headed over to Woolworths, a couple of streets back from Todd Street Mall, and on the way from a nearby camera store I purchased a $200 pair of binoculars. A fair bit of money, but I figured a worthy investment into my new life as a twitcher. As I wandered through the supermarket aisles, I called Adam to find out what he was doing for dinner.

'No plans,' he said.

'Great! Let me cook for ya. Do you like salmon?'

He hesitated but said, 'I'll eat whatever.'

'It's cool if you don't like that, I can cook whatever.'

'I don't really like seafood.'

Of course, we were a million miles from fresh salmon. I considered my alternatives: a couple of T-bone steaks? Lamb sausages? Then I spotted what I felt confident was the perfect meat to cook for a Central Australian.

Having bought groceries for the coming week, I drove back to Adam's house, a stone's throw from Todd River. It was pretty much a river by name only: if you saw it with water more than three times, you were considered a local. Currently the riverbed was a long sand-filled trail, lined with gum trees that had powder-white trunks.

I unlocked Adam's front door with a key he'd given me, then walked in lugging my bags of groceries. I found him in the kitchen texting on his phone. I dumped the bags on the countertop and said gleefully, 'Hey, guess what? I have kangaroo steaks!'

His face fell.

'Oh no!' I said.

'It's just that usually I like it fresh.'

'Shit.' I stared at my sad steaks in their styrofoam trays wrapped in plastic. 'This is like you saying, "I'm going to cook you Chinese", and then breaking open a packet of two-minute noodles.'

As I unpacked the groceries, Adam told me how his people cooked kangaroo. After the roo was gutted, its carcass was stitched up using a sharp-tipped stick and secured with some intestine. They singed all the hair off in a fire, and cut the feet and tail off, discarding the feet but cooking the tail. The rest of the roo was also prepared in the hot coals.

'It's so tasty when there's a lot of fat on it,' said Adam. 'So delicious. No garnish necessary.'

All of a sudden his cat Diddle leapt onto the counter. I'd woken up that morning to her prodding me with her clean white paws, looking at me curiously with yellow-moon eyes. She was named after the nursery rhyme 'Hey Diddle Diddle', and her fur was imprinted with a tortoiseshell saddle on her back.

'Hey, Diddle,' Adam said to her, as she collapsed into a lazy heap on the counter.

She immediately meowed as if to say, 'Not bad, Adam, you?'

He swore she never shed fur, even though she slept on his bed and on their charcoal grey couch. She was the perfect housemate.

'Do you eat the eyes of the kangaroo?' I asked Adam as I stroked Diddle's silky fur. She rumbled like a motorcycle engine and wore a satisfied look.

He nodded. 'And we drink the blood. We believe it makes your blood thick.'

That way of thinking was familiar to me. In traditional Chinese medicine, a tiger penis boiled in soup enhances virility, and bear bile is used to fortify the liver. I found it novel to discover how our respective cultural worlds overlapped.

We let my second-rate, store-bought steaks remain on the dinner menu. As Adam told me of how his mob put a tin can underneath the kangaroo's slit throat to drink the blood hot, I prepped the veggies I would roast to accompany the roo.

Adam's favourite meat was emu. 'I would do anything for emu meat,' he said wistfully, explaining it's more of a hassle to prepare than roo because you have to pluck it first, and during hunting the emu always shit themselves, leaving a mess of green poo.

He shook his head slowly. 'I wouldn't know what to do if emu was my totem.'

As with many Aboriginal groups, Arrernte people are forbidden from eating their totem, which dictates hunting Law and the protection of breeding grounds—to the point that a totem can be regarded as kin. I'd once met a Wiradjuri woman who told me her dead brother occasionally visited her as his totem: a glaring crow, making clear his disapproval with whatever she happened to be doing. It didn't annoy her; she was glad to still have his guidance.

Arrente creation stories that feature ancestral beings with the ability to morph in and out of animal form loom large on their cultural landscapes. Such stories are invoked in song, art, ceremony and dance, the animal attributes portrayed with a startling likeness. They help keep human existence anchored to the natural world—people, species and Country are interlinked in a divine trinity.

A totem is usually an animal or plant, but there are also totems of wind, sun, water or cloud. 'In fact,' wrote anthropologists Baldwin Spencer and F.J. Gillen in 1899, 'there is scarcely an object, animate or inanimate, to be found in the country occupied by the natives which does not give its name to some totemic group of individuals.' Among the more unusual entries on their list of totems collected from across the Central Desert were 'monster or mischievous spirit', 'uncircumcised youth' and 'laughing boy'.

'What's your totem?' I asked Adam.

'The cockatoo,' he said, as he put the kettle on so we could drink the Chinese tea I'd gifted him. Turns out, it's possible to have totem-envy. 'My grandfather's totem is the wedge-tailed eagle—I wish that was mine,' said Adam.

I asked if he'd read a recent story in the local newspaper of a wedgie trying to make off with a young boy at the Desert Park's famous bird show. The paper included a dramatic photo of the eagle wearing a fierce expression, wings spread like a fighter plane's and talons sunk into the hoodie of a terrified six-year-old. Luckily the kid only suffered superficial injuries, but the eagle was retired from performing.

'Those birds are incredible,' said Adam. 'They can take down whole kangaroos. Americans are so obsessed with their bald eagle, it's even their national bird, but it only hunts fish.' He added contemptuously, 'It's just a glorified seagull.'

With two steaming mugs of green tea, we opened up my paper map of the Northern Territory. Adam pointed out spots of interest: this was where the annual Finke Desert Race was held that he had participated in, this was the Granite Gold Mine where he and Chris worked, and here was his home community of Wallace Rockhole.

Adam's grandfather was born out bush, the traditional way, then as a young man moved about a lot for work before founding Wallace Rockhole. Around a hundred people now lived there permanently, most of whom were related to Adam. He'd come to Alice for high school, living at the house of an aunt and uncle who had a son around the same age.

'You might have to send me more of this stuff,' he said of the tea, taking another appreciative sip. I was glad—not everyone finds Chinese tea palatable.

Adam was taking a year off from the mines to spend time with his young son. He partly blamed the breakdown of his marriage on the long periods away from home and admitted working at the mines wasn't sustainable long-term. He had grown up horseriding—his grandfather was a former stockman—and harboured dreams of establishing a tourism venture in which he would take visitors for rides out on Country. 'We'd point out different things from our culture,' he told me.

'Sounds like a fabulous idea,' I said sincerely.

In the meantime, during his sabbatical Adam was picking up other career skills: working as a teaching assistant at his son's school and now, during school holidays, as a park ranger. Soon they would head out bush for a few days to do a controlled burn.

'Scary, right?' I asked.

'Yeah, those fires can turn on you any minute.'

The other day on duty he'd watched a legless skink die in the fire.
'Did you feel bad?'
'Nah. Pretty soon after a wedgie swooped down and collected it.'
Takeaway barbecued skink.

Having popped a tray of cut-up potatoes, garlic, brussels sprouts and carrot in the oven, we decided to take the short drive to Anzac Hill or Untyeye-artwilye (corkwood story) while dinner was baking. We took my car, with Adam in the passenger seat pointing the way through suburban streets and then onto a road that wound up a steep hill covered in ghost gums. From the car park it was a few steps up onto a platform at the hill peak where an Anzac memorial had been erected. Both the Australian flag and NT's orange-and-black flag, bearing Sturt's desert rose, flapped about in a restless wind. We were just in time to catch the cooling sun turn the mountain ranges purple. The Ntaripe gap was thrown into dramatic relief.

'There are a few Dreaming stories attached to the gap,' said Adam. He told me one speaks of the ranges as the bodies of two ancestral caterpillars that will touch one day; another says the gap is a chunk of caterpillar bitten by a dingo.

All up, we could see more than a dozen land features—hills, rocks, swamps and rivers—that were the battlegrounds, cocoon sites, dance grounds and campsites used by the caterpillar ancestors: Yeperenye, Ntyarlke and Utnerrengatye.

In *First Australians* I'd learned of another gap further south which was a men's site forbidden to women. There, in 1883, one of the area's first constables William Henry Willshire, accompanied by three 'lubras' (Aboriginal women), encountered a group of Central Desert men. The men demanded the party clamber over the 500-foot range. Willshire wrote in his journals: 'at first they assumed defiant and bellicose attitudes, but they were cleared out and passed on, followed by the lubras, who picked up some rags, bushes, and grass, and made coverings over their faces, and walked blindfolded, led by the sound of the horse's footsteps and the black boy's voice through the Gap'—such was the care that the women took to avoid infractions on such sacred Law.

Willshire was a nasty piece of work who summarily executed Central Desert men who interfered with herds of cattle. At least thirteen deaths can be attributed to him, although the true number is likely to be higher for he was not fond of official paperwork. In contrast, his personal journals are filled with memorable passages revealing his sadistic streak. In one description of an encounter with 'cattle killers', he wrote:

> It's no use mincing matters—the Martini-Henry Carbines at this critical moment were talking English in the silent majesty of these great eternal rocks. The mountain was swathed in a regal robe of fiery grandeur, and its ominous roar was close upon us. The weird, awful beauty of the scene held us spellbound for a few seconds.

As is often the case with the cruellest of men, he applied twisted logic to his treatment of the fairer sex. He wrote perversely of Central Desert women: 'Men would not remain so many years in a country like this if there were no women, and perhaps the Almighty meant them for use as He has placed them wherever the pioneers go.' These proclivities finally triggered a chain of events culminating in Willshire's exit from this region of Australia.

In 1891 Willshire ordered his Central Desert troopers to shoot two men in cold blood at Tempe Downs Station and wound one of the men, Ereminta, allowing Willshire to personally cut this man's throat. Historians believe Willshire was infatuated with Ereminta's partner, Nungoola. After the murder, Willshire took Nungoola to his camp at Boggy Water. Only with these atrocities were higher authorities alerted to the fact that the intemperate Willshire was not well placed in his role, and he was removed. He later spent twelve years working at an Adelaide abattoir as a nightwatchman.

There is still a street in Alice named in his honour.

✳

As I travelled through the Tjoritja (MacDonnell Ranges), having left Adam's house and headed west from Alice, I realised I had never before seen such beautiful rocks. Some are smooth and pink like raw steak or have the sheen of cold roast beef; others are stacked in layers like a lasagna; and there are car-sized rocks like square scoops of melting ice cream or jelly cut cleanly with a knife.

The caterpillar humps of the Tjoritja were visible wherever I drove, a sweep of shadow-streaked ridges. Winding through the Tjoritja is the Larapinta Trail, beginning at Alice. Over several weeks it takes walkers through 223 kilometres of arid, stony, mountainous terrain. I was driving it over several days. Here and there I stopped at secretive pools of cold, dark green water guarded by rock walls. Ghost gums were growing, impossibly, from sheer cliff faces, and their smooth, skeletal limbs ended in hands of gumleaves reaching up to the sky.

The ranges are that particular Australian shade of orange-red. Having sustained an eternity of weathering, much of the continent is laced with iron oxide lending the land such a distinct hue. Yet this colour doesn't appear much in the lands upon which Sydney is built; there the views are coloured by blue-green gums growing in a thick cover over yellow soil and dark rocks. To me, the orange-red is exotic—there's something novel about being in a place that feels like postcard Australia. It is the Australia of tourism ads and Outback westerns.

On my third day in the ranges I camped at a picturesque spot by the venerable Larapinta (Finke River). The water was so clean and clear that it reflected the long strip of land and its huddles of elderly gum trees, sculptural rocks and fringing reeds, like a Rorschach inkblot test. Larapinta is touted by tourism literature as 'one of the oldest rivers in the world'; scientists say it has followed the exact same course for at least the past fifteen million years. 'If Uluru symbolises the nation's heart, the Finke must be its ancient artery,' a journalist once wrote.

In the distance I could see the climax of Tjoritja's ageless ridges: the towering Mount Sonder. For a few minutes at the beginning of each day, it is lit up with licks of pink sunrise.

I drove down a dirt track that meandered along the course of the river. Eventually I found a spot back from the riverside, nestled among some shady gums and a patch of metre-high, drought-hardy buffel grass. After getting out of my car and doing a long catlike stretch, I ran my palms over the cylindrical seed heads of the grass and found them furry to the touch.

This invasive species hitched a ride to Central Australia with Afghan cameleers, as they were known, beginning in the 1860s. In truth, the cameleers not only hailed from Afghanistan but also parts of what today we call Iran, India, Pakistan, Egypt and Turkey. They weren't strangers to land dominated by harsh, hot sands and rock. In a time before highways and monster road trains, these camel riders were the sole cross-country transport line for supplies, tools, produce, surveying equipment, mail and sometimes even water. While diverse in nationality they shared the Muslim faith and across the Outback built mosques and special places facing Mecca where they prayed.

As is often the case, one innovation begets another. Their obsolescence was sealed as they helped build major infrastructure projects including the Overland Telegraph Line, linking communication from Australia's north to south, and The Ghan (the Afghan Express) railway named in their honour.

Despite the decades their community had spent living and working in Australia, the White Australia Policy was to ensure they had no permanent place here.

More than once over the past few days, I had spotted a line of footprints in the sand, each print the shape of a giant apple cut in half. Reportedly 750,000 feral camels are wandering throughout the Australian Outback—the largest wild population of camels in the world—sprung from the founding population brought by the cameleers.

Their saddles were stuffed with buffel grass that left a bread-crumb trail across the countryside. Later the grass was deliberately planted for dust control, after local cattlemen noticed it could with-stand heavy grazing. Like so many introduced species, buffel grass is an aggressive coloniser; it steals nutrients from native grasses and sedges. A day ago at Ellery Creek I'd read park signage explaining how native lizards, mammals and birds seem to like the grass less than native flora, and where it grows their populations drop. The grass also feeds very hot, long-lasting fires that kill river red gums and other native plants. Sandy creek beds once acted as firebreaks, but lined with buffel grass they're like detonating lines that spread the flames; most sinisterly, the grass is quick to regrow after these intense fires, like a zombie that just won't die. Slashing it only increases its growth rate. The weed is so pervasive, there's no hope in hell of hand-pulling or chemically annihilating it from the entire vast, unpeopled Central Australian desert. One expert called the grass 'the botanical equivalent of the Cane Toad'.

But I struggled to regard the grass as objectionable, while this sea of nodding, golden heads bobbed in the wind and caught the afternoon sunlight. I sat back in my camp chair almost feeling drunk. Fluttering moths spelt out lucky figure eights in the air, and a friendly magpie lark pecked for crumbs by my feet. I wanted to catch that amber light spreading like honey over everything, because I knew when it trickled away the dreaded cold returned, as it had each evening of this trip.

Later on, keen to change up my usual routine of huddling around a fire in the wintry night, I left my tent set up and drove through the darkness towards the highway. After a short drive up, I took a left turn onto a road that ended at the Glen Helen Homestead Lodge—a long, low building with a corrugated iron roof—one of the few resorts in this far-flung patch of country.

Inside, the lodge was busy with tourists who, like my father, did not consider camping or caravanning their idea of a holiday. Seeing as it was only 7 p.m. and outside the bitter chill had already set in, I could see their point of view. I felt cosy in this heated, wood-panelled lodge, divided into a restaurant and pub. Framed paintings by Albert Namatjira and his extended family hung on whitewashed walls.

After ordering a beer, I sat on a burgundy leather couch with my diary, hoping that if I took slow enough sips I might draw out a few hours here.

A middle-aged woman piped up from the other end of the couch. 'What are you writing? Is that a journal?'

Her husband, sitting on a sofa adjacent to her, looked up at me for a second and then went back to reading his newspaper.

The woman smiled. 'Are you writing a book?'

'Yes, I *am* writing a book!' It was the first time anyone had presumed this of me.

'Fiction or non-fiction?' she asked, taking a sip of red wine.

'Non-fiction.' I hoped my smile seemed mysterious and in keeping with the aura of a travel writer. I told her about my trip and how young people from Sydney know little of the country outside our main cities—how I wanted to change that for myself. I hesitated before explaining the other key driver of the trip, because I couldn't read which way it might land. 'Also, I want to learn more about Aboriginal Australia.'

She smiled. 'I've been absolutely blown away by the Aboriginals!'

She and her husband were at the tail end of a trip in which they'd driven down the Stuart Highway from Darwin to Central Australia. As a horticulturist she responded strongly to the philosophy 'you give to the land because it gives to you' and had been fascinated to learn about their complex marriage system. And to her own surprise, she'd been impressed by the ancient rock art at Kakadu National Park.

'I never liked Aboriginal art before. But now that it's been explained to me, what the different symbols mean, I can look at an artwork and understand it.'

Didn't that say it all? It's much easier to appreciate someone else's culture once you had stepped inside of it and had someone from that culture, or someone in the know, guide you through it.

I breathed a sigh of relief.

Then she veered straight into the badlands of political incorrectness. 'We have Aboriginals in Tassie but they're not full-blooded like up here. This trip completely changed my views on them! I'd always thought they were nothing but druggies and alcoholics.'

I held my tongue. Out of habit I kept my cards close to my chest when first meeting someone, as I knew my views were considered 'extreme' by many Australians and could rub people the wrong way. I didn't see this as self-censorship so much as healthy self-moderation. Although I wondered, as well, if I was simply justifying taking the less confrontational, less courageous option.

She told me her husband had visited the Territory some thirty years ago, and he felt that the severe legal restrictions on alcohol had transformed these communities for the better. 'I mean we still saw some drunk ones, but otherwise I was blown away. I have a new-found respect for them.'

As she took another sip of red wine, I thought how easy it would be to make the case that if some Aboriginal people had terrible drinking habits, who did she think they'd learnt them from? But I didn't want to throw her off. She wasn't exactly a poster girl for anti-racism, but she'd taken an encouraging step in the right direction. Were our trips so different? We were both eager to learn more about someone else's world while navigating a minefield of cultural faux pas. She was a good illustration of the transformative potential of travel.

I asked her about the buffel grass, wanting her take as a horticulturist. 'I know it's a weed but I can't help but find it beautiful.'

'A weed is simply a plant that isn't wanted,' she said. 'Every plant is native in one place and has the potential to be a weed in another.'

I was reminded of the havoc that certain types of eucalypt has wreaked overseas. It's a distinctly Australian plant—for hundreds of thousands of years, our continent hosted hundreds of eucalypt species with only a handful moving up into Asia as an endemic species. But after colonisation, humans took this fast-growing, swampland-draining, versatile hardwood across the oceans, and now it has become one of the world's most widely planted trees—though not without problems. Take Portugal, where the eucalypt is the most abundant tree, covering a quarter of all forested land. Thanks to the natural oil in gumleaves, the country now suffers the sort of ferocious bushfires Australians are all too familiar with. And as a Portuguese environmentalist once said, unlike the gum forests of Australia theirs are deathly quiet: 'Our fauna can't feed on it; they can't find refuge in it. Our insects can't eat eucalyptus, so there are no birds. We should introduce koalas. At least there would be something cute to look at.'

Australians are used to thinking of our country as being uniquely vulnerable to invasive species. The spread of foreign animals such as foxes, cats and rabbits, as well as pastoralism, has left Central Australia empty of many native animals that once roamed here: the desert rat-kangaroo, the bilby, the numbat, the western quoll. So it's startling to remember that Australia's native flora and fauna could behave as aggressively as the buffel grass does here.

✱

My drive to Mungo National Park had been child's play compared to the two days I now faced on the Tanami Track: a notoriously remote, thousand-kilometre stretch of corrugated dirt-and-gravel road that heads north-west through isolated country. By road's end I would finally leave Central Australia, having spent several weeks in the region, and find myself in the Kimberley region of Western Australia. Along the track were a couple of communities, the first of which I hit three hundred kilometres north-west of Alice Springs. I passed two days in the lively, creative 759-person community of Yuendumu. It had a buzzing art centre where local artists sat cross-legged on the floor dabbing paint on canvasses in intricate patterns. Several Yuendumu artists had international reputations and through their art travelled widely.

Once I left Yuendumu I was destined to pass through a 600-kilometre-long gap: no town, no store, no petrol station, no mobile phone reception. A phenomenally expensive place to break down—good luck finding a tow-truck driver who wants to make that journey.

Before heading out into this long uninhabited stretch of the Tanami, I filled up my petrol tank plus two jerry cans, and prayed disaster had no plans to strike. Then I set off.

It was warm enough for me to roll my windows down. This let plumes of dust roll in, but I was happy to feel the sunshine on my elbow. Waves of elation passed through me—how liberated my life was right now, on the road again.

There were hardly any trees, mainly shrubs. Occasionally I spied birds as big as dogs sitting hunched and ominous on deadened tree branches. But the main feature of the landscape were countless termite mounds that mushroomed the further I went, eventually growing so tall that they looked like villages of mud huts.

I'd knocked 250 kilometres off the Tanami Track when I passed the Granites Gold Mine Airport. I thought of Adam in his truck, driving through a lifeless tunnel city.

After five hours of steady driving, I slowed at a vehicle-related roo death on one side of the road. A gang of scavenging birds were taking advantage of the fatality. I knew if I got too close they would immediately fly away, so I pulled over to spy on them through my binoculars. One bird of prey was bloodying his beak in the carcass while two smaller birds of prey played henchmen, keeping a pair of riffraff crows away. The fidgeting crows reminded me of a pair of impatient junkies; it was the definition of 'pecking order'. Eventually a car approached, and the larger birds cleared out. The crows, however, desperately leapt on the roadkill with little regard for their lives.

Thanks to my trusty bird guide, I was getting better at identifying birds of prey, a distinct type of large bird that feeds on flesh and has a hooked bill and sharp talons. Often the quickest way to identify a bird of prey in flight is by its tail: for the wedge-tailed eagle it's in the name; black kites have the forked tail of a fish; the brown falcon's tail is striped and rounded; and the nankeen kestrel has a thick band of black at its tip.

I started up my car again. So far, I hadn't faced any major obstacles. Most of the track was in reasonable condition. It was dusty and usually orange, sometimes red or white, and wide enough—just—for two trucks to pass each other. Whenever road trains passed me, the billowing dust kicked up by their human-sized wheels was so thick I pulled off to the side rather than risk crawling through it. The ground mainly felt compact and gravelly, but some patches were sandier, and there were some large dips and ruts that made me slow down. Of course, with a prodigious distance to be covered and only so much fuel and human energy to cover it, there's such a thing as driving too slowly.

Everyone in the Outback spouts their own tried and tested methods for driving these remote roads. A youth worker once told me that the faster you drive, the less teeth-chattering vibrations your car will suffer as it sails over sections corrugated as an iron roof. Another believed in swerving into sharp dips and hugging the road, rather than riding roughshod—*ker-chunk, ker-chunk*—over them. I took all this advice with a grain of salt, although occasionally it made good sense. Such as: when a roo gets in the way, don't hit the brakes but squeeze gently and then run it over if necessary—otherwise you risk spinning out of control. Also, don't keep skidding in soft or wet sand; instead find something to place under the wheel to create friction.

At Yuendumu's art centre I'd told one of the hippie volunteers about the road train that had kicked up rocks and damaged my windscreen.

'When that happens you should put your thumb on the glass,' he said and mimed the action. Ryan had said something similar to me back in Alice.

'When I had my windscreen fixed in Alice,' I said to the hippie, 'the guy installing it told me that's an urban myth.'

'He's not a scientist,' said the hippie contemptuously.

'No, but he is an expert in windscreens. Are you a scientist?'

Another volunteer, overhearing us, shouted, 'He's nothing!'

After another hundred kilometres, feeling I'd reached my day's limit of nerve-rattling driving, I stopped for the night. I was more than halfway up the track, and what with plenty of fuel remaining I decided the next morning I would take a detour and spend a night at the immense Lake Gregory, or Paruku to the Walmajarri people— I'd heard it was an excellent place for bird-spotting.

The calendar had just ticked past mid-July, the dead of winter, but as I was travelling north the temperature was quickly growing warmer. The nights I'd spent in Yuendumu were the first of my trip that weren't hideously cold. I decided that tonight I would roll out my tent instead of sleeping in the cramped car. I set up in a dry riverbed some distance from the road. There were still a couple more hours of daylight, so I explored the area and spotted a flock of Major Mitchell's cockatoos the colour of pink fairy floss with sunset mohawks. Afterwards I watched the day come to an end from my camp chair while writing in my journal.

By the time I was ready to cook dinner, a round, golden biscuit of a moon had slid up from the horizon, and I took it as an omen that all was well and would be well.

PART THREE

The Kimberley & The Pilbara

23 JULY
Day 48

The ranger in Mulan handed me a sticker that read: 'I <3 the Kimberley Ranges.'

I looked down at it. 'Am I in the Kimberley?' I asked with a jolt of surprise.

'Yes, on the eastern edge,' she said.

After spending the night on the side of the Tanami Track, I had continued on my way and soon crossed the border into Western Australia. Another hundred kilometres later I'd taken my detour: a left turn that led me to the hundred-person community of Mulan. This pinprick of human settlement—in the midst of desolate, dry, silent land—makes a startling contrast to the dense and cacophonous urbanisation where most people live.

Visitors to Mulan were required to apply for a permit from the local ranger. I arrived at the ranger's timber house expecting an Aboriginal man, but was greeted by a tall, strawberry-blonde woman around my age with a friendly demeanour. She was the sole ranger on a considerable swathe of parkland, and I admired her constitution for such lonesome, remote work.

I was so happy to hear I was in the Kimberley. For me, the Kimberley was imbued with a mythic quality. It's one of those rare regions of Australia that has yet to be permanently altered by large-scale, invasive agriculture or the resources industry. Stretching all the way to the northern coast of Western Australia, it's three times the size of England but only hosts a population one thousandth of England's. If you broke down that immense landmass per capita, each person in the Kimberley could sit perfectly isolated on their very own thousand hectares, baking under the sun and humming into an indifferent wind.

Two years earlier I'd interviewed a biologist who had discovered a new species of fish in the Kimberley and named it after the much-loved Western Australian novelist Tim Winton. The thirty-centimetre-long, gold and silver grunter is one of two species discovered by this scientist and his team within five minutes of reaching the Prince Regent River by helicopter. He and his team went on to identify twenty new species of fish over just nine months. This is likely the tip of the iceberg regarding unidentified biodiversity in the Kimberley.

I planned to spend one night by Lake Gregory. From Mulan I drove for thirty kilometres through fields of eucalypts with very white, crooked limbs, standing quietly in a knee-high carpet of dried yellow grass. Strewn throughout the grass were hundreds of tomb-stone-shaped termite mounds made of brown mud. These mounds are ubiquitous in the Top End, occasionally reaching six metres in height and always the colour of the local soil: burnt orange, brown, yellow or charcoal grey.

The day had nearly departed by the time I caught my first glance of the lake. Only a month had passed since I'd seen such a broad body of water, yet so accustomed had I become to the dry scrub that to me the lake glittered like a mirage on the horizon. Its waters were receding, and so it was buffered by a wide strip of mud the bluish colour of wet concrete. When I parked the car and went for a walk, the mud felt squishy and cool oozing between my toes.

As the sun began its final descent to the horizon, a flock of ash-coloured brolgas suddenly took flight, in such numbers they filled half the sky. I watched them sail: long, graceful, feathered ships, headed for some place already clothed in stars to dock for the night. Through my binoculars I saw each was born with a red mask and circular cut-outs behind their cheeks. Their long, slender necks and bone-thin legs contrasted with a luxuriant layer of flight feathers, the tips dipped in black.

I looked up the brolga in my bird guide, and beside the entry wrote 'Lake Gregory 2016'. There was something nerdy and addictive about birdwatching, similar to collecting Pokémon cards. In the past two days I had added fourteen birds to my set, including a zebra finch, a grey-headed honeyeater, and one rare creature, the Major Mitchell's cockatoo. In the pursuit of my targets, I had to attune myself to the movement, colour, sound and light of the land. There were parallels to hunting—except it was bloodshed-free and, thinking of Adam and his penchant for emu meat, didn't lead to the delicious smell of roasting flesh.

It already seemed like a former life that I was in Mungo, asking the Barkindji ranger if brolgas were real. Now, observing a flock of these wonderful, unhurried creatures, I felt embarrassed I'd been so ignorant, but also blessed that I had awakened to this world of birds around me. As members of the crane family, the brolga—which often turns up in Dreaming stories—seemed to me the Australian cousin of the white crane so heavily featured in ancient Chinese tales. I watched until each bird had disappeared over the horizon.

The sun set like an egg broken over the cold, blue glass plate of the lake's surface, the yolk pouring out in a hundred colours and smearing the sky and water. Soon after, scattered seeds of starlight sprouted one by one.

I would have liked to have spent more time at Paruku. However, I had many kilometres left to drive and not much time before I was due at a town on the west coast called Roebourne. It lies just to the south of the Kimberley, in the neighbouring region of the Pilbara. Extensive tracts of the Pilbara have been claimed for industrial use by iron ore companies such as Rio Tinto and BHP Billiton.

Over the following four days, I covered 1625 kilometres. The Tanami Track ends in the Kimberley town of Halls Creek, where I saw many swollen boab trees shaped like bottles and hung with round, furry brown fruit. I had read the trees are spiritually significant to the local people and been used as ossuaries (a keeping place of human bones). The largest of them were hundreds of years old. I headed west on the Great Northern Highway until I hit Broome on a coast lined with picturesque beaches, then I followed the coastline south until I entered the Pilbara in the approach to Port Hedland.

I expected to find a sleepy seaside village and a surfside cafe in which I could order a vanilla milkshake. But as I came closer to the town, the highway grew crowded with loud mining trucks and white SUVs bearing a neon-yellow stripe, the archetypal vehicle of the resources industry. The land was devoid of greenery and architectural charm, with crane-like machinery creating gargantuan piles of raw materials. Crisscrossing roads were bordered by overhead powerlines, cold and bare as deciduous trees in winter. *Perhaps some people find this beautiful*, I thought. *Maybe they see money, power and potential.* Port Hedland has been described as 'the engine room of the Australian economy'. But to me, the roads leading there felt dystopian; this was *Mad Max* but without the leading man in steampunk attire—just fire, fuel, dust and machinery. I felt assaulted and dwarfed by a landscape so dominated by industry. Humans were invisible here.

I decided to skip Port Hedland. I would find my vanilla milkshake elsewhere.

❋

I was headed to Roebourne, two hours from Port Hedland, to meet filmmaker and digital artist Tyson Mowarin.

We'd first met a few months earlier at *The Guardian* office, which Tyson had been visiting to discuss a possible collaboration. When he told me he lived near a place containing a million petroglyphs (rock engravings), I wondered how I had managed to go my entire life without so much as hearing the word Murujuga or its English name Burrup Peninsula. I'd been to the Eiffel Tower, the Great Wall and the Empire State Building, but I hadn't known anything about this Australian site of natural and historical significance, one that every Australian citizen has a responsibility to protect. I mentally added it to the top of my list of places I wanted to visit on this trip.

Now Tyson and I would be meeting on his home turf rather than mine. I was 3714 kilometres from home, as the crow flew—about as far as you can get from Sydney without leaving the country.

It was the tail end of July when Tyson collected me one morning in his pick-up truck, from the holiday rental where I was staying courtesy of friends-of-friends. We took the hour-long drive down the coast, talking all the way. He seemed like a serious and thoughtful person, and I liked serious and thoughtful people. He wasn't only a filmmaker and digital artist but also a teetotaller and single dad raising an eight-year-old daughter.

At the town of Karratha, we came off the highway and headed to the peninsula by driving through a three-kilometre strip of mud-flats, disappearing under the shallow tide. The peninsula arrived as a series of low green hills, and soon after landing on it Tyson took a left turn and sent our four-wheel drive jumping on an unmarked gravel track. Ten minutes later we stopped at a spot on top of a hill and climbed out of Tyson's car.

We were surrounded by colossal mounds of squarish red rock. It was as if a single towering monolith had been blown to smithereens, and the rubble that showered from the heavens had landed in mountain-sized piles.

'Doesn't look natural, does it?' said Tyson.

I shook my head.

It was an alien, industrial-looking setting, weirdly harmonious with the Woodside Pluto liquified natural gas plant constructed on a distant plain—a stupendous tangle of grey tubes and white cylinders.

As we were on one edge of the archipelago, beyond the plant were miles of flat and shining azurite-blue water.

Murujuga means 'hipbone sticking out' to the local Yaburrara and Ngarluma people. It was once the largest of a chain of forty-two islands and islets, laced by a coral reef off the coast of the Indian Ocean, before a causeway joined the island to the mainland in 1963. I could see a metal plaque attached to a heavy red-orange rock, sitting on the edge of where the road dropped off and led to the shallow valley before us. It read: 'Hereabouts in February 1868, a party of settlers from Roebourne shot and killed as many as sixty Yapurarra [*sic*] people in response to the killing of a European policeman in Nickol Bay. This incident has become known as the "Flying Foam Massacre".'

'The whitefellas say only ten or fifteen died, but we reckon more than eighty,' said Tyson, flatly. His black polo shirt bore the logo of his digital agency, Weerianna Street Media.

The killings were the climax of a series of deaths that had taken place over several months. In one version of events, the string of violence began when a Yaburrara man took some cattle, and local police killed the offender. The Yaburrara people fought back, killing a police constable, an Aboriginal police assistant and a pearling labourer. Local pearlers and pastoralists then armed themselves and, with the approval and support of the government resident in Roebourne, R.J. Sholl, descended on the clan's camp and carried out the reprisal killings. In another version of events, the policeman who was killed had kidnapped a Yaburrara woman.

I was reminded of the prescient words of Surveyor-General Sir Thomas Livingstone Mitchell, who in 1836 wrote in his journal while exploring the interior of New South Wales and Victoria:

> the kangaroo disappears from cattle runs, and is also killed by stockmen merely for the sake of the skin; but no mercy is shown to the natives who may help themselves to a bullock or a sheep. Such a state of things must infallibly lead to the extirpation of the

aboriginal natives, as in Van Diemen's Land, unless timely measures are taken for their civilisation and protection.

The killings decimated what remained of the Yaburrara people, who had already suffered many deaths from an outbreak of European-introduced smallpox two years earlier. But Tyson said he knew at least one Yaburrara family descended from survivors and assimilated into his nation, the Ngarluma people, who occupied adjacent land on the mainland.

Tyson pointed at a hill behind us. 'Do you see that?' he asked, tracing the ridgeline with his finger in the air.

At first it appeared no different to all the other piles of red rock that surrounded us. Then I noticed something: on the crest, a line of stones was carefully planted upright in the gaps between boulders. They were longer and thinner than the others.

'They're standing stones,' he said. 'They're all over Ngarluma Country, and when you see them, it probably means a burial site or a waterhole is there.' I would never have noticed them if not for Tyson. And now I wondered how many times throughout my life had I failed to notice evidence of human life? I was reminded of when I first moved to China and, not yet speaking Mandarin, felt as if my head were wrapped in invisible cotton wool: I couldn't communicate or understand the words that surrounded me. And when you're in a culture not your own, are you not blind as well? It was so easy to traverse a landscape or human settlement and fail to understand or even misinterpret what you were seeing. How many manmade messages, indicators, warnings and sacred sites, just like these standing stones, were embedded in our landscape over several millennia of human occupation, but as an Australian not versed in the ancient cultures of the land, they had gone over my head?

And which is worse: to be a Chinese Australian blind in China, or to be a Chinese Australian blind in Australia? It seemed no matter where I went, I was alienated and a stranger from the land.

'Look, this is the only form of protection,' said Tyson, pointing at a small square sign on a metal pole held upright with rocks and streaked with orange rust. It asked visitors to respect the site and said causing damage was an offence against the *Aboriginal Heritage Act of 1972*. Most of Murujuga had been included on the National Heritage listing since 2007; the site easily qualified for a UNESCO World Heritage listing, and advocates and traditional owners were leading a campaign to have it added.

'Maybe there should be a fence built around these standing stones?' I suggested.

'Our people don't like fences. We think it might just make someone curious and want to jump over it.' He thought for a moment, then conceded, 'Although like this someone will probably crawl all over this one day and knock the stones over.'

He said hardly anyone was prosecuted for vandalism anyway. In 2008 a cement company had destroyed some rock art on Murujuga in a heritage-protected zone. They were punishable for a five-million dollar fine but in the end were only required to pay $280,000. The Western Australian Greens called that figure a 'slap on the wrist'.

Tyson claimed recent changes to the *WA Aboriginal Heritage Act*—including an increase in prison times and fines for vandalism—were nothing but whitewash. Most worrying to him and his people was how the Western Australian government had narrowed the definition of what constitutes a sacred place, and consequently wiped more than a thousand sites from the records, including some on Murujuga.

I mulled over the dilemma. 'Maybe it's better to simply make people appreciate the importance of the site.'

Didn't more non-Indigenous Australians need a strong dose of reality? Didn't we need to come face-to-face with the terror and horror of our past? For too long we'd kept dark secrets from ourselves. Was the country still a child, lacking in the psychological and emotional resilience to confront these shameful aspects of its history?

'Okay,' I said to Tyson, hesitantly, 'I don't know how you're going to feel about this, but what if this were to be developed into a proper tourist site?'

I hypothesised: yes, there would be all these people gawking at the memorial, more foot traffic and a higher risk of vandalism. On the other hand, this was an important story. If we were to memorialise the dead *together*, we might really feel as a country the impact of the frontier wars on the lives and communities of this continent.

Tyson seemed conflicted and didn't immediately reply. I couldn't read his expression from behind his wraparound sunglasses. 'That's a tricky one,' he said finally.

I looked at the standing stones—red and bone-like, pointing to the sky—and my heart felt heavy as I thought of the Yaburrara lives that had been taken by colonial forces. The blood of those men, women and children had seeped into the soil as they passed into the after-life: a family who'd laughed, fought, eaten, bathed, cried, grown up and grown old together, who'd sung the land into good health and paid their respects to the spirit beings that had created it; a clan with a name and a history and, so they had believed, a future—all those lives, evaporated.

'Thank you for showing me this,' I said quietly to Tyson.

He nodded, and we got back in the car.

We drove north to Withnell Bay where boulder-covered hills tumble into perfect blue waters. The bay shares its name with local pioneer John Withnell, one of the 'special constables' from the killings. Sholl, the government resident who approved the killings, continues to be honoured with a street name in Roebourne and a paver on St Georges Terrace in Perth.

Throughout Australia are countless examples of dubious place-name choices, and generally the insults escape the notice of the non-Indigenous populous. Further inland, near the iron ore hotspot town of Tom Price, is a seemingly sarcastically named Mount Nameless—about which Yinhawangka elder Lola Young said, 'They didn't ask the Aboriginal people here if that place had a name already. And it had. Its name for thousands of years has been Jarndunmunha: there's nothing nameless about that.'

One of the most baffling to me was a name further north in the western Kimberley region: the King Leopold Ranges. In 1879 the hills known as Milawundi by the Bunuba people were renamed by explorer Alexander Forrest to honour the Belgian monarch. King Leopold II had recently carved out an expansive colonial empire in the African continent on behalf of his minuscule European nation; under his cruel regime, millions of Congolese people died, and copious quantities of ivory and rubber were pilfered.

Other sites on Bunuba Country were bestowed with European names that, while not honouring colonial tyrants, pay homage to notable Brits with very tenuous connections to Australia. Alexander Forrest, or possibly his brother John, decided a gorge in the Kimberley was as good a place as any to tip his hat to Scottish geologist Archibald Geikie. Historical records indicate Geikie never once set foot in Australia. At the time of my trip, the gorge's name was formally being reverted back to Danggu.

There had been some rain recently, and as we drove over the low hills of the peninsula I saw spinifex of a very light, pleasant green growing in clumps—the only daubs of softness on a severe and cubist landscape. Contrary to appearances, the archipelago is rich in biodiversity and hosts over a hundred bird species. Beneath its dark turquoise waters, reef beds are decorated with brittle-stars, sea cucumbers and sea urchins, while plenty of crab, fish and other sea life call this region home.

As we drove I asked Tyson about his abstention from alcohol. He said everyone he knew drank. When he went hunting with his mates, he'd bring the guns and they'd bring the beer, even though he wouldn't be drinking any of it. And they couldn't watch the footy without drinking; in fact a game had just started, so they'd be drinking now.

'The first and last time I ever drank was on my twenty-first birthday, and I didn't even have a chance to get drunk because by the time I reached for my fourth can they were all gone—everyone else had drunk them.'

'Not drinking is pretty unusual in Australia,' I said.

I told him about my unhealthy lifestyle while working at *The Guardian*: the Friday night piss-ups and how messed up it was after a hard week of work to need a drink that badly, to unwind and blow off steam. But I never had the urge to drink on this trip. I was already drunk on the beauty of this country, swimming in open horizons. All those show-stopping sunrises and sunsets, the sky, the rivers, the sea, the land—my body was alive with it all. It was a different kind of intoxication.

'I'm not a purist like you, though,' I said. 'I'd be okay to have a drink every now and then, but it's great to not need to. Why do you think you're like that?'

'I dunno, I must be stupid or something.'

'More like the opposite.'

'I've seen what drinking has done to the community and prefer to be healthy. I'm not even tempted.' Tyson paused. 'Although I reckon that's why it's hard for me to meet a woman. Because everyone else drinks.'

We drove to a section of the peninsula that had been developed for visitors to view rock art. The boulders exist due to millions of years of weather battering away at volcanic rock. Despite its broken-up appearance, this type of granophyre is highly resilient—'hard as diamonds', as archaeologist Peter Veth once put it—so it makes for a canvas that, once carved, 'never forgets'. The archipelago is covered in art: the largest and most diverse collection of rock engravings in Australia, if not the world. Among the works are, purportedly, the world's oldest representations of the human face.

Australia's scientific community is still uncovering Murujuga's full breadth of work. From at least two hundred site-specific studies—generally commissioned by mining or industrial companies to fulfil licence agreements—are hints of a dizzying array of imagery spread out across the archipelago, in a variety of styles, techniques and subjects, and almost certainly of global significance. It seems paradoxical that much of this archaeological record exists essentially to chronicle what Australians are destroying. A handful of large-to-medium surveys not done for industrial purposes, including one by Veth and his colleague Jo McDonald in 2009, give a minimum estimate of one million engravings; although Veth believes that across the entire chain of volcanic islands, the figure could be double that.

Tyson parked his pick-up truck at the entrance, and on foot we approached a path that snaked up between pyramids of orange boulders the size of washing machines. These are the canvases upon which Yaburrara life and creation time is depicted.

It was a cloudless day and the sun was out, but it remained cool enough that I wore a pair of denim jeans and a black sports jacket. I peered through my binoculars, scanning rocks twenty metres away, and spotted a boulder scratched with light lines. 'It looks like, maybe, three carved boomerangs stacked atop one another?' I said excitedly.

'That's the Ngarluma symbol,' Tyson explained. 'You can see it all over our Country.'

I pulled my phone from my back pocket to take a photo, but he stopped me.

'It might be a men's site where an elder was instructing secret men's business,' he said.

We walked up the path bordered by hundreds of engravings—a gigantic, permanent outdoor gallery—and frequently stopped to allow me to look through my binoculars. Tyson said that visibility was best in the late afternoon and it was late morning, but we saw plenty of petroglyphs, depicting fish, eggs, human figures, bird tracks, and other icons I didn't recognise. We had the whole place to ourselves, yet I felt the presence of many thousands of art makers throughout history.

We'd seen dozens of petroglyphs when I spotted the carving of a long, four-legged creature. Its tail was curled in the air and head bent down; most notably, it had stripes on its back. 'Look!' I said. I knew what those stripes meant: it was either a numbat or—'Might be a thylacine,' said Tyson. This extinct animal is more commonly known by the misnomer 'Tasmanian tiger'; in fact, it roamed the mainland before the population receded, with the final three thousand years of its existence spent isolated to Tasmania. The last of its species died in Hobart Zoo in 1936.

I felt a special thrill at seeing a thylacine in ancient rock art, as if a match had been struck in the dark room of history and the animal's ghostly presence had flared up. 'Must have taken ages!' I exclaimed, conjuring in my mind the image of a man with a sharp, weighty flint in his hand, painstakingly chipping away at the rock; the artworks displayed a range of techniques including pecking, battering, scoring and incising.

'Yeah,' said Tyson, 'that's some of the hardest rock you can get. Those would all take at least a few days.'

'Isn't it amazing the way humans have always wanted to leave their mark?'

The path continued to meander between hills, large and small, and soon we reached wet areas where the rocks were fuzzy with green moss. There were piles of tiny, broken white shells that I recognised as middens; they're found all over Australia, even in built-up, colonised-way-back places like Sydney. Most Aboriginal people in pre-colonial Australia hadn't been in the habit of wearing shoes, so after eating they had fastidiously discarded sharp leftover bits of shell and bone.

Tyson pointed at some dry sandy rocks adjacent to the puddles. 'See that yellow? All the rocks around us are actually that colour. Those boulders only turn red after they've been exposed to the sun a very long time, and it's just their surface that's red. The darker the colour, the older the rock.'

'Oh wow, look at that one.' I pointed at a particularly lovely portrait of a kangaroo on the face of an elevated rock, positioned as clearly as a shop sign. As with most of the other engravings, to create this image the maker had scraped away the darker top layer exposing the paler colour beneath. I lifted my binoculars to take a closer look. The perfectly proportioned kangaroo had been carved from a single outline with two spots for eyes. It was captured side-on, its ears flattened back, all limbs visible and a thick tail curving to the corner of the rock. Despite being frozen in stone, it was as full of life as if it were about to leap out and bound away.

No one is sure of the meaning behind each petroglyph. Perhaps this one indicated the presence of kangaroo, or perhaps 'increase ceremonies' had been conducted here to boost kangaroo numbers, or this was the site of a Kangaroo Dreaming story.

Tyson explained that the older carvings of land-based animals, such as the fat-tailed macropods and thylacine, contrast with the newer carvings featuring sea creatures, such as fish, turtles and dolphins. Studies show that such thematic changes synced with the rise and fall of sea levels. When humans first arrived in the Pilbara, sea levels were lower—twenty thousand years ago they hit their lowest point, at 130 metres beneath today's levels—so what are now islands were mountain peaks rising out of a flat plain, and the coastline lay more than a hundred kilometres from where it lies now. Naturally, seafood wasn't on the menu back then. Over several thousand years, the coastline crept closer until reaching its present level seven thousand years ago.

How startling that through all these climatic and dietary changes, Tyson's people have sustained life on this land.

'Do you ever feel like carving more of them?' I asked Tyson from behind him, as we leapfrogged single file across some rubble. 'You know, as a continuation of this cultural practice.'

He spoke over his shoulder. 'People have thought about it, but elders would get upset. Anyway, we have new ways to express our culture, like painting on canvas and making films.'

I nodded. I was no purist who advocated for cultures remaining frozen in time and quarantined from outside influence. 'It's the same thing but on a new medium, isn't it?'

Tyson seemed to juggle more projects than was manageable for one man. He was working on a virtual-reality film, a card game based on the Ngarluma kinship system, a location-based welcome to Country app, and a short film starring Balang T.E. Lewis. Tyson's work is compelling and beautifully shot, and has picked up awards at film festivals. In his office he'd shown me recently captured drone footage for his hour-long documentary *Connection to Country*. The landscape shots were gorgeous, saturated with the rich reds, lemony yellows and spinifex green of the Pilbara, drizzled with the soft light of dawn.

Like so many people living in regional Australia, he had mixed feelings about the industrial development of his land. On the one hand it was driving the destruction of local heritage; on the other, many community projects had been funded by mining money as part of compensation agreements with the companies.

As we made our way back to the entrance, Tyson explained that when the gas giant Woodside had funded one of his own projects, they'd exerted no creative pressure. 'They said to me I could use their money to say, "Fuck Woodside", and there's nothing they could do to stop me.'

Someone as talented as Tyson had limited choices in a place like Roebourne. He had less access to the mainstream arts industry and corporate sponsorship than people in our capital cities. At the same time, Tyson seemed wary of city life—he loved the bush. And not just any old bush, but *his* bush, *his* Country. That's what happens when you have two thousand generations of Ngarluma life in your bones. 'I know this fella that lived in Roebourne for a few years, but eventually he and his family moved back to Perth because his girlfriend couldn't find a decent place to have a cup of coffee—I thought that was the dumbest fucking thing I'd ever heard,' Tyson said drolly, as we climbed back into his truck.

I laughed at how stupid it sounded, but also wondered if coffee was just the straw that broke the camel's back. That woman probably missed a whole host of distracting city playthings: multiplex cinemas, whisky bars, yum cha, literary festivals, yoga classes, Saturday markets, dinner parties and, most of all, lots of other white people. Tyson had his Country; she had her town.

We got back in Tyson's pick-up truck, and it didn't seem to matter where we drove on the peninsula, the visage of a chemical plant appeared around every corner like a caped villain, flare stacks spewing fire and gassy fumes.

At the nearby peak of a low hill, we parked the car. Before us the land spanned out as a flat plain, then rose again in a series of hills. There was another one, roaring and burping: a giant liquefied natural gas processing plant. Beyond that, two hundred kilometres out to sea, Woodside machinery was extracting five trillion cubic feet of dry gas that for millions of years had been trapped underwater and underground in the Pluto and Xena gas fields. The gas was then piped through to the facility before us and shipped to Asia.

'Meanwhile we can't even get gas in our homes, we have to buy it in bottles,' said Tyson, with crossed arms, shaking his head.

Elsewhere on the peninsula were Rio Tinto's iron ore leases and railhead, a port, salt production, a liquid ammonia and fertiliser plant, and a quarry—all jostling for space with the rock art.

'They had to use a diamond saw to cut the petroglyphs out,' Tyson said.

Since 1980, thousands of rocks had been relocated and many more carefully traced, cast, photographed, logged in records by archaeologists, then promptly destroyed and turned into bedrock. Rock art advocate Rebecca Hossack, speaking on ABC radio in 2013, claimed she talked to an electrician who witnessed ten thousand petroglyphs crushed for road fill. She accused Australia of hypocrisy—we'd been 'vociferous' in signing the UN declaration against the destruction of cultural property when the Taliban destroyed the Bamiyan Buddhas in Afghanistan, 'and yet here in our back garden we are doing something so much worse'.

Among the salvaged rock art, 1700 pieces had been transported to a nearby ridge. Tyson pointed at the spots where the rock art had been dumped: women's rocks over here, men's rocks over there, and the animal rocks in between. He told me his people believe the rocks and their carvings have lost some of their special meaning. 'They're still sacred and important but,' he struggled to find the right phrase, 'a little less so.' (Woodside say that in 2010 they worked with the Department of Aboriginal Affairs and senior Aboriginal law holders to rehabilitate the site.)

'I think I get it,' I said. 'It's like taking the ruins of Pompeii and chucking them a few hundred kilometres west in a nonsensical jumble.'

'Yeah, or Stonehenge.'

Hossack had likened the piecemeal destruction of the archipelago's rock art to 'putting your finger through a giant spider web'. In her opinion, to remove one rock was 'tantamount to destruction of the whole'; they could not be viewed as individual works, or even as sites or collections—they were a connected body of work stretching across the islands and spanning epochs.

That uniquely hard rock and its indestructible memory, into which the Yaburrara people carved, has left us with something incredibly rare: an uninterrupted record of a group of people over tens of thousands of years. In those symbols are expressions of their religion and worldviews, customs, history and knowledge of the land, possibly reaching back to their arrival some fifty thousand years ago, right up to that terrible day in 1868 when the settler militia murdered most of the remaining traditional custodians.

And now Australia's resources industry, with the permission of our government, has pulverised parts of this million-stone chronicle into dust.

How imperious the Commonwealth of Australia must be, I thought, that it could decimate a people and then continue that act of destruction by smashing their rock art—carvings that had survived so many turnings of the millennia and dramatic climatic changes.

I slipped into an existential funk, disturbed by the notion that even after fifty thousand years of order, an invader can sweep in and completely upend a culture's reality. What a distressing experience it must have been for the traditional owners to have the Law underpinning their existence challenged so profusely by the colonisers. Was it the equivalent of waking up one day and being told the Earth was flat, 'e' no longer equalled 'mc squared' and the forces of gravity had been reversed?

Roads ran from the factory to the main highway, and for a few moments Tyson and I watched gleaming Toyota HiLuxes scurry busily like white ants in a neat line. They carried workers, many of whom had flown in from Broome, Perth or further afield.

'Do you think all the miners know whose land they're mining on?' I asked Tyson.

'They wouldn't know anything.'

❋

My plan was to head inland and camp a few days in a couple of national parks. Before I left, Tyson gave me the contact details of his aunt in Broome. 'She's married to a guy who is Malay and a blackfella—you'll probably find that interesting,' he guessed correctly.

The quickest route from Roebourne to Millstream Chichester National Park was via a road privately owned by Rio Tinto, built to provide them maintenance access to their railway. It was unsealed, and before driving it I had to watch a short video at the Roebourne visitor centre and apply for a thirty-day permit. Every day the railways moved tonnes of iron ore from inland Pilbara to the seaside ports at Dampier and Cape Lambert, where it was loaded onto ships for delivery to the rest of the world. The 1400 kilometres of track made it the largest privately owned railway in the world, or so I learnt from the training video.

The dusty road curved alongside the railway, and a couple of times I was overtaken by long trains presumably carrying iron ore. I stopped to watch one and noted it took three minutes to pass by.

In the landscape nothing was taller than the green bushes growing on the side of the road, giving me a clear view to the distant mountains. Some were gently sloping, while others were ridged or flat-topped. They were all covered in a fuzz of green desert grass and spinifex, but beneath you could see the Australian red of iron ore.

I'd now spent a few weeks driving with the windows rolled down, and the interior of my car was covered in dust. You could see my fingerprints where I'd touched the screen to switch tracks on a CD. Outside, the back window of my car was also covered in red dust, except where an anonymous passer-by had scribed 'clean me :)' with their finger.

It's only ninety kilometres from Roebourne to Millstream Chichester National Park. With that, my trip meter clicked over to eleven thousand kilometres—I'd driven an average of two hundred kilometres per day.

The park is a green oasis set in a bed of hard rock, in the lands of the Yinjibarndi people. It has several spring-fed natural pools, drawing water from an underground aquifer held in porous dolomite like a sponge.

I headed to Python Pool, just a short walk from the main road and lined with a pair of tall rock walls sloping to make an 'M'. In the middle of the 'M' I saw a strip of rock bleached white—traces of a waterfall that probably ran in the wet season.

I wasn't alone. A mother was with her three exuberant young kids who were making as much noise as they could, skipping and jumping on the dusty ground towards the water's edge. 'Shush, stop it,' said their weary mother, strands of her blonde hair sticking to her face. Alas, the children weren't to be reined in quite so quickly. That sheer rock wall curved around a body of very dark, still water, and to the children's delight was a natural amphitheatre. Their shouts pinged off every surface. The oldest kid yelled, 'Cooee!' and the younger kids followed suit, oblivious to the peace and quiet that fled like a flock of startled birds.

Their beleaguered mother kept trying to quieten them, until one kid paused his play to ask, very innocently, 'But why?'

By then she had plonked herself on a rock and had her head resting on one hand. 'Because it's a sacred spot,' she said flatly. By her intonation I assumed she didn't know or care if that was true, but I thought it quick-thinking of her to pull out *that* card.

I headed to a lookout, where I was lucky to see a Sturt's desert pea growing spectacularly out of the stony earth. Each flower had several shiny black snouts from which long triangular petals, red and bright as chilli, unfurled horizontally.

Other than some scraggly snappy gums, the mountains looked bald to me, covered in spiky spinifex that resembled a vast gathering of echidnas. I thought back to how Tyson had told me of his visit to tropical north-east Arnhem Land, which is thick with vegetation and relatively flat; being from arid country, he felt claustrophobic. Not surprisingly, I was feeling homesick for river country in the interior of New South Wales, with its carpets of waist-high golden grass and its wise old red gums. I thought they provided the perfect amount of cover, in contrast to the ridiculously impenetrable jungles of the tropical north. In my part of Australia you were offered real privacy: good, solid trees you could set your camp next to, with room to park your car and enough cover that no one would know you were there. Everything here was so exposed—no use trying to hide between spinifex bushes when you were anything larger than a blue-tongued lizard.

I drove for another couple of hours further inland to Karijini National Park. Eager to go for a hike, I settled on a section of the tightrope track up the steep ridgeline of Punurunha (Mount Bruce). The rumbling of trains echoed across the plain. Even in WA's second-biggest national park, I couldn't get away from the clanking hubbub of the mining industry. The mountain is part of the Hamersley Range, containing eighty per cent of Australia's identified iron ore reserves and one of the world's major iron ore sources. The banded iron formations of the Hamersley Province are the thickest and most extensive rocks of this type in the world, deposited 2400 million years ago when the continent was turbulent with volcanic activity.

The rocks along the track were long and sharp-edged, shaped like giant crystals. As I traced the thin mountain ridge, to the left I saw miles of open, flat, untouched stone country, splotched with spinifex and stunted mulgas. To the right was Rio Tinto's Marandoo mine site, which the WA government excised from within national park boundaries in 1991. I wondered how useful it was to designate land as national park when a cashed-up mining company could draw a chalk line around the bits they needed. Karijini National Park: home to the Banyjima, Yinhawangka, Kurrama and Rio Tinto peoples.

A platform overlooked the mine, beside a sign that explained how the ore was processed, transported and delivered to Rio Tinto's port on the Burrup. Iron ore is a key component of steel production, but it was hard to sit there in the middle of the desert, when I hadn't seen a building taller than six floors in almost two months, and envision the Pilbara's red rocks winding up as all those highways and highrises erected across Asia.

In another section of the park, I was surprised when the land abruptly plunged a hundred metres. The gorges were formed when, according to the traditional owners, 'the earth was soft'. A drop in sea levels tens of millions of years ago caused the land to dry out, and over time the rivers—created by great serpents called Thurru—chiselled through cracks in the rock, carving out the gorges of Karijini. The rivers now flow north-west across the coastal plain, always striving and searching for the quickest route to the ocean, pining for a reunion.

While most of the Pilbara is hot, flat and baking, at the bottom of these thin, deep splits it is wet and cool. Ice-cold waterholes grow paperbarks, figs and ferns. These plants are relics from around sixty-five million years ago, when the climate was tropical and rainforests flourished; over time they retreated and became isolated sanctuaries.

Bird life is also concentrated in these oases, with spinifex pigeon and zebra finch fluttering in and out of them each day for a drink.

I slipped about on cold, wet rocks in places where the gorge became so narrow it was only wide enough for one person. From this place of shadow, I found it hard to remember that the world above was an arid plain filled with sunlight and sky. But that's Australia for you: a country of extremes, where even the vastness of the horizon can all of a sudden be tipped sideways and hem you in between steep gorge walls.

After two nights at the park, I drove to its north-eastern corner and walked a track that would lead me to Fern Pool. I went down a long metal staircase that wound along the side of a red rock gorge and then clambered over a section of slate. Eventually I came across a tourist-free bit of mermaid-blue water; it was too small to be the main pool but was so pretty I decided to stop awhile. The creek was lined with paperbarks and a thick fringe of reeds as tall as me.

The traditional custodians believe the Thurru still lives in these watery hidey-holes—*Little wonder,* I thought, *if they all look as magical as this*—and everyone is supposed to take care not to offend them.

I quietly knelt down, my knees pressed into the damp riverbank, and spoke in a self-conscious whisper. 'Hi, my name is Monica Tan. I come from Sydney on Eora Country. My Chinese Malaysian parents are Ven and Kim, but our ancestors come from Fujian province in Southern China. I promise I am only passing through your lands.' And, having learnt of a local practice from a display at the park's visitor centre, I scooped up a handful of water and held it to my mouth, slurped, and sprayed it into the air.

Earlier in the year, I had gone to Perth to interview Yamatji actor and television presenter Ernie Dingo. He told me about how in the summer of 1976, he and the Noongar/Yamatji musician Richard Walley had performed what is believed to be the first contemporary welcome to Country for non-Indigenous Australians. We spoke about traditional welcomes and acknowledgements of Country, and he compared the latter to a 'knock on the door': a simple, courteous way to alert traditional owners or the spirits of the land of your presence. He said that traditionally, if you were visiting the sparse mid-west Country of Western Australia from which his people hail, to perform an acknowledgement of Country you first headed to a vantage point, such as a hill, and lit a fire. 'That plume of smoke would indicate that you had been sitting there,' he said. 'That's just like the knock on the door.'

At the time of our interview I was already formulating my road trip, and I sought his advice on how I should acknowledge each place I travelled.

He said, 'When we go for a swim in a waterhole that we've never known before, we get some sand and rub it in our hands. Then we say our name, where we come from and what we're doing in the area. So wherever it is that you're travelling, just say: my name is so-and-so, I come from such and such, or your family name, I'm daughter of so-and-so; I'm a visitor, I'm just travelling through and I accept your blessings.'

Throughout this trip I had done as he'd advised. Sometimes, when I'd been nervous about my safety, I had even asked for protection. But generally I kept it to a short, respectful, verbal assurance that I meant no harm and would soon be on my way.

I got back on my feet and continued up the track, which was crowded with healthy green trees. I passed one particularly impressive specimen with several muscular bone-white trunks reaching this way and that like a many-armed Hindu deity, and hundreds of tendril-thin roots reaching towards the earth. It was odd to see such a robust tree in the middle of the desert. And unlike in the hot and deathly stillness of just about everywhere else in the Pilbara, plenty of birds and insects were flitting and buzzing about.

Looking at a shrub, I noticed a nest. Upon seeing how elaborately it was constructed, I corrected myself: this was no nest, rather a bower of the eponymous bowerbird. I had never before seen the bird or its bowers, only their illustration in my bird guide. I was astounded that a bird was capable of such designed beauty. The bower was made with sticks placed upright but curling so that together they were shaped like two powerful ocean waves facing each other and poised at the moment before collapse. The ground at both ends of the bower was covered in white decorative items: stones, shells, bones, and bits of glass and plastic.

Moments later, I met its maker. He was the size of a magpie but spotted and brown, with a splotch of lilac on his neck that somehow flared independently of the other feathers. He strutted back and forth in the vicinity of his construction, making all sorts of un-song-like, crunchy, raspy, mechanical noises. I peered around for a female bird, for why else would he put on such a display? I should not have been so surprised that a bird with such exquisite taste in architecture would be a flamboyant dancer. It was all very postmodern. He'd fan his wings out low, in the shape of a stiff tutu, and the next moment be hunched over so that they were up and spread wide like Count Dracula's cape.

Later I read that both the performance and the striking—albeit impractical and vulnerable—home are only for the purposes of seduction. Once mating has taken place, the female is solely responsible for egg incubation and chick-rearing. She's even denied use of the love-palace he built. According to Morcombe, a male bowerbird will leap onto any female tempted to go between the bower's strong walls, leaving her no room to flap her wings and escape. Next she must build 'a little cup-shaped nest in a tree'. For weeks she tirelessly feeds their chicks while below her lover has moved on to other tail feathers, mating with several females over one breeding season. On the other end of the spectrum are the many monogamous Australian birds— magpies, wedge-tailed eagles, cockatoos, corellas and brolgas—that mate for life or extended periods.

A five-minute walk later, I emerged at the main pool where a dozen other tourists were gathered. It was almost as large as an Olympic swimming pool, penned in by a tall vegetation-covered hill and a rock ledge with two small waterfalls. At the start of the track I'd seen a sign notifying tourists that the pool is a 'special place' and a 'significant Aboriginal site'. It asked visitors to respect the pool by not jumping from the waterfalls, and advised them to avoid making loud noises and to use the ladder provided to enter the water quietly.

No such luck. Among the tourists at the pool was an old man running a dive-bomb competition with two adolescent boys. I watched him take several steps back from the water to give himself a decent run-up, then leap off the wooden platform. With a giant 'WOO!' he went cannonballing into the water.

Two young women were stripping down. 'I love your bikini!' one squealed to the other. The one with the nice bikini began yelping about how freezing the water probably was.

The tourists weren't the only animals making a racket. At first I assumed birds were responsible for all the squawking, but it was a colony of bats that had roosted in an enormous tree drooping over the pool. Using my binoculars I could see in glorious detail their furry bodies and leathery wings, hanging upside down like miniature folded-up umbrellas. Apparently they fed on the fruits of a rock fig clinging to the gorge walls.

The old man's wife, wearing a broad-brimmed hat and a sun-sensible, long-sleeved paisley shirt, stood on the wooden platform in the shade looking on with a watery smile. Her obnoxious husband seemed giddy with delight that he'd found more rambunctious company and was working hard to keep the lanky teenage boys entertained. 'Watch this!' he told them. He mimed holding a shotgun and pointed it at the bats. 'POW-POW!'

We all watched as the bats kept on squawking, paying the fool no attention.

He seemed disappointed. 'They're really not bothered by us, are they?'

I had forgotten to bring my swimsuit so quickly undressed and slipped into the water, hoping no one would notice I was in my underwear. Surprisingly the water wasn't at all cold like the bikini woman feared, and I swam away from the tourists to a small set of waterfalls, almost as warm as a shower. I stood under the water so that it massaged my head, shoulders and arms. When I went entirely through the water, I found a cave dripping with green ferns and hair-like moss. I sat on a rock happy to be away from everyone else. With my fingertips I touched soft tendrils of green moss and felt depressed at the way the tourists had treated this church like the pool of a flea-bitten motel. I wondered how they would feel if someone pulled out a deckchair at an Anzac memorial, plonked themselves into it and slapped on a bit of coconut oil.

I believed there should be holiday spots where you could scream with joy; likewise I understood that mining had become part and parcel of the modern economy. At the same time, I thought, *Isn't it not just reasonable but vital to regard certain places as sacred? And that as sacred places, they are elevated from our base daily needs and wants.*

Such places in Australia are sacred, first and foremost, because they are sacred to the traditional custodians. If a Christian was to enter a Buddhist temple, she would follow the lead of the believers, first taking off her shoes, then respecting the silence with which those around her burnt incense. And when a Buddhist walks into a Christian church and sees believers kneeling at the pews, quietly murmuring words of prayer, that feeling of holiness and spiritual power translates. When we treat places and traditions as sacred, over time they become sacred to us as well. Is that cultural appropriation? Or do the ancient laws of these lands rule supreme, applicable to everyone who walks this country?

What would happen, I wondered, to us non-Indigenous Australians?

I thought of a quote from Kurrama elder Peter Stevens I'd read in the park's visitor centre. It had chilled me to the bone. 'Law and culture never change. You can do what you like in this land, but whatever you do, this land never change. They think they can do anything with it . . . but in the end, maybe this land might turn on us. One day he got to turn on us.' The words seemed particularly ominous in the context of Australia's addiction to coal, while the clouds of climate change were closing in and darkening our horizon.

I slid into the water and ducked under the falls to swim over to the wooden platform. It was time to get back on the road.

✳

In the first hour of the day-long drive I faced to reach Broome, I passed through stunning country studded with giant orange peanut-shaped rocks. I was no longer surprised to see them defaced with graffiti. I suspected the words 'Milo 4 Missy', written in white spray-paint, were destined to outlive the author's romance—then again, maybe the mining companies would get to these rocks first.

After that, the scenery became an interminable stretch of unbroken, unmusical spinifex country. I tried to keep all my senses open and not fall into 'tunnel vision', as Tyson had warned me city folk were apt to do when driving country roads. But the longer I drove, the deeper the desert penetrated my brain as a low, dull thrumming. The unrelentingly flat horizon was cutting me in two, and the hot, dusty air of the Pilbara blew through my car like a hairdryer. My palms began to sweat. When I hit hour nine on that long drive north, my vision began to blur, turning discarded tyres into perentie lizards and mammoth semitrailers into sparkling dots. Those road trains seemed to have force fields that sucked my car in. In my dreamy state, I had to steel myself to grip the wheel and stay on course.

I pulled into Broome as the heavy hem of the night sky dropped over the horizon. Fine-boned adolescent wallabies, barely visible, kept skittering dangerously into view. With my windows rolled down, the warm night air drifted in. It had the tropical scent of frangipanis and the briny finish of the sea.

Broome is spread across a fishtail-shaped peninsula in the Kimberley region, along a coastline speckled with thousands of islands and ringed by shallow reefs teeming with sea life. I felt there was something ramshackle and balmy about the town that I liked. Elsewhere in Australia, the first few days of August remained in the depths of winter, but here, even in the evening, the weather was temperate. And judging by the residents and visitors I saw walking its streets, Broome reminded me of Hawaii—a melting pot of Asian, black and white cultures.

I had been to many Chinatowns around the world. But as I headed to the caravan park where I planned to spend the night, I drove through the first Chinatown that I had ever seen whose buildings were made of corrugated iron and streets lined with palm trees. A century ago it must have been crowded with bazaars, long soup shops, pearl dealers, brothels and emporiums. Now tourism is its main industry: hostels have replaced boarding houses, restaurants and bars replaced gambling dens.

Broome is synonymous with the pearling industry. The largest species of oyster in the world is found along its shores, growing up to thirty centimetres in length and weighing up to five kilograms. From the outside, the fan-shaped *Pinctada maxima* is no beauty: the surface of its shell is rough and chalky to the touch, and a drab, dishwater grey. But after you crack open its tightly shut lips, you find that inside it is coated in smooth, hard, radiant, very white and very thick mother-of-pearl. Some grow silver pearls, like luminescent moons locked up in underwater jewellery boxes.

Many saltwater nations on the north coast have cultural links with pearl shell. (Saltwater refers to those Indigenous Australian nations or clans situated by the ocean, with other geographically based identifiers including 'freshwater people', 'spinifex people' and 'desert people'.) According to Bardi and Djawi Elder Aubrey Tigan, here in the Kimberley those iridescent shells belong to Aalingoon (Rainbow Serpent) who 'came down here . . . and lives beneath the sea. He comes every full moon, when it's a big tide. As he floats on his back . . . the scales fall off his back and turn into goowarn (pearl shell) as they drift down to the seabed below.' This belief aligns with those of other ancient cultures: during the Chinese Tang Dynasty, scaled dragons were depicted clutching or chasing a flaming pearl, while the Gnostic text from Syria, *Hymn of the Pearl*, tells the story of a boy asked to retrieve a pearl from a serpent in Egypt.

Trading pearl shell began in Australia long ago, first with inland nations where the shell was associated with water, rain and life. Incredibly, a 22,000-year-old pearl shell fragment was found in a West Kimberley rock shelter having travelled two hundred kilometres from shore. Later, Macassan fishermen from present-day Indonesia made annual voyages to northern Australia in search of trepang (sea cucumber), pearl and turtle. And finally, from the mid-nineteenth century onwards divers leapt from European pearling boats, called luggers, to collect shells lining the seabed of Broome's Roebuck Bay.

After a night at the Broome Vacation Village, I called Tyson's aunt Caroline and she suggested I come over. She lived not far from the town's famed Cable Beach, in a suburb consisting of tidy, one-storey brick bungalows. I found hers on a quiet cul-de-sac made shady and inviting with flourishing tropical trees.

A woman with a soft, friendly face opened the door. 'Monica?' she asked.

'That's me.'

Caroline stepped onto the porch, and we looked at each other awkwardly for a moment. She didn't seem to know quite what to do with me—not the first time on this trip my presence alone was baffling.

'So, do you want to chat inside or outside?' she asked doubtfully.

'I really don't mind.'

'I suppose inside might be better—it's cooler.' She opened the flyscreen door and led me down a short hallway into a kitchen and dining area. Framed photos of children and grandchildren stood upright on a cabinet. 'This is my husband, Ismail,' she said, pointing to a wiry man in the kitchen preparing a meal. He looked up at me and, smiling, asked how I was. 'And this is Ismail's mother, Tina,' Caroline added. An elderly woman with a frizz of curly grey hair and owl-like spectacles was sitting at the dinner table.

'Take a seat,' said Caroline, pouring us glasses of water.

I talked about my book and how I'd met Tyson, hoping this would adequately explain why a strange Chinese Australian woman was in their home. 'Tyson mentioned to me his great-grandmother was married to a Chinese pearler?'

'His name was Timothy Lo Sum Chai,' said Caroline. 'He went to Onslow on a pearling lugger. He loved it in Australia, so he just jumped off and stayed rather than going back to China.'

The luggers were handmade wooden vessels up to nineteen metres in length. They rode low in the water with canvas sails that harnessed the galloping winds. Over a century ago, fit, young Asian men like Timothy Lo Sum Chai—with an eye for adventure and dreams of making their fortune—were a common sight on the streets of Broome.

'I was surprised on the drive here to see street names like Taiji Road, Fong Way and Bin Sallik Avenue,' I said. Not only surprised but also impressed. For all of Sydney's visible multiculturalism, it has few street names or suburbs without Anglo names. It sends a subtle signal that only British Australians warrant honouring, even though a Mahomet, Ying or Moowattye may be just as deserving.

'That's a relatively recent thing—it wasn't always like that,' said Caroline. She recalled many years ago meeting her father's captain from his days in the army, a man called Jack So. 'When he drove around Broome he had tears in his eyes. He said, "There are no street names honouring my men."' His soldiers were more or less all former pearlers enlisted from Broome.'

Caroline was a Ngarluma woman who had grown up in Onslow, a coastal town further south from where I'd visited in the Pilbara. Her mother-in-law, Tina, was Yawuru from her mother's side, and Tina's father was a pearler from Borneo, Malaysia. Tina's husband,

Ismail's father, had also been a pearler from Borneo before he passed away thirteen years ago.

'Did your mother know all the tribal ways?' I asked Tina. 'She grew up bush?'

'Yeah, and she spoke Malay. Fluently.'

I calculated Ismail's racial makeup, and with a small jolt of surprise said to him, 'So, you're actually three-quarters Malay!' Come to think of it, he definitely looked Malay. But it wasn't exactly the most politically correct thing to say. The last group to tally up racial makeup were Australian government officials attempting to breed Aboriginality out of the country.

'People don't believe me, but we got Irish in us too,' said Ismail, his eyes twinkling. I had to admit that with his dark skin he didn't look the slightest bit Irish.

'Ismail's only got about that much,' Tina mimed a pinch with her fingers, 'white in him from my great-grandfather.'

I said to Ismail, 'Imagine if you went to Ireland and met someone who looked just like you.' I liked the idea of the grinning, brown-skinned Ismail standing on a rain-slicked pavement in Dublin, face-to-face with his grinning, pink-skinned distant Irish cousin.

'I'd love to go to Ireland to meet Mick Flavin, the country music singer,' Ismail said. He was mad for country music.

Malay, Irish Australian and Yawuru—it was terrific that such a stir-fry mix of countries and cultures could coalesce in a single human being as it did in Ismail. I found it uncanny to meet a family with both Aboriginal and Asian ties: they spoke with a blackfella accent, said Aboriginal English phrases like 'speak lingo', loved to go fishing, could cook beef rendang and had family in Malaysia—and in the case of Ismail, at least, joked about 'slopes' with self-deprecation.

They blurred the racial categories to which I was accustomed. It was a refreshing change to be put off balance by their hybridity—usually it was *my* hybrid Chinese Australian identity that startled those I met.

I reminisced with Tina and Ismail over visits to Malaysia: those afternoon walks through the steamy jungles, eating pungent, sweet durian, the rubber plantations and family reunions made challenging by language barriers. Something felt good about having this in common with a blackfella family and the way it sat outside the domain of British colonialism. We could put the burdensome pack of history down, breathe easy for a moment, and just speak as guileless children of the Asian diaspora.

I knew that throughout Australia's past, blended Asian and Aboriginal Australian families weren't uncommon. Throughout the nineteenth century, young Asian men, and rarely women, immigrated to Australia for work. Most of those men returned to China, but some married into white or Aboriginal families. As a consequence, it isn't unusual to meet Aboriginal people with Asian surnames.

'The Asian people like the Malays, the koepangers, the Japanese, the Chinese, they all mingled with the Aboriginal people on the pearling boats,' explained Ismail, cheerfully. Koepangers were those recruited from Kupang on the Indonesian part of Timor.

Although the ten-person lugger crews differed in culture, religion and language, they became close-knit families during their weeks out at sea, working from dawn to dusk in gruelling conditions. A century ago in Broome, no one would have blinked an eye at meeting Aboriginal people who could speak some Japanese, Chinese or Malay, with them having taught their Asian coworkers English in return.

How exciting to learn of Asian-Aboriginal relationships characterised by friendship, romance and cooperation. Quite unlike that of my generation, best characterised as one of displacement when Aboriginal public housing in Sydney's suburb of Redfern was being knocked down to make way for apartments catering to Asian uni students.

However, throughout the first half of last century, Australia had a markedly different attitude to all the dusky-skinned babies being born in Broome. The town—or 'Mongrelia' as it was called by one newspaper in true tabloid fashion—was even highlighted during parliamentary discussions in the lead-up to the *Immigration Restriction Act 1901*, framed as a doomsday look into what the country should expect if non-white immigration was to continue. The act became the first major piece of legislation for newly federated Australia and halted almost all non-white immigration into the country. Across the nation, population numbers in Asian communities plummeted. Ironically Broome's well-known Asian flavour was preserved thanks to the town's master pearlers, who petitioned for exemptions from the regulations due to their industry being so heavily reliant on cheap labour from our neighbours to the north.

I asked Tina if she knew much about the pearling industry during her dad's time.

'Back then they wore the full diving dress with the big helmets,' she said.

In town on a display, I'd seen photos of the lead-weighted boots, baggy, rubberised, canvas suits, and fishbowl helmets, that could total over eighty kilograms—impossibly bulky, yet worn by divers while collecting pearls. It was incredibly dangerous work; before World War I, up to a third of indentured divers were dying on the job or from related disease and injury.

'Did your father ever get the bends?' I asked.

Decompression sickness, or 'the bends' as it's commonly known, has symptoms that are the stuff of nightmares: the feeling of insects crawling all over your skin, paralysis, and itching, mottled or marbled skin. And of course, if the bends doesn't get you as you surface from the ocean's depths, there are still sharks, rip-tides, whirlpools and cyclones to contend with.

'No, but my cousin Sali's husband took the bends,' said Tina. 'Just looking by the way his eyes were sticking out of the sockets, we thought he was going to die. It was scary.'

In 1913—in response to grumblings about Broome as an Asian hotspot blighting white Australia—the federal government hired twelve divers from the British Navy to work for the pearlers. Many died within a couple of seasons. That was the last time a white man put on the hard hat. It was such a difficult and dangerous profession, and for such little pay—'the life incompatible with that a European worker is entitled to live', noted a royal commissioner later.

I had read in a paper looking at Asian and Aboriginal pearlers in Australia, by historian Julia Martínez, that among the pearling masters were the good, the bad and the ugly. The industry was rife with stories of brutal twelve-hour shifts without breaks, insufficient food, and cramped and unhygienic living quarters. When there weren't enough Aboriginal serfs to go around, indentured labourers from Asia filled out the crews, sometimes working an entire year just to pay off a debt incurred in transport costs to come to Australia. If subsequent debts arose, the unpaid work continued. Indentured labour was used in the Australian pearling industry right into the 1970s.

And rarely was the work a path to citizenship. 'My father fought for the Australian Army and he was a pearl diver, but still he couldn't be naturalised,' said Tina. Though she was nearly eighty, her sense of indignation hadn't subsided. 'I'm still waiting for his war medals to come.'

Her father hadn't just been in the army—he'd belonged to a top-secret Allied forces unit, Z Special, dedicated to covert recon-naissance and sabotage operations. It was made up, in part, of Asian Australians, hand-picked because their appearance and language skills assisted them in infiltrating enemy lines in Japanese-occupied parts of Southeast Asia. I was struck by the irony that the same racial element that saw these men excluded from Australian society had been exploited for the country's war effort.

According to Tina, her Yawuru mother didn't have it much better. 'Coloured people weren't allowed on the streets after dark, so before six o'clock you had to be behind the common gate. In the early days, the white man was boss over the Aboriginal people. We weren't treated as humans.'

'If you were found, what would happen?' I asked, in half disbelief. A few years ago I had learned that in America's dark past, the slaves of the south were cruelly punished if caught beyond the plantations they were assigned to. It was a deeply disturbing notion that such curtailing of personal freedom of one group of people by another had taken place here, too.

'My mother was caught that many times, they send her to Beagle Bay, away from Broome. About three times she went to Beagle Bay. The last one was they sent her to Moola Bulla out at Halls Creek. It was like a,' Tina chuckled, 'well, we called it a concentration camp.'

It seemed, to me, a particularly dark family joke.

Later I read that Moola Bulla had been set up in 1910 by the Western Australian government to train Aboriginal people to work in the pastoral industry, against a backdrop of increasingly violent confrontations between locals and the European newcomers over land and cattle. But Moola Bulla quickly degenerated into an institution where Aboriginal 'troublemakers' were detained and 'half-caste' children sent for a European education. I learnt of a particularly haunting story about a man sent there, named Ballymungen, whose son had been taken away. Every night Ballymungen would still make food for his son and speak to him as if he were there. His story is one of many heartbreaking accounts of parents who pined for their Stolen Generation children.

I mentioned that in a couple of days I'd be walking out of Broome up along the coast, on a nine-day guided tour called the Lurujarri Heritage Trail. Apparently there was a chance we'd go fishing, which I was particularly excited about. 'Do you know of a good fishing store in town?' I asked.

Caroline gave me the name of a place and said Ismail and Tina were related to those families in charge of the tour. 'Salmon is running now. And they do a lot of reef fishing up that way, so you need a lot of tackle!'

Like so many Aboriginal families they loved to fish, and their repertoire in the kitchen had lots of seafood dishes cooked in Asian flavours: steamed fish with chilli, lemongrass and coconut milk; dugong with soy sauce. The NITV show *Kriol Kitchen*, filmed in Broome, celebrates Aboriginal Australian home cooking that uses native Australian foods with Asian recipes, like goolil (turtle) chilli tamarind sambal or magpie goose curry with pan-fried damper.

'It's almost two o'clock,' Ismail said to his wife, pointedly.

Caroline gave me an apologetic look. 'We have grandkids we got to pick up.'

'I'll get out of your hair,' I said, with a smile.

But before I got up to go, Ismail opened the freezer and came back to the table to show me a sandwich bag of salmon. 'This is my salted fish!' he said proudly, opening it up so I could have a sniff. 'Oh, one's gone mouldy,' he said, peering at it. 'I'll have to chuck it out.'

'No, you soak it,' his mum said.

'Or you wanna cut that piece off?' his wife suggested.

'Just carrying on the tradition of what the old man taught me,' he said, happy as a clam.

*

In Broome, through the media grapevine that can follow you to the ends of the earth, I learned that a prominent Indigenous man I'd once interviewed had learned of my trip. Apparently he had exploded with irritation. He was sick of Australians who used Indigenous Australia to 'find themselves', blustering to a mutual acquaintance, 'Why can't they just leave us alone?'

When I heard about this, I burnt with humiliation.

And I was frightened that my trip had attracted the animosity of such a powerful man. I had assumed my relationship to Indigenous Australia was different to that of a white Australian—that when I entered Indigenous communities, I didn't wear the ugly historical mantle of coloniser.

Colonialism? *That's white people's problem.*

But no. There it was—being a non-white Australian did not automatically make me an ally of Indigenous Australia. A few months earlier I had been interviewed by ABC Radio and after they posted the recording online under the wince-inducing headline 'Monica Tan's Indigenous Odyssey', someone responded sarcastically on Twitter: 'I am waiting to be discovered.' Now, to this prominent Indigenous man I was simply another damaged Aussie having a life crisis, bags packed tidily as a Mormon's, wandering the Outback in search of blackfellas. I was reminded of a cynical saying: that every whitefella who heads to a remote blackfella community can be classified as a 'missionary, mercenary or misfit'—or, arguably, a combination of the three. How naive I'd been to believe that as a non-white Australian I would be considered an exception and entitled to an exclusive all-access pass into Indigenous Australia. He wanted no bar of it.

All of this played on my mind as I drove to Roebuck Bay, having left Caroline's house. I parked in an almost empty lot. The bay is known as Nalen Nalena to the Djungun and Yawuru traditional owners, its crimson sands marbled with the blue veins of an outgoing tide.

It was quiet now, but a century ago this had been the parking lot for hundreds of pearling luggers. The air would have been filled with the sound of creaking wood as they swayed in the sea. During the lay-up season from December to March, torrential rains shut the industry down; it was said you could jump from lugger to lugger, from Dampier Creek to Town Beach, without touching the ground. Before the ubiquity of plastic, Broome was supplying the world with mother-of-pearl that was cut into buttons or inlaid in cutlery handles, combs, knives, buckles, cufflinks, musical instruments, revolvers and furniture.

From there I took a lazy stroll; the only pace acceptable in a holiday town like Broome. I wandered up Dampier Terrace until I hit a short strip of upmarket jewellery stores—Cygnet Bay Pearls, Jewels of the Kimberley—and in their windows I saw, on velvet stands, marble-sized pearls hanging from gold pendants or set into diamond rings. There was nothing new about the pearl's association with luxury and extravagance. One store had printed on a sign the 2000-year-old folkloric story of Cleopatra who, in an attempt to impress Marc Antony with her lavishness, took off one of her enormous pearl earrings, dropped it into a glass of vinegar and then drained the glass.

In the wild, the pearl is an aberration—a minuscule irritant trapped in the soft tissue of the mollusc. To neutralise this rude invader, the mollusc forms a pearl sac of tissue and steadily secretes the material that coats the inner surface of its shells. Eventually, the irritant is rendered an inert and rarely perfectly round ball.

Eventually I took a left turn, heading to the centre of town, and at a crossing saw a small metal plaque. It was set in reddish stone and honoured the city's Aboriginal pearl divers in English and the local Aboriginal language of Yawuru: 'To our old peoples, coastal people, river people, desert people. You were blackbirded, forcibly removed from your traditional Country to work, to serve the early pearling trade. You had the first cultural links to the pearl shell.'

The early European Australian pearling companies, often in cahoots with pastoralists further inland, invaded these lands by gunpoint, killing people who resisted and forcing the rest into a life of serfdom. The Yawuru, Karajarri, Nimanburru, Jabirr Jabirr, Nyulnyul and Bardi are all nations whose cultures and ways of life were upended as their young men and women were ripped from their traditional lifestyles and blackbirded—forced or tricked—into the industry as pearl harvesters or sex workers. With the industry came jetties, shops, road and towns; the land was blasted then forged into new shapes.

Broome boasts of having the world's longest-running outdoor cinema, Sun Pictures, which opened in 1916. I came across it in the middle of town. From the outside it was a combination of timber and corrugated iron, painted in cream with sky-blue and earth-red detailing. The words 'SUN PICTURES' were set in light bulbs, in the fashion of Hollywood's golden age. Inside, the floorboards were made of warm jarrah, and many rows of beach-style canvas chairs faced a missing wall and an outside section with a movie screen. Being an outdoor cinema, it only showed films after dark. But some tourists were milled about, savouring that sense of having stepped back in time.

I wandered over to a wall covered in film posters and historical photos. Immediately I was struck by one framed, black-and-white photo, taken in the 1920s. The photographer had been standing in front of the screen, facing a full house packed to the rafters. The audience was almost exclusively men and boys, all dressed in their best white shirts and some with snappy fedoras. The youngest in the room were three identical little Asian boys in the front row, with one brother sitting on probably their father's lap. But the most fascinating aspect of the photo was also its most obvious. The best seats in the house—cane chairs with cushions, in the middle of the cinema— were occupied exclusively by white men. Almost everyone else, sitting higgledy-piggledy on hard wooden benches and in deckchairs around them, was dark-skinned.

The fact that Australia had colour bars in hospital wards, movie theatres, RSLs, hotels and swimming pools—until as recently as the 1960s in many parts of the country—was something I'd only learnt of while working at *The Guardian*. And I'd never before seen a photo that so clearly documented the segregation. Standing in a cinema whose audience was once discriminated against based on race, and seeing such undeniable proof of it, made this ugly part of our history much more real for me.

It made me wonder: why has this so rarely been portrayed in our depictions of Australian history? In our national consciousness, the word 'segregation' is associated with somewhere else: perhaps South Africa or the United States, with images of 'whites only' drinking taps and Rosa Parks so famously taking a stand on that bus. Genocide, slavery and segregation—do these words apply to Australia?

As I stood there in front of that photo, I could hear the conservative historians and right-wing media pundits foaming at the mouth at the mere suggestion. *What bullocks, what a crock, don't try and make me eat your black armband history turd.* And so strongly were those words linked in my mind to the brutality of countries far away (not here) that even while faced with such incontrovertible evidence, I still felt as if it was an act of semantic extremism to describe Australia in such a way.

I plonked myself in one of the canvas chairs, where I guessed the Chinese and Japanese section would have been located. From here I would have seen a row of white men, just the backs of their heads, hair neatly combed and shiny with Brylcreem. Those men would have been the less moneyed Europeans, while sitting further in front were the white master pearlers, medical officers, merchants and officials.

The largest contingent was the remaining 'coloured people'. Malays, Timorese, Filipinos and Aboriginal people would have sat smooshed together behind a mesh wire railing on stadium-style benches close to the noisy projector at the back of the cinema, or on the neck-craning seats up front. They entered via a separate door on the right-hand side of the theatre.

Darwinism had gripped the imagination of the Western world and seemed to give scientific credence to the notion certain races were superior to others. Conveniently, the palest skin tones were positioned at the apex, while Indigenous Australians were regarded as little more than a dying breed. Back then this cinema was a perfect diagram of Australia's social hierarchy, carefully carved up by both race and class.

And where were my people? Literally, sandwiched in the middle.

Not only were east Asians considered to be mid-tone in skin colour, our society was familiar to Europeans. We had merchant culture's commerce and currency, officialdom, taxes, bureaucracy, military, written language, mathematics, built architecture, private land ownership and agriculture, cities and dominions. To the colonial rulers, these were markers of civilisation that elevated us, somewhat, from the 'primitive cultures'.

Considering white Australia's attempts to definitively demarcate what constituted a 'civilised' and 'uncivilised' Australian, no wonder they were so horrified by the rampant 'miscegenation' in Broome. Such populations were considered 'unstable, directionless and altogether inferior to racially pure communities' and 'a threat to cohesion', wrote historian David Walker in his 2013 essay 'Broke Narratives: Reflections on the history of Australia's Asian connections'. In the early twentieth century, William Gay wrote the popular poem 'Australian Federation', about the Australian people belonging to 'one dear blood'. But the more babies being born of mixed descent—a quarter this, one eighth that—the harder it was to know what type of prejudice to apply to someone.

At a time when young Australia was forging a new national identity, a town like Broome was a blemish on our reputation. In the heady years around the time of Federation, Australians wanted to wean themselves off the tit of Mother England but still regarded themselves, dutifully, as an extension of her flesh and blood. Virtually every parliamentarian feared that Australia might be viewed as a mangy, mongrel dog of a country—white was right, but white was not yet might. This piece of Britain—broken off and plonked onto the other side of the world, thinly spread on an enormous continent—remained vulnerable to the depraved morass of almond-eyed, dark-skinned 'Orientals' and Pacific Islanders to the north. You can't control what you don't understand, and Broome's proper mixed-up racial jumble must have looked like a disaster in the making.

As I sat there in the canvas chair, I began to mull over what Tina had said about her mother being sent to Moola Bulla just because she was out on the streets after dark. Could that really be correct? Surely it wasn't the full story. It felt wrong. It sounded too extreme. At most, perhaps, it was the result of a scoundrel policeman gone rogue. I pulled out my phone to see what evidence I could dig up online that might support her story.

It didn't take long to find. I brought up a copy of Western Australia's *Aborigines Act of 1905*, section 40 of which states: 'any female aboriginal who, between sunset and sunrise, is found within two miles of any creek or inlet used by the boats of pearlers or other sea boats shall be guilty of an offence against this Act'.

I shook my head and felt ashamed. Not only for what had happened but also for being so sceptical of Tina.

How many times have non-Indigenous people doubted Indigenous horror stories because, just like an oyster faced with a foreign irritant, we find it easier to take troubling pieces of information and coat them with doubt, over and over and over, until they disappear altogether and are rendered benign to us? But this legal document proves, unequivocally, that my country once legislated such demeaning treatment of Western Australian Aboriginal people. This document makes a mockery of the Australian 'fair go'.

However, despite the racist legislation, despite this cinema's old border wall, Aboriginal Australians with Asian heritage—and a dash of Irish, like Ismail—continued to be born in Broome. After all, for much of its history, the town was just a remote dot in a vast swathe of wild, wild Australian west, where police presence was patchy at best. A town where coloured workers were exploited, and audacious Chinese and Japanese pearlers used white 'dummy' owners to make good on the paperwork. And under cover of night, on boats and cattle stations, Asian and Aboriginal lives remained intertwined.

As the Chinese proverb goes, 'Heaven is high and the emperor is far away', and Broome will forever remain a town of fusion food and fusion families.

PART FOUR
Lurujarri Trail

7 AUGUST
Day 63

Roger, one of many baby boomers on our trail walk, pointed at our Goolarabooloo guide and whispered to me, 'He looks like he's walking slowly, but I can barely keep up!'

It was day two of the Lurujarri Heritage Trail and our guide, Edward, was leading our line of walkers on a narrow track. He was dressed in a baseball cap, white singlet and shorts; on his feet, he wore thongs with a single thick band around the forefoot that reminded me of what my cousins in rural Malaysia shuffled around in. Kind of hilarious considering how this morning, among the walkers, a subject of much consternation had been optimal footwear for today's 22-kilometre walk through changing terrain.

The Goolarabooloo guides deliberately refrained from giving us too much information, encouraging us to 'be present'—with mixed success. We'd been told to shut off our brains and lead with our hearts: no easy task for a thirty-odd party of urban professionals. We were here to experience 'living Country' not conquer a trek. That said, not everyone had been able to resist bringing their Fitbits along.

Edward's insouciant choice of shoe and the way he almost slouched along with a natural gait, straight-backed yet relaxed, made a mockery of us all and our top-of-the-line, abrasion resistant, antimicrobial sandals (and the spare top-end sneakers in our packs). An old cordial container filled with water swung from one shoulder on a rope, a walkie-talkie and first-aid kit from the other. A packet of smokes stuck out of his back pocket.

'I'm practically running,' panted Roger.

Later I asked another walker, a physio, about whether the Goolarabooloo guides used a particular movement we should be emulating. She didn't think so; she just thought they were comfortable in the environs. They weren't working hard like we were having to—in uncertain territory, alert, anxious, taking note of everything, with information overload. 'Not in your own body, somehow,' she said. They were acclimatised to the heat, to walking the soft, undulating sand, that with every step seemed to disappear underfoot with a sigh.

The Lurujarri Trail wasn't the first multi-day walk Roger and his wife had done. There had been the Portuguese section of the Camino de Santiago, which leads to the shrine of the apostle St James the Great in north-western Spain. In Japan they'd walked the Kumano Kodō, with its three ancient shrines; over the centuries many of the villages it passes through have grown accustomed to the pilgrims, accommodating them with affordable traveller inns.

'I guess this is a bit of a pilgrim's walk too,' I said.

'Yes, I guess it is!' Roger replied, sounding surprised.

Now in August, mornings on the Lurujarri were cool as south-easterlies swept over the landscape. Then temperatures would climb as high as thirty degrees in the afternoons, before quickly cooling off in the evenings as sea mist came prowling on dry land.

Our 72-kilometre hike over nine days was along the bottom third of a 450-kilometre Dreaming track that follows the Ululong Law cycle. It begins at Ardiyaloon (One Arm Point) on the coast of the Kimberley, then traces the coastline south to Wabona, about two hundred kilometres south of Broome. The Ululong links the lands of the Bardi-Djawi, Nyulnyul, Jabirr Jabirr, Ngumbarl, Djungun, Yawuru and Karajarri peoples.

On the Ululong, the Dreaming is known as Bugarregarre. The ancestors in these stories were not ordinary flesh-and-blood men and women. Rather they were powerful beings that lived when the land was unformed—half-dream, half-reality, a thick primordial soup. As they lived and journeyed, their actions and interactions with one another gave the land its shape—the very mountains, rivers, rocks, waterholes, stars, trees, animals and birds we could see today—and through their wisdom and follies laid down the patterns of life and Law, showing all subsequent generations how to live.

In a story shared on the SBS series *Songlines*, Goolarabooloo man Richard Hunter spoke of his people's Naji spirit beings. 'These first people come out from Dabberdabbergun, the birthplace. They used to walk up on to the beach. It was a silent world. The first sound was created and wake everything up. Now they have to drink. So Bugarregarre they dreamt that there is water, but it's inland. So they made their journey.'

All over Australia, Dreaming stories coalesce around physical tracks, known in English as songlines, songcycles or Dreaming tracks. Each has a birthplace and an end place, and in between many, many sites that are the settings for these stories. Over the millennia the sites have remained spiritually charged thanks to countless ceremonies conducted by human caretakers. Because the stories describe the land in immense detail, they can be used as oral maps and allow story keepers to navigate tremendous distances.

Australia's vast lattice of Dreaming tracks simultaneously acted as trading routes upon which shells, ochre, axes, spears, boomerangs, shields, narcotic plants, songs, dances and even wives were once dispatched.

Some of these tracks cover mind-boggling distances. The Eaglehawk Dreaming track, for instance, connects Heavitree Gap in Alice Springs to Byron Bay on the east coast, while the Black Snake/Bogong Moth Dreaming track connects Normanton in the Gulf of Carpentaria to the Snowy Mountains near Canberra. Many of today's highways are upgrades of colonial-era dirt roads that were built on Dreaming tracks, including one that starts in Darug Country in western Sydney, goes through Sackville and then along the current Great Western Highway to Little Hartley just beyond the Blue Mountains.

We passed by a large and shallow pool of water, so still the vain sky bent down and filled the surface with a perfect likeness of itself. In less than a day of walking, we had left behind the hustle and bustle of Broome town life. Out here evidence of human occupation was still tangible but more muted and melted into the non-human world: a few footprints, the ashy smudge of an old fire. This was a landscape dominated by an infinite sky and imperial ocean, and I was immediately humbled by it.

Somewhere in the tidal flats of Ngunungurrukun we stopped for a break. To my delight, a guide gestured towards the horizon at a mixed flock of gudurlwarany (brolgas) and lindalinda (jabirus or black-necked stork). I pointed my binoculars at the birds, watching as a lindalinda gave a small flap of its wings, lifted into the air and performed the folk dance for which its species is famed. The bird was dressed formally: black and white feathers, with a head and neck that from certain angles shone with the shifting bluish-purplish-greenish iridescence of a soap bubble. All of the birds moved with slow-moving elegance—avian world royalty. Edward said they were pecking for yarrinyarri, a type of bush onion. He plucked one growing shallow in the sand and showed it to us. It was tiny and light-brown, the size of a child's fingernail.

One of the senior patriarchs of the Goolarabooloo community, Phil, pointed out a water soak in the distance. He had a croaky, commanding voice and an impressive belly on two solid legs that made him look stately. I squinted at a patch of dark green that, seemingly to him and the other guides, was clear as a neon sign reading 'HERE BE WATER'. He said you could dig or, 'When the tide comes in, it pushes the water up, fresh as.' Such secret stores of freshwater were once crucial to survival. I was struck by how much I took water for granted. On this trip it was delivered in plastic tanks on trucks; if I were here alone with no supplies, I would be dead in three days.

Phil was guardian to 'living history' and of these lands through which the Dreaming track passed. He had a duty to keep making this same journey as the ancient ones, and to ensure through cere-mony—song, dance, ritual, painting the body with ochre, stories, language—that the land was kept in good health. The more know-ledge an elder has, the more status and power they are bestowed in their clan. In this part of Australia, the most senior men burdened with guardianship of the Dreaming track and their lands, and with responsibility for the smooth transmission of knowledge and transfer of duties to the next generation, are known as maja (Law bosses).

The very existence of the land is dependent on that transmission. In the Goolarabooloo world the divisions between past, present and future often merge. Guardians aren't so much repeating the past or upholding tradition as they are actively *maintaining* living history. In a documentary I'd watched, one of the key non-Goolarabooloo members of the Goolarabooloo community—a wiry, suntanned Dutchman called Frans Hoogland—illustrates the Dreaming by pressing a handful of sand into an amorphous shape in his hand, then letting it crumble: a metaphor for a reality that isn't fixed as it is in Western thought, but rather a creative, ongoing, flexible process, constantly reshaped and 'kept together through interactions between people, animals and the Dreaming'.

We walked 'long-way' on the beach, and in parts the hike grew tedious. To pass the time I took note of marks in the sand: the spotted scuttling of hermit crabs, the two-feet-and-a-tail marks of wallabies, arrow-like bird tracks, snakes, car tyres, what looked like dingo tracks and, of course, human footprints. Stare at something long enough and details will emerge; I'd never noticed how distinct a footprint is. Humiliatingly, a couple of walkers pointed out that I was 'duck footed'—something I was aware of but was ordinarily concealed.

I thought back to my visit to Lake Mungo, where I'd seen on display a replica of a series of Pleistocene-era footprints discovered there in 2003. It was the largest such collection anywhere in the world. Some twenty thousand years ago, the twenty-five individual trackways—mostly human, but also some marsupial and emu—were made on a damp claypan. In 2006, park officials invited a group of highly skilled Pintubi trackers from Central Australia to take a look. The trackers concluded that among this family group traversing the claypan was a child who walked, paused, turned and ran away from the group but then walked quickly back. A day or two later another group, likely men, crossed the same area while running. The trackers also deduced that a spear was thrown, missed its prey and skidded into the ground. Most intriguing was a single line of right footprints, which the trackers said must have belonged to a one-legged man capable of hopping very quickly with the other hunters.

At the time I'd read this, I'd been incredulous that the trackers could extract such detailed knowledge from footprints alone. Only now did I have an inkling of just how much information footprints betrayed.

We veered onto a narrow track through dense vegetation, spreading out along a line so we were walking in small groups. One of the guides, Tay, and I found ourselves separated from the rest of the pack, but he continued to identify for me trees, fruits and birds, and the porpoises swimming in the ocean. His hair curled in tight black coils that from the sun had become coppery red at the ends. He, too, suffered from duck feet and I thought, *Boy, we must look like a pair of dopey Charlie Chaplins.*

He pointed out one of the region's best-known plants, the gubinge tree. Also known as the Kakadu plum, it's tropical-looking with broad paddle-shaped leaves, and it has one of the highest concentrations of vitamin C of any fruit in the world. At this time of year its branches were barren, but back in Broome at a market I'd sampled a dried piece—unsurprisingly it had an extremely citrusy taste, almost like orange sherbet. A local industry was shipping boatloads of the stuff overseas, and countries like China were requesting volumes forty times what northern Australia could supply.

The trees here had so much personality. The morrells around me seemed to grow horizontally, spreading out with low branches like opening beach umbrellas. Wavy-edged leaves quivered in the wind.

Among the Goolarabooloo people, married men and their mothers-in-law have an 'avoidance relationship': if one walks into a room, the other is obliged to walk out. And so the shrubby jigal tree, with leaves like butterfly wings facing back-to-back, became known as the mother-in-law tree.

Oddest to me was the manujen with perky orange fruit like Jaffa lollies, currently ripe. Earlier one of the guides, a white woman who'd been a friend of the Goolarabooloo people for many decades, had mentioned the fruit 'leaves your tongue feeling furry'. I plucked one and popped it in my mouth; it tasted like sweet potato and, sure enough, the strangest sensation soon followed, as if my tongue had sprouted a layer of fuzz.

Tay and I rejoined the rest of the group and walked through a section of Lurujarri covered in middens and flecked by thousands of colourful, triangle-shaped rock shards, mainly cast-offs from stone toolmaking. We continued to walk, through an expansive ocean of sand, and were eventually directed by our guides to gather around some pale stones. The hot sun felt like a cattle prod against the backs of our necks.

I gasped as I stared at the ground: these weren't stones, rather bones bleached blindingly white from years of sun.

Tay crouched by the bones, and with large and gentle hands lifted up an intact skull, sand pouring out through the gap in its cranium.

'Was that person from this trip or the last?' joked one of the walkers.

Edward didn't immediately reply, rather gave a secretive smile and then explained these were the bones of their elderly people. 'They just go here and die. If they old and crook they camp here, have a drink of water until they can't go any further.'

It was easy to picture: an old lady sitting cross-legged in the sand, stoking a small campfire. The sun rises, then sets, and the moon does the same. She watches quietly and waits, fading with every hour. All around her are the lurujarri—coastal dunes for which the trail is named—and the yanijarri—red pindan cliffs—the last things she will ever see.

It was haunting to think about, and for a moment none of us said anything. I listened to the wind on the sand, like the shuffling footsteps of silent congregants in a cathedral. So often Indigenous Australians reveal a majesty in their relationship to the land that makes us non-Indigenous Australians feel ashamed of our boorishness.

Along the trail, we passed by ancient burial sites dotted between water soaks, bush food pantries, dinosaur prints pressed into the rock and rock tool workshops. We were camping in spots that had been camped at for thousands of years, and would soon be fishing on reefs that had been fished on for thousands of years.

The trail was first opened to the general public in 1987 by Paddy Roe, the former head of the Goolarabooloo people, in an effort to 'wake up' a relationship between non-Goolarabooloo Australians and the land. The trail is unique in the way it welcomes non-Goolarabooloo Australians to directly experience healthy Goolarabooloo Country. This coastline was mostly left untouched by pastoralists, industrialists and urban developers, and throughout colonisation had been kept in good spiritual condition via song and ceremony. As one of the non-Goolarabooloo members of their community said to me, 'whether black, white or brindle' they were bound by one simple, guiding principle: 'maintain Law, culture and the buru (land)'.

One of the walkers asked how old the human remains were, and Tay said that nobody knew—archaeologists weren't allowed to touch them. On every walk along the trail they covered the skull back up, and by the next journey it had been exposed by the wind again. Here, preserving and respecting something meant leaving it where it was, as it was, rather than erecting a fence around it, collecting it for scientific study, or sticking it in a hermetically sealed glass cabinet in a museum thousands of kilometres away.

Tay scooped up a few handfuls of sand and reverentially spread it over the skeleton until all traces of it were erased.

*

With exhilaration I spotted camp on the horizon. Together with other walkers, I gave a weary cheer. Our group dribbled in at different times, having done the last section of the walk at our own pace. We'd left last night's camp at seven in the morning and it was now four in the afternoon.

A plastic mat had been rolled out over the sand. Too tired to do anything else, I dropped my pack and plonked myself on it with a satisfied grin. Tarps had been strung up on a nearby tree for extra shade, and adjacent were long trestle tables that served as a makeshift kitchen and buffet area.

The Goolarabooloo guides were assisted by some non-Goolarabooloo volunteers—sun-dried nomad types—and over the many hours we'd walked they had been busy transporting gear on a truck, including two heavy fridges, our luggage and bits of furniture, to set up the camp. One volunteer was feeding logs into a fiery pit, over which stood three huge blackened pots with ladles: one with drinking water, the second to refill the dish-washing station, and the third with steaming black tea.

Those nomads were a better cultural fit with the Goolarabooloo than us urban professionals. Their laissez-faire attitude tried our patience. We wanted to know what, where and when things were happening, and the replies from the Goolarabooloo could be maddeningly vague. *When can we go crab hunting?* 'After lunch sometime,' they'd say, with a shrug. *Yes, but when precisely after lunch?* The Goolarabooloo were only specific when it mattered, and I had to admit that had advantages. Plans were adapted to shifting conditions; we could choose the best thing to do when the time and weather was right.

The nomads and Goolarabooloo families were close. Between them were long-standing friendships, some spanning decades. Together they had erected their tents away from us walkers in a huddle of nylon and polyester, with four-wheel drives, big as bulls, parked nearby. I marvelled at the way both groups never seemed to give off any sense of needless busyness. Even when they were working hard—stirring cooking pots, gathering firewood, washing cutlery, passing around chubby babies dusted with pindan—they maintained the impression of sustained repose. Those who weren't working or out fishing or crab hunting sat about in their campsite on weaved mats or camp chairs, chewing the fat in a low, quiet drone, now and then shooing away a fly with an easy wave.

Some of the paying walkers felt too intimidated to breach the divide and interact with the Goolarabooloo families. To me it was like being back in school and rapping nervously on the staffroom door—there was an air about the place that shifted when I entered, and I instinctively felt it was out of bounds. I also suspected that the Goolarabooloo families were a bit shy.

I erected my tent between two paperbarks on the edge of camp. Unlike those I'd seen in other parts of Australia, the paperbarks here were stunted and hunched over. Their flaking-bark boughs reached towards my tent like the thin arms of protective grandparents. I made things extra homely by hanging my water bag on a branch and using my sarong to create extra shade.

Getting to the bathroom required a bit of a trudge through a long sandbank. The path was lined with red ribbons tied in bows to tree branches and solar-powered lights planted in the ground. Finally I reached a small water tank with hand soap, where the path split and led to two drop toilets. Each had a bamboo curtain strung up to provide some privacy and a container of toilet paper labelled 'shit pit kit'.

I was weary and sweaty, definitely ready for a swim. The entrance to the beach was west of the campsite, so I took the path curving along a small sand dune that blocked any ocean views. I could hear the waves, so knew I mustn't be too far back. To my left grew mangroves so impenetrable they seemed bewitched to guard something precious. I passed a flock of parrots, the neon green and red of a traffic light, decorating a bush.

I was carrying a knife borrowed from the kitchen in a bucket with some tackle. I had optimistic intentions to kickstart my new fishing career.

A group of children came down the path. They walked barefoot, and all their hair was wet and plastered to their heads. Having spotted me, some of them grinned.

'Hello!' I said. 'Do you know how I can get to the beach?'

A girl in a bright pink shirt offered to show me. 'C'mon!' she said, slipping her dove-like hand into mine. Without conferring, the rest tagged along like they were a bunch of helium balloons connected by string. They were full of exuberance and so generous with their affection—not a scrap of self-consciousness. You'd have to be pretty cold of heart not to fall in love with them.

One by one they introduced themselves: James, Rowena, Melanie, Lee-La, Trevor, Julio. 'Hi James, hi Rowena,' I said, going around the circle. They looked to be between eight and twelve years of age.

As I repeated each name, a cheeky smile dawned on their faces. Some put their hands over their mouths to smother laughter. Only one of the boys, who appeared younger than the rest, looked around the circle with a confused expression. 'No, it's not,' he said in a small voice.

The others hissed, 'Shut up.'

But the jig was up, and no one had the discipline to keep going. They erupted into a fit of giggles and immediately confessed their real names.

'My name is Sally,' I said. *Hey, that was fun.*

'Sally, do you know how to speak Chinamen?' a boy with a mohawk asked, as we continued up the path.

I taught them how to say ni hao (hello) and, when my mind temporarily and inexplicably drew a blank on every other Mandarin word I knew, blurted out, 'Niubi.'

'That means "awesome",' I said quickly, and prayed they'd instantly forget. It actually means '*fucking* awesome'.

The children spoke a fusion of English, Kriol and local languages. In the old times their ancestors were polyglots, not only speaking their own language but also those of neighbouring nations.

At twelve, Kallista was older and more thoughtful than the other children, and wanted to know more Mandarin. She and I traded kou for yawa (mouth), jiao for yiniburu (foot), shui for aba (water), and cai for mayi (food).

Sal, the kid who'd asked if I could speak 'Chinamen', asked if I knew Jackie Chan.

'Know him?' I said. 'He's my uncle.'

The path meandered up a hill, and the children scrambled lightly to the top while I trudged through the sand.

Sal's nine-year-old cousin James (or was it Sebastian?) was whip smart like his sister Kallista and shot me a look heavy with suspicion. 'I don't believe you.'

'You ask him if he has a niece called Sally in Sydney, and he'll say he does,' I assured him, confident there was no way they could do that.

All but James were suitably impressed. 'What's he like?' someone asked.

'He's short in real life,' I said.

James wasn't budging and continued to stare at me with narrowed eyes, scrying for lies in my face. 'Where is he right now?'

I didn't skip a beat. 'He's in New York shooting a film.'

'What's his Chinaman name?'

I used to know that. What was it again? *No time, better make something up.* 'Chong Long.'

'I still don't believe you,' said James.

'I believe you,' said Sal, nodding his mohawked head. He was looking at me so trustingly that I knew, then and there, I was destined for hell.

The girls headed back to camp while the boys settled on another swim.

I followed them as they clambered up the sand dunes that blocked the beach. The dunes ended abruptly with a wall of rock several metres wide that was like nothing I'd ever seen before: a sandy pink colour, nobbled and scratchy as sandpaper, with the imposing spikiness of a gothic cathedral. It was painful to walk barefoot on the spires.

After a nervy hand-over-foot clamber down the rock turrets, I jumped the last section and my feet landed on sand.

I faced the open sea, and what I saw made my heart sing: a wide circle of sand, protected by that thorny hedge of rock and stealing a hint of pink from the setting sun. We stood on the wet sand and looked to the sky. Banks of fairy-floss clouds fanned out, their woolly edges glowing gold.

The boys were already turning into little ruffians but hadn't entirely lost their peach-fuzz sweetness. Seeing the diary in my hand, one of them offered to draw me a picture. 'Don't stare my work,' he kept saying, putting a protective arm around his drawing until he was finished. He had drawn a pointy Stüssy 'S', a classic schoolyard doodle, decorated with wavy lines, circles, triangles and zigzags. Putting the final stroke on his masterpiece, with a flourish he wrote: 'from Sally'. Another boy jeered, telling him it should say: 'to Sally'.

One of the boys asked me if I got jalla. 'Yes or no?'

'Yes,' I replied.

All the boys cracked up laughing.

'Do you know what jalla means?' the boy asked. He had a buzzcut and a toughboy look.

'No, don't tell her!' the other boys shouted.

'Do you have jalla?'

'Yes,' I said again, smiling to myself.

They cracked up again.

The toughboy was gasping for air with laughter, clutching his stomach. 'Do you know what kaka is? That's what jalla is—it's shit! *You said you have shit!*'

A figure appeared from the rock hedge and came striding down the beach. It was one of the walkers; I remembered him introducing himself as a retired film and media pilot. He was in his swimming trunks, silver hairs standing to attention from his barrel chest, looking every bit the ageing action hero.

'Let's go swim with the kartiya,' said the toughboy.

The boys zeroed in on the pilot, followed him into the ocean, and were soon splashing and jumping all over him.

I was amazed that this word for whitefella, kartiya, was used here. After first reading it in Kim Mahood's essay, I'd then heard it in conversation over a thousand kilometres away from where I stood now, at the Yuendumu art centre while chatting with a Warlpiri artist. I'd asked him if I would be considered a kartiya. Perhaps the term had been derived from a Warlpiri word for 'white' (kardirri), and clearly I wasn't literally white in skin colour—or did it just mean a non-Aboriginal person?

'No, you like us. You Yapa from China,' he replied, using the Warlpiri word for 'native person'. 'Chinese, Indian—you been colonised like us.'

I wasn't sure if I felt like a colonised person, but I appreciated his reply and took it as a gesture of solidarity.

He told me he was familiar with China, having visited when his work featured in a Shanghai art show. He had fallen in love with the city's soup dumplings and made a good friend, a Shanghainese guy and Aboriginal art lover, who had promised to introduce him to Jackie Chan. (I wondered how many Chinese people were, at any given moment, out in the great, wide world chatting to a local in a sleepy countryside village—in, say, France, Peru or South Africa—claiming to be a relative of Jackie Chan.)

'He's got connections to the Chinese Communist party,' the artist added about his Shanghainese friend, who was apparently 'very rich'.

'Everyone who is rich in China has connections to the Communist Party,' I replied.

After watching the boys have fun in the water, I decided I should swim too. The water was bracing and refreshing, cool but not cold. I sank low enough that the soft waves gently slapped my face, and rubbed fistfuls of wet sand over my grimy skin. Swimming further out, I allowed the crushing arms of the ocean to take hold of me and toss my body about. I propelled myself with long, even strokes, then indulged in the childish joy of duck diving.

It felt so good. After all that time wandering the desert, I realised how much I'd missed this.

Afterwards I walked back up the beach and gathered my fishing gear. I wandered over to where the rock wall curved and then dropped like stone steps into the ocean. What did I know about fishing? Next to nothing—but enough to guess that fish didn't just hook themselves. I needed bait. Fairly quickly I spotted a crab gripping the wall of a rockpool. It was a beautiful thing the size of my palm, orange with turquoise-blue streaks on its side. I almost felt annoyed at it for I knew I'd now have to kill it. I'd never killed anything larger than a mosquito in my life.

For a moment I just stood there, knife in my hand, geeing myself up, and both dreading and hoping it would just go away.

Then I lunged for it.

The tip of the knife connected with the crab's shell but failed to penetrate. The crab scuttled away, but it was cornered in a rockpool where the water was draining out.

I lunged again, and again the knife failed to penetrate.

My stabs were too half-hearted. I found it extremely difficult to kill this thing so fervently trying to escape death.

I was one beat too slow in delivering yet another feeble blow. The crab—no doubt profoundly thankful and amazed by my incompetence—ducked under a heavy-looking rock. Was there any point in me lifting that rock and trying again? Both the critter and I knew perfectly well I was incapable of executing the kill.

Deciding it was better to end the charade, I gave up on fishing.

I drifted up the beach and joined a row of my fellow walkers sitting on the sand. They were looking out to sea at a pod of humpbacks playing as the sun set. The whales had swum thousands of kilometres from the Antarctic to these relatively warm waters off the Kimberley coast—an ideal nursery to calve and care for their young. Through my binoculars, the whales were framed in a cinematic black circle. With incredible power their bodies exploded out of the water and then crashed down, splintering the calm of the ocean. Occasionally just the dark curve of a spine, slicked with water, would slide out and disappear moments later.

As the sun sat on the lip of the horizon, the colour of the water deepened. Lines of white birds crossed my field of vision like airborne ballerinas. Larger black and white birds, with very angular wings, dive-bombed into the ocean. Meaty fish, maybe mackerel or salmon, were circling schools of whitebait and forcing them to the surface—meaning the whitebait simultaneously became prey to the birds. I laughed with utter joy at such a performance. It was hard to identify which party was better at fishing, but I knew for sure that I wasn't in the running.

I hadn't expected to be so impressed by the beaches of the west coast. After all, I'm a saltwater person; I grew up by some of the most beautiful beaches in the world. So how come I was dumbstruck by this ocean? The template was the same: sand, sea and sky. Yet there was something different I couldn't put my finger on.

Perhaps it was the water—it had never occurred to me that something as vast and imperishable as the ocean might have a different personality elsewhere in the country. Around Sydney, waves spend longer in the open Pacific; by the time they ram themselves into the coastline, they are tall walls of roaring water that collapse dramatically into piles of ice-cold whitewash. But here in the Top End, the coastline is fringed by islands, local bays, headlands, reefs and gulfs; by the time they reach the shore, the waves have dissipated and roll sluggishly in. Here the water seems paler, calmer and warmer than the water down south. When the gentle waves sweep up and over the low slope of sand, they swish like a ballgown.

But that wasn't what had struck me—it was something else.

I laughed aloud when it came to me. On the east coast, I'd never once seen the sun set over the ocean. Here the setting sun sat like a pendant on the shimmering deep blue evening gown of the water. It had a drama and pageantry not found in the meditative sunrise, with regal pink and molten gold clouds gliding across the sky.

Is that what the Goolarabooloo people meant when they said here was 'Sunset Country' and the Naji spirit beings had headed for 'Sunrise Country'?

One of the other walkers, Lauren, was also from Sunrise Country and had seen plenty of them across the ocean of her home suburb of Bondi. She was around my age, with curly dark hair, and we spoke of a few awkward encounters throughout the trip.

That afternoon she had set up camp, only to have one of the Goolarabooloo families pull up in a mammoth 4WD.

'Is this your spot?' she asked them.

'Yes,' said one of the men.

'Uh, do you want me to move?'

'That'd be best,' he said, with a grave nod.

Lauren got ready to move until they saw it would be a hassle for her, and relented.

'Just for one night?' he asked her.

'Yes,' she promised.

To me, she wryly described the incident as 'a microcosm of the entire land rights issue'. She didn't like the fact she was occupying

someone else's land, but damn was it hard to give up such spectacular ocean views.

She also said that information wasn't exactly being served to us
walkers on a platter, and she'd dealt with this the only way she knew how.

'So, are there any sacred sites around here?' she'd asked Phil as he
cooked damper scones over a fire. In her mind, she was just making
small talk. Western culture teaches children that if you want to understand something, just ask. Questions are considered a sign of one's
curiosity or concern and quite often respect.

Yet Phil looked uncomfortable. 'Yeah,' he said, turning over the
scones.

'Whereabouts?'

He cocked his head inland. That day we had passed many
impressive red anthills.

'Ah,' she said, 'is it in the anthills?'

He looked even more uncomfortable. 'Nah.'

There was an awkward silence.

Lauren thought perhaps she wasn't making herself clear. 'So, where
is it, then?' she asked, more directly.

He looked peeved and burst out, 'Look, I can't tell you.'

That amazed her—the level of secrecy. I wondered if it was the
same place Edward had told some of us about: an area where no one
was allowed to camp or light fires. A powerful Bugarregarre snake
lived there, and it was forbidden to say his name. 'How do you know
what the name is if no one is allowed to say it?' a walker had asked
Edward, in the same vein as Lauren asking Phil. Edward had said
only the very old people were allowed to discuss the snake and its
place. This snake was a symbol of one of the kinship groups whose
responsibility was controlling social relationships. Members of the
group had the power to control living snakes and, by extension, controlled society. I later read the last man to inherit this special power
had died in a leprosarium called Bungarun in the nearby town of
Derby. In fact, hundreds of Aboriginal sufferers had spent the end

of their lives at Bungarun and were buried in its graveyard. The man who died had no living descendants and since then, alarmingly, no one had control of the snakes.

I told Lauren that throughout my Australian travels I'd had several experiences similar to hers: evasive answers to my questions or brilliant stories that ended with 'that's not to be repeated'. Knowledge in Aboriginal Australia seemed as tangible to me as a solid gold watch or a wooden chest of letters and photographs. Like family heirlooms, these stories are passed down through the generations, and their keepers have to be careful about who handles such precious things. There's also secret men's business and secret women's business, which are restricted by multiple levels of 'security clearance' that non-Aboriginal Australians more commonly associate with governmental spy agencies. Generally the only stories—or even versions of stories—shared with us are those few that have been 'declassified' by the powers that be.

In the old days a person could be speared to death just for looking at a sacred object or place that was forbidden to them. I hadn't heard any contemporary tales of capital punishment, but plenty about bone-chilling curses administered to those who failed in their caretaking of sacred sites or revealed secrets to those lacking in proper clearance.

The actor Balang T.E. Lewis had left his Ngukurr Country—Roper River, about three hundred kilometres from Katherine in the Gulf of Carpentaria—after his film *The Naked Country* was released in 1985. Elders had accused him of revealing secrets in the name of fame and put a death warrant out for him. 'Bit like Salman Rushdie,' he once told me in an interview, referring to the Islamic fatwa issued against the British Indian novelist in 1989, 'but an Australian version.' Eventually, however, the prodigal son returned. 'I am lucky I sobered up an' come home to face the music. I am still here.'

After the sun dropped behind the west coast horizon, almost everyone picked themselves up off the sand to head back to camp.

Only a young nurse called Andy and I decided to hang around for a little longer and savour the very last droplets of light.

I felt incredibly relaxed, as if every nerve in my body was a door flung open. Just by being out on Country, I was getting stronger and healthier—in the body, yes, but more importantly in mind and heart. My life back in Sydney had been poisoning me. This time last year I would have been sitting at my computer in the office, elbow deep in fizzy news headlines and angry tweets.

Andy and I took turns using my binoculars. She had thick waves of amber hair that matched a sprinkle of red freckles on her nose. She was mad for whales and told me that a few years ago she'd spent weeks here whale watching as a community volunteer for a survey. I could see how they were an easy animal to love, but after a while I grew tired of watching them and let her take over my binoculars.

I said to Andy that an Adnyamathanha person had once told me even non-Aboriginal people had totems, even if we didn't realise it. Perhaps the whale was hers.

'This is definitely my happy place,' she replied, her eyes still glued to the binoculars. 'What I like the most about the whales is that nobody can ever own them.'

The sky was still dramatically changing colour. I was enjoying feeling the sea wind brush against my skin and lips, and my feet half sunk in the wet sand, far too much to leave yet. That remarkable cliff wall stood sentry behind us, encouraging us to turn our backs on the rest of Australia and do nothing but relish the slow death of day.

✱

I was determined. Today, I would catch a fish.

It was the morning of day six on the trail—one of several rest days interspersed between the long walk through sand dunes, wet beaches, thickets of endangered monsoon vine and plains dotted with paperbarks. The day before, on the beach, I had met Sophia

Roe, matriarch to one of the Goolarabooloo families, and she had kindly invited me to go fishing with them.

Now I was in a Toyota HiLux being driven by Sophia at a good clip, kicking up clouds of powdery pindan on a corrugated track that traced the coastline. She was the proud mum of four kids, two of whom were currently in the car: seventeen-year-old Raelyn and nineteen-year-old Imani. Next to Sophia was her mum—introduced to me as 'Nanna', so I called her that too—who held tight to a pretty, chubby toddler on her lap. The toddler belonged to a cousin living in a town a few hours east of Broome. Imani was the main one who took care of her, although everyone in the family seemed to pitch in.

'Looking after babies is my thing,' Imani explained, tucking her mobile phone into the strap of her bikini. 'Especially newborns, just a few weeks old.'

She didn't have a baby of her own, and I found her logic a bit curious.

'Babies sleep a lot,' she said. 'That's why I like looking after them.'

I was raised in a typical nuclear family: a workaholic dad, stay-at-home mum and three kids in a suburban, two-storey brick home. But the Roe family seemed to operate a lot more like my extended family in Malaysia, where it wasn't unusual for children to be sent to live for periods with adult siblings, grandparents, uncles or aunts. Especially during my parents' generation—my mum and dad came from large families with seven-plus siblings, and efficient child rearing involved shifting kids to whichever relative had space in their house or time to spare, or lived near a good high school. It kept the internal bonds of these clans strong.

Every time I went back to Malaysia, I noticed how enmeshed the lives of my extended family were. My cousins laughed and joked with one another like best friends, and treated our aunts and uncles as second mothers and fathers. Whereas with me and my siblings, their rarely seen Australian cousins, they were warm, sure, but unable to breach the courteousness that separates strangers. I'd always feel a stab of jealousy and regret we were so disconnected from our kin.

How lonely our nuclear family was in Australia! And yet, among a nation of immigrants, how common was our story in Australia? Only Aboriginal families hadn't suffered this type of isolation—although through decades of forced child removals, the Australian government had done its best to inflict on their people that same fracturing of clans.

Everyone in the car had cans of fizzy drink, and the seats smelt of day-old squid, something Raelyn complained loudly about. I was surprised by the way she barked out driving instructions to her mother: 'Go to first!' 'No, fourth!' 'Put them locks on.' She was as mouthy and brash with her family as she had been shy and sweet to strangers back at the campsite. 'If you had any brains, Mum, you'd driven on them right side o' road,' she said. I waited for her mum to blow her top, but Sophia was utterly Zen. A calm smile spread across her face like melting butter. She just kept trucking along, bumpety-bump. She wasn't a tall lady, yet seemed in her element commandeering this burly car. Her hands gripped the wheel tightly, and she leant forward, peering through the front window.

'And what if them car come up that side from around the corner?' asked Raelyn's older sister Imani, sensibly. 'If is you drivin' us we'd all be killed!'

Well, Raelyn didn't have anything to say to that.

A blanket of orange pindan and thick vegetation whizzed past my window, broken up by flashes of sapphire ocean. The beaches looked desolate of animal life. Many of the resident wader birds had left for their annual voyage to northern Europe.

I did glance a black kite making easy glides on an updraft. For the Goolarabooloo, their forked-tail appearance chimes with the forked-tail salmon being 'fat' and good to eat. Pelicans, mullet, catfish, dugong and kangaroos should also be fat now. It's a different way to mark time: not via clocks and calendars, more like an elaborate yet reliable Rube Goldberg machine, in which components are linked and produce a domino effect.

'Do you know how t' tie your hook?' Raelyn asked me, pointing at the handline I'd brought.

I shook my head. She gently retrieved it from my hands and unlaced the end of my brand-new fishing line from the plastic wheel it was wound around. After threading a metal ball sinker, she tied a knot and threaded it through the eye of a hook; holding the hook in place with her teeth, she wound the line back around itself before knotting it. 'There you go,' she said with a smile.

It had been so neatly and deftly done, I was certain Raelyn could tie hooks in her sleep.

She looked out the window to the sea, eyes glittering. 'I'm goin' spear all them fish!'

As the family spoke, they seemed to me fixated on the tide: what time it was high, what time it was low. Raelyn pulled out a laminated chart from a car seat pocket, looked up today's date, and said that later this afternoon the tide would peak at seven metres. Only now, at low tide, was the reef exposed enough for us to fish. The dramatic high tides along this part of the coastline meant water levels were always rising or dropping at a rapid rate. Sophia explained to me that when you were perched on an elevated section of the reef platform, it was easy to forget the water was closing in from behind you—and that could leave you trapped in open water. 'You've always got to be moving backwards,' she warned.

She pulled off onto the side of the road, and another truck appeared and parked beside us. It was manned by her husband, Warren, and carried more family members including their two young sons. Both cars had their windows rolled down, and everyone argued boisterously in the gap between about where they should park: up along the cliff where the vehicles would be out of the tide's way or more conveniently down on the beach.

'On the beach!' yelled Raelyn. She made it clear that should the family make the mistake of parking on the cliff, she wouldn't help carry any of their gear.

Eventually the group arrived at the same preference.

Raelyn smiled at me, haughtily. 'In the end, they all follow Raelyn's plans.' She was careful to say it just loud enough for only me to hear.

We veered off the track and down a crumbling, treacherous path onto the beach. The car rocked from side to side as it careened up and over the collapsing waves of sand. We landed with a thump, all four wheels now safely on the flat beach. Sophia had barely put the car into park when Raelyn swung the side door open and started running towards the water. She clutched a spear gun in one hand and pulled on a snorkel with the other.

We were at Dugal, one of the most picturesque spots on the trail. The rocks looked like a model-sized, crumbling lost city painted in curry-powder yellow, coral pinks and reds. It was named after its rich deposits of white ochre, and I could see white chunks sandwiched between the rock like a layer of crumbly feta. I was given the okay to try some—white only, though, as the red was strictly for men. I mixed it with saliva and painted the back of my hand and fingers with it. It had a dazzling, almost metallic sheen; I bet it would practically glow in the night by a bonfire. Before application it would be mixed with animal fat or grease and used medicinally, decoratively on ritual objects and on the body in ceremonies and initiations, enhancing the wearer's spiritual power and causing them to enter a transcendental state.

I looked out and smiled at the sight of Raelyn terrorising fish in the water. All I could see was her back and the top of her head, floating above the waterline. While the kids went spearfishing, the rest of us—Sophia, Warren and a couple of adult cousins he had driven in his car—walked along the rocks, headed to a section of exposed reef that during low tide jutted into the ocean. To the right of us was gushing water, and to our left a long and low pindan cliff wall, fluted like the folds of a scarlet curtain drawn across this stretch of coast.

Someone cried out, 'Octopus!'

Sophia snatched the creature out of a nearby rockpool with her bare hands—a slimy, purplish, liquid thing. Its sucker-covered tentacles immediately wrapped around her arm. There was something night-marish about seeing her hand disappear under that serpentine mass of translucent skin. It was like glue you couldn't get off your fingers, and every time Sophia peeled one tentacle off another had taken its place. After some wrestling, she clutched the octopus by its sucker-free head and threw it onto the rock with great strength—*splat*, like runny egg on a frypan. The legs still squirmed weakly. She took it by the head and threw it down again. Now it was well and truly dead. We had our bait. I was impressed by her coolness.

'Do you like oysters?' asked one of the sister-cousins, turning to me after peering at the waterline.

'Do I ever,' I said.

'Plenty o' them oysters here.' She pointed at some nearby rocks encrusted with frilly shells, mauve and white. Taking her knife, she banged in the tip so she could pry an oyster open; inside was a slug of beige mussel that she passed to me on the snapped-off shell.

'It's okay to eat?' I asked tentatively. I'd only ever eaten oysters washed and sitting on a tray from a fish shop—not cemented to rocks, doused in ocean water.

'It's good. Real fresh!' She nodded encouragingly.

I popped it into my mouth. It was smaller than commercially sold oysters, but oh it tasted good. A creamy liquid full of flavour, natur-ally seasoned by salt, burst in my mouth.

With not enough knives to go around, another cousin began smashing oysters with a rock, so I did the same. Part of me could have happily done that all day.

Over on the reef platform, Sophia was prepping her line. When I joined her she cut an arm off the octopus for me, and I threaded it onto my hook. She showed me how to swing my line so that the hook circled in the air like a lasso, and throw it as hard as I could into the ocean. On my first cast it dropped feebly into the surf, tumbled back and promptly snagged on the reef. I had to clamber down into the water and unhook it. Five minutes in, and I was already soaking wet. On my second cast the hook swung wildly back towards me. Sophia said I should make sure my finger was off the line. 'But it *is* off the line,' I said with a sigh.

For the next hour the others proved they could cast their lines twice as far as mine, beyond the whitewash. Every time I thought I had the hang of it, the next cast I'd mess it up. My line would catch on the plastic wheel or under my finger then swing erratically towards me and my fishing buddies.

'Darn it,' I said, as my hook almost took out one of the sister-cousin's eyes.

She picked up her bucket. 'I'm fishing over there,' she said and moved a few steps away.

'Monica's still learning!' said Sophia, trying to be supportive.

But eventually even she shuffled away to a safer distance, because when I looked up again I saw the entire family squashed in a tight heap on the furthest corner of the reef. I laughed hopelessly.

Another thirty minutes passed, then there was a commotion. I turned towards Sophia. She was in a tug of war with a fish, her feet steady on the rocks and her face contorted with concentration. Her thin plastic line was jerking and yanking all over the place, but she held on tight. Finally, in one heaving wrench, she pulled the fish free from the almighty hands of the ocean and sent it flying through the air. It landed with a thud on the rocks by her feet. Fate sealed. It was a sizeable blue bone groper, shaped like a paddle. For a while it flipped and gasped, one visible eye staring at me mournfully.

We'd been fishing for nearly two hours, and I still hadn't caught anything. I told myself it didn't matter. I was brimming with joy just being out in the wind and water and sun.

As we fished—or as they fished and I fed our bait to the ocean—my buddies pointed out things that were barely visible to me but to them 'was legible as a newspaper', to borrow a phrase from Thomas

Mitchell's surveyor journals. 'Monica, look, a mob of fish!' I saw a blurry flash of silver. 'Monica, look, a gullal!' I saw a pointed dark thing that was possibly the snout of a giant turtle, or gullal as they called it. I really only half believed them until that mob of fish and gullal came close to shore, proving their keen eyesight correct.

But when a metre-long sea snake appeared, it was obvious even to me, as if someone had drawn a giant white-and-yellow 'S' onto the ocean. Was it moving? It must have been, for it was growing larger every second, yet its movements were so imperceptible it gave the impression of floating. I couldn't tell which end was its head, as sea snakes have flattened tails that help with swimming. They're generally considered non-aggressive, although they come loaded with toxic venom like many Australian snakes.

We were entranced. Even the kids, who by now had rejoined us, hushed for a moment.

Then Raelyn shouted, 'Go away!'

Her younger brother picked up a rock as large as his head and was poised to hoist it like a caber toss when his mother stopped him. 'Leave it alone,' she said. 'It looks injured.'

We watched, feeling tense, as the snake swam to within just a few metres of us.

Then it started to grow smaller—it was swimming parallel to our reef platform and away. Sophia's son, unable to resist, heaved the rock into the water where it plopped with a splash. The snake was long gone.

Everyone relaxed and resumed fishing. One cousin asked Raelyn to hand back the knife. She stood up and threw it, and her cousin caught it adroitly by the handle midair. I looked at them, amazed, with Raelyn giving me a cheeky grin.

I turned to Sophia. 'Are there things like snakes in the water all the time?' I'd never seen a sea snake before. Unlike snakes on land, they weren't something I'd given much thought to. Now I gulped, looking back on all the times on this trail I had swum in the ocean so carelessly.

'Yeah, but have you noticed we're always looking around?' she said, referring to her keen-eyed family.

'But shit, us walkers don't! Sometimes we just go swimming and we don't pay attention to anything.'

'Don't worry. One of us mob is always watching. It's like with our kids—we're always watching them, keeping an eye out for danger.'

We stopped fishing when the rising tide swept over much of the reef platform, forcing us to island hop back to shore. It was already afternoon but I was running on so much adrenaline I'd failed to notice we hadn't eaten lunch. We walked further up the beach, past our parked cars. From a distance I could see a boat being moored by a group of young Goolarabooloo men, mainly in their teens, dressed in board shorts and baseball caps. They'd just come back from sea. Some of them were already on shore, crouched over something I couldn't quite make out. Then I saw the blood-splattered carnage.

Two gullal had been carried off the boat and placed further up the shore. I had never seen such giant gullal. Their shells were the shape of satellite dishes, mottled with olive and brown splotches and quartered by long, white lines. Parts of the shell were broken— hunting wounds through which bloodied flesh oozed.

One gullal was tipped over, stomach-side up. Nearby were its dismembered front flippers, one atop the other like a pair of leather gloves. A man stood barefoot in a growing pool of cherry-red blood, slicing at the edges of the gullal's hard underbelly until it was pried open; the lid on a can of muscles and organs. Disconcertingly, the gullal's head and amputated stumps were still moving in soft, slow jerks as a man pulled out its entrails and spilled them all over the sand. Its eyes were dark opals, now dull, and its nose ended in an almost sharp-edged beak. They hadn't yet cut off the back legs, which unlike the front flippers had the flatness of a duck's webbed feet.

Soon more young men were giving the other gullal the same treatment.

I recognised Tay, who smiled at me shyly. 'Today we let some of the boys have a turn at hunting,' he explained.

Hunting gullal the traditional way isn't easy. From a moving boat the men and boys had thrown a wooden wongami spear and a wire harpoon with enough strength and accuracy to penetrate the swimming animal's shell. Tay said the young men had done well and proved their mettle to their older male relatives.

Even a novice like myself could identify the gullal organs, which didn't seem too different from a human's: a bean-shaped stomach, dark liver, and thick red heart and lungs. Sophia began emptying a stomach of thick, fibrous stuff she said was seagrass.

'Can I help?' I asked her.

'Sure! Do like what I'm doing but with the intestines.'

I picked up one end of a steaming pile of pink intestine, encased in yellow skin like uncooked sausages. I slid my thumb down the skin as directed, creating a long tear, and used my fingers to scoop out the fibre that became more like poo the further down I went.

I found the slaughter provocative but not distressing—which surprised me, considering my weak tango with the crab. Because I didn't grow up in the bush or on a farm, none of this—blood and guts, two half-dead animals—was in my vocabulary. But in this context, surrounded by so many old hands, I felt comfortable. And I think some deeply rational part of my brain felt that to regard the animal as food, or better yet as sustenance, was not a form of disrespect. Far from it.

In traditional times gullal lived good, long lives because saltwater people took care of the seas, the coastline, and all the animals who lived there. Sustainability was embedded into their entire worldview. Outsiders, not blackfellas, discarded into the ocean masses of fishing nets that tangled up and slowly drowned gullal. Outsiders, not blackfellas, first polluted marine environments with plastic debris and toxic agricultural, mining and coastal development run-off. And outsiders, not blackfellas, took the world and sent it off the cliff of climate change into rising sea levels and rising sea temperatures, drastically altering ocean environments.

Of course, the right of Goolarabooloo people to hunt gullal as they have for tens of thousands of years, in an era of high-speed tinnies and the bald reality of dwindling marine life, isn't a cut and dried issue. But for these nine days, when it came to respecting and connecting to the land I chose to trust that my hosts knew best.

All the gullal bits were loaded into the ute, leaving behind only the heart and lungs on the beach. The tide was closing in, the strip of visible sand getting skinnier by the minute. Every year at least one photo went viral of some dipstick's car floating in these seas, and none of us wanted to be this year's dipstick.

I followed Sophia and Nanna back to our car. Her husband was already in his truck, with Raelyn and Imani in his passenger seats.

'We gotta go fast, okay?' said Warren to Sophia through his open window.

She nodded and climbed back into her captain's seat.

I smelt terrible. A piece of squid bait had squirted horrible brown shit all over me, and I was sure I'd stink of squid, gullal blood and seagrass poo forever.

Sophia grinned at me through the rear-view mirror. 'Hold on, Monica!'

We were off—leaping and crashing up and down over the lurujarri. Inside the car we pinballed about, and I grasped the armrest. Nanna swore a few times, not enjoying the rough ride. Sophia cranked up a country music mixtape, which yodelled away on the car's bass-heavy sound system. 'Ride 'em, cowboy!' she cried.

Among all the violent bucking, I was amazed to see the family dog, Lady, snoozing without a care in the world on the seat next to me; she was wheezing loudly. The car was littered with empty fizzy-drink cans, and puddles of Sprite and Coke sloshed about in the cup holders.

We quickly fell behind the other car, and Nanna growled.

'I'm going as fast as I can!' Sophia cried.

We were still a good hundred metres from dry land when the car suddenly slowed as if a giant foot had dropped from the sky and was crushing it. We sank dangerously low in the sand. Sophia revved, then revved again. The wheels skidded wildly, shooting jets of wet sand into the air.

Just as all felt lost, on the third rev the car shot out from the sucking sand like a champagne cork. I breathed a sigh of relief. The car jounced along gleefully. When we reached the end of the beach and wet sand gave way to compact earth, we all whooped with joy and laughed at one another.

'The four-wheel-drive gods were looking out for us!' I said.

We pulled up alongside the other car. Raelyn was in the front seat, Imani in the back, and they both looked at me grinning the same, cute Mona Lisa grin. 'You get bogged?' asked Raelyn.

'Almost!' said Sophia. She turned to me. 'How'd you find that, Monica?'

'Pretty wild,' I said.

She laughed.

'Like a rollercoaster ride,' I said.

Nanna chortled. 'We'll have KFT tonight: Kentucky Fried Turtle!'

Back at camp the shell was immediately thrown over hot coals. Minutes later the thin layer of meat still hanging from the shell dripped with its fat, sizzling and darkening. Tay seasoned the meat with salt and pepper.

Many of my fellow walkers squirmed at the sight of the butcher's mess of gullal organs sitting on the trestle table. Out of politeness to their hosts, they tried to hide their discomfort. But when Sophia spoke of how they were preparing the gullal for dinner—stir-fried and deep-fried, with the tripe marinated in soy sauce and vinegar— one of the walkers replied she was 'going vegetarian' that night.

I thought of how the Goolarabooloo people had a more intimate relationship to those gullal than any of us urban walkers had with our store-bought steaks. To me the Lurujarri Trail was an opportunity to physically dissolve into the processes of the land: the gullal eats the seagrass, I eat the gullal, my poo fertilises the plants. Rather than an extractive relationship, it is a cooperative one—links in a complex web; humans as active agents within, not over, the natural world. The trail was our chance to integrate into these natural processes, and the deeper and longer I did that, the more I became a child of this country.

Tay cut a shred of meat off the shell and passed it to me to try. I found it tender and full of flavour, like pork but oilier.

'Catch anything today?' he asked me.

'Came close to catching some of your family members,' I said, after swallowing a mouthful of gullal.

*

It was that sublime time of day when the light became coy, disappearing then reappearing from behind dark slats of tree trunks. Some of us walkers were meeting Phil atop a sand dune near camp.

On one side of the dune, the sun was slowly sinking into the ocean to a score of soft booms and crashes from the waves. On the other, the yellow wall of lurujarri abruptly became a shallow pan of soft, red yanijarri flour from which grew thick vegetation—lardik (freshwater mangrove), garnboor (freshwater paperbark), gunuru (white gum) trees, and a vine known as wilga with heart-shaped leaves— across the pancake-flat land to the horizon.

Phil pointed out a nearby hill, indistinguishable to me from the other hills. 'The old fella, Walmadany, who lived and owned this part of the turf, that's where he's laying.' Phil said that his grandfather, Paddy, had buried Walmadany right there: a serene spot at the top of the lurujarri with a postcard-worthy view of the sunset. 'You see that rock?' he said, pointing to an oval-shaped piece of sandstone, smooth and flattish. 'That's the headstone.'

All up Paddy had buried seventy-eight people in the dunes of the coast. He wasn't from here but had been left with this duty because the young men and women who belonged to these lands were no longer here. They should have taken over the reins from their elders as the land's custodians, but colonisation had dealt a heavy blow. They had died in frontier violence or from introduced disease, or white authorities had ripped them from their land, family and culture, imprisoning them in distant missions and forcing them to work on pearling boats or pastoral stations far from their homelands.

By the beginning of the twentieth century, the Djungun and Ngumbarl elders had nearly all died, and custodial care of their lands had been passed to the most senior elder of the neighbouring Jabirr Jabirr people to the north, Walmadany, and two other elder Jabirr Jabirr Law-keepers, Narbi and Kardilakan. But Walmadany could see the writing on the wall: that the fate of the Djungun and Ngumbarl peoples lay ahead for the Jabirr Jabirr people. Without any young people left in their clans, what would happen to the lands when they, too, died?

Then, in the late 1920s, a young man called Paddy Roe came to Jabirr Jabirr country. Just sixty to a hundred elderly people remained. As Phil told it, 'My grandfather came—he was a Nyigina man. He came from the other side of Roebuck Plains. And this old fella, because they knew his mother and his family, so they welcomed him to this country and they taught him a lot about this country.'

Paddy came with his partner, Pegalilly. When Pegalilly became pregnant, the Jabirr Jabirr elder Narbi foretold she would give birth to two daughters; their rai (spirits) had been waiting in the paperbark of Bindingankun, hoping to enter Narbi, but as she was too old they had entered Pegalilly instead. It was believed the moment of conception is linked to a physical place, tree or animal, and a person's spirit returns there after death.

Although they weren't Jabirr Jabirr by blood, Pegalilly and Paddy Roe were brought into the fold. The passing of custodianship is no simple affair: Paddy was walked through the land multiple times, from beginning to end, and taught via song and storytelling the many names of key features and their significance. Through the singing of these songs and telling of these stories, in the correct order while traversing the land, Bugarregarre was sustained. That duty now fell solely on young Paddy's shoulders.

I thought about the human remains we'd seen on the trail and was struck by the implication. Perhaps an old man had died heartbroken by years of watching the members of his clan be cast into the wind; or a woman whose children, grandchildren and great-grandchildren had died or been taken away, and all hopes quashed of a reunion before her death. They were the keepers of ancient knowledge, essential to care for the soul of the land and keep apocalyptic imbalances at bay.

Paddy had spent years working in the Kimberley area as a station hand and windmill contractor, before establishing the Goolarabooloo Millibinyarri Community in Coconut Wells, north of Broome, in 1979. The word Goolarabooloo is derived from several Yawuru words meaning 'a western coastal people living in or near Yawuru land'.

Before Paddy died in 2001, he passed on custodial duties to three of his grandsons: Richard Hunter and Phil Roe, and Joseph Roe who passed away in 2014.

A few years ago, at the serene and spiritual spot where Walmadany was buried, the Australian oil and gas company Woodside Petroleum had planned to build a $45 billion liquefied natural gas precinct. Had things gone their way, this land would have been imprisoned in concrete and its thicket of endangered monsoon vine cleared for the construction of a monstrous gas plant. I thought of what might have been: a huge building sleeplessly belching noise, light and gas emissions, much like the ones I'd seen devouring Murujuga. To make way for the tankers, up to twenty-one million tonnes of ocean floor would have needed to be dredged, clouding the waters and affecting local populations of whale, fish, turtle, snubfin dolphin and other sea life.

It was no small sum that the Goolarabooloo people walked away from: $1.5 billion in benefits to the local Aboriginal communities over the coming thirty years. And by no means was this a universally backed decision. For some, including living members of the Jabirr Jabirr people—descendants of those young people who had been forced off their lands—the plant didn't necessarily symbolise the destruction of Country. Rather, it represented jobs, financial independence and a stronger community, as well as a possible circuit-breaker on the cycles of alcoholism, violence, depression and suicide that had racked their families for decades. Also between the groups of local Aboriginal people were disputes over the nature of the authority offered to Paddy Roe by Walmadany all those years ago.

I wondered what Walmadany would have done had he known that within a few decades Australian attitudes regarding his people would change and his descendants would return to their lands.

A warm wind swept over the sandhills and over our skin, and the sun was quietly extinguished by night.

I turned to Phil and said I'd seen on a trail sign that Walmadany had been a maban man. 'What does that mean?'

'Like a medicine man, witch doctor,' he said, looking at me meaningfully.

'Do they have special powers?' I asked.

'They can cure you better than when you go to hospital. They can look straight through you; they'll tell you what's wrong with you.'

Another walker, a middle-aged dark-haired woman, asked, 'And was he just born that way or did he learn to be a witch doctor?'

'Well, most likely his father before him and his ancestors just passed these things onto him.' Phil paused for dramatic effect. 'I'm learning the same way as him.'

'Oh,' the woman said.

Phil was staring at her hard, not blinking.

'I'm a bit nervous now,' she squeaked, and everyone laughed.

I couldn't resist sliding in a wisecrack. 'Hey, can you fix blisters and midge bites? Because we got a few of them going on right now.'

As we walked back to camp, I contemplated the fact that for tens of thousands of years custodianship of the land had been passed through the generations and regulated by strong laws, with serious infractions punishable by sickness and even death. Shared Dreaming tracks and extensive kinship webs had kept these laws consistent across clans and nations spread over hundreds of kilometres.

Then came colonialism—a grenade thrown into this time-old system.

The battle over this stretch of coast was symptomatic of one of Australia's most contentious and challenging questions: who has ultimate authority over the land now? Anywhere in the country, a piece of land might have multiple parties staking a claim: the government, freehold landowners, corporate leaseholders, and sometimes multiple native title claimants. Each party had different rights, depending on how you viewed history, sacred Law and modern law.

The Lurujarri Heritage Trail doesn't seek to answer that question but instead poses an equally important one: can a sense of land 'adoption' not 'possession' be cultivated among those who lack the deed given by birthright?

In a cross-cultural four-year campaign to preserve James Price Point—as this region is known in English—Goolarabooloo families had joined forces with non-Goolarabooloo conservationists, scientists, local residents, and activist ferals. The campaign had attracted a few high-profile names. 'Me and ol' Bob Brown walked along the beach here,' said Phil, of the charismatic former leader of the Greens political party. There was also the billionaire entrepreneur Geoffrey Cousins—'He landed in a chopper'—and Australia's favourite hippie muso, John Butler—'He stayed out at Coconut with us. He part of the family. He lived out of Coconut Wells for a long time.'

What I loved about this trail was that the Goolarabooloo people seemed to understand that although I was a stranger, I too could care deeply for this land.

Dusk had melted into an indigo evening, fragrant and lit by the moon. The volunteers served dinner, comprised mainly of fish caught that morning and leftover gullal. After dinner, as the walkers prepared to watch documentaries about the campaign to save James Price Point, Raelyn came looking for me. 'They want you down at the beach,' she said, with a smile that reminded me of her mum.

I picked up my fishing gear and followed her barefoot up and over the dunes. We reached a gazebo by the ocean where the Roe family were camped. Everything was glazed in silver moonlight. Tay was fishing by the water's edge and nodded when he saw me. Sophia smiled at me; her teeth seemed to glow in the dark. She said they had a fridge full of blue bone and mackerel. She told me she'd hooked another big something, but a shark had come along and with one chomp stolen her prize catch.

When she offered to throw another fish onto the coals for me, I said I'd eaten and wasn't too hungry. It smelt delicious, though. 'Maybe I could just have a taste of yours?' I asked.

'Make sure you give her a bit with the fat,' said Raelyn.

Sophia passed me a good-sized piece that had a sliver of orange fat, garnished with a pinch of salt and nothing else. It was so delicious I said maybe I would like more fish after all, but could share it with someone. They individually wrapped a couple more fish in alfoil and stuck them on the hot coals.

The family were fishing differently tonight—from the shore, rather than perched on a reef that jutted out. They had to use thicker lines with heavier sinkers that could be hurled over the wall of pounding surf.

As Sophia told me some of their future plans for the trail, she pulled on her line, letting it loose in a spaghetti pile by her feet. Once enough was loose, she took several steps back. In a short run towards the ocean, she powerfully pitched the line. It was bloody fantastic.

'Do you know which sport you'd be mad good at?' I asked her.

'Javelin?' she said.

'Oh my god, exactly.'

Raelyn and I shared the cooked fish, although she kindly let me eat most of it. When I tried to offer her more, she shooed me away. 'We always eat them up, this fish. It's all we do, is eat fish.'

Imani finished off the bits I didn't eat, including the cheek and eyes. 'We always eat the whole thing. See them eyes?' She poked her fingers into the head, scooped them out and licked them straight off her fingers. 'There's this real hard white bit and then it's gooey.'

For the next few hours we yarned, fished, and drank from plastic cups.

When we tired, Sophia said to her cousin, teasingly, 'Tay, let the lady have a seat.'

He quickly got out of his seat and took it over to me. For himself, he overturned a plastic bucket to sit on. I accepted the camp chair, feeling embarrassed.

Sophia was impressed by my road trip and said she'd always wanted to travel but it was too hard with the kids. 'The furthest I've been is Perth,' she said flatly.

'If you could, where would you go?'

'Everywhere,' she said.

'Which country?'

'Oh, not overseas.'

'Why not? Don't say because of terrorism.' I'd heard that too many times on this trip.

'No . . . all those planes being shot down.'

'I knew it! Terrorism! That's crazy, you know?'

'I'd go to Bali, maybe.'

I decided not to mention the 2002 Bali bombings that had killed eighty-eight Australians.

Eventually Sophia headed back up the beach to the fire, around which the rest of her family had gathered in slumber. That left me and Tay on the edge of the black ocean, half-heartedly fishing, with the dirty-yellow half-moon very low on the horizon. I asked him what he did for work between trail walks, and he said, 'Not much. I was a driving instructor for a while.' The trail was everything to him. His father, who had passed away a few years ago, had chosen him to carry the mantle of their culture and to look after their country. Now Tay also cared for his mother in their home. He spoke as a man carrying grave responsibilities. 'I love my Country and I love doing this,' he said.

My toes were wrinkled from being in the wet sand for so long. Ice-cubes slicked with moonlight swam around in my Coke to the tuneless blowing of the ocean.

'What's that?' Tay said, pointing at something washed ashore. We got out of our seats and crouched over it: a small shark, no longer than the length of my forearm. Tay picked it up with his bare hands, holding it just behind the gills so it couldn't bite him, and flung it towards the ocean. It spun in the air, *womp-womp-womp,* and then was swallowed by the frothing mouth of the sea.

Every few minutes, comets were making silvery rips in the sky. Tonight was the first on this trip I'd been up late enough to see the sky in full brilliance.

Many Bugarregarre stories illuminate the creation of the constellations. Like a mnemonic device, Dreaming stories encode knowledge of animals, foods, weather, land features and water sources vital for survival. Where literary cultures store knowledge in libraries, oral cultures use a network of elders carrying in their minds a prodigious body of stories, dances, art motifs and songs. Each time such knowledge is drawn upon and reproduced, it is etched deeper into the memories of other family members. It was commonplace in Aboriginal Australia to have complex systems of checks and balances to ensure that in this transmission of knowledge from one generation to the next, no aspect of the information is corrupted. Western science is continually uncovering consistencies between these stories and empirical evidence of dramatic climatic and geological events that took place tens of thousands of years ago, pointing to the possibility the stories are equally as old.

Looking at the night sky over Goolarabooloo Country, I could see the stars that traced the outline of Marrala (Emu Man) with his head near Jina (eagle's claw prints, or the Southern Cross). Two stars near what Western astronomy called the Hydra constellation are Naji sisters who emerge from the reef in Minyirr to pick yarrinyarri, when they are unlawfully touched by a reclusive bushman; later he is weighed down by remorse and, sitting in a meditation pose, changes himself into a rock wallaby. Each year, when these stars show themselves in the night sky, it's the right to time to pick bush onion.

My own people, the Han Chinese, have one of the most romantic visions of the night sky. We call it Yinhe (Silver River) from a story that's at least 2600 years old.

The story is literally of star-crossed lovers. The youngest and prettiest of the Goddess's seven daughters, Zhinü, encounters on Earth a humble but kind-hearted cowherder, Niulang. The pair fall in love and have two children. Up in the heavens a day is equal to a year in the world of mortals, and when the Goddess eventually discovers the illicit relationship she orders her daughter to return home. In her anger she takes off one of her hairpins and uses it to scratch a silver river in the sky, to prevent her daughter and her love from ever reuniting. Every night Zhinü is visible as Vega in the sky, wistfully weaving on her loom, separated from Niulang and their two children. All the magpies in the world are so touched by their devotion that every year, on the seventh night of the seventh moon, they fly into the air to form a bridge, and the pair are reunited for that evening.

I sat back in my camp chair. As I looked up at the stars, I was overwhelmed by gratitude for the opportunity to be here and experience Country. Walking this trail I had felt the soft lurujarri sands under my bare feet, eaten its mackerel fresh from the ocean, listened to the muffled booms of waves disintegrating on the shore and slept soundly under its paperbarks. I had left tracks in its sand; it had blown sea salt over my skin. We had become accustomed to each other's scent and grown less afraid of each other. Country needed me as much as I needed it—I saw that now. The health and happiness of the custodians depended on the land, and the health and happiness of the land depended on the custodians. Separated, we were lonely.

The Goolarabooloo people have a word for this sense of connection: le-an. Your le-an is intuitive and emanates powerfully from your gut. The longer you spend out on Country acquiring its knowledge, the more your body and mind become attuned to its sounds, patterns, movements and energy flows—that's your le-an deepening. When the ancestral beings sang the universe into existence, humans and Country were created simultaneously. They were notes in one musical score and, as with any song, the individual notes mattered less than their arrangement; their rai, or spirit, was made of the same essence. Le-an is the way in which humans and Country reconnect and become one, as they were in the beforelife and will be again in the afterlife.

I had been afraid I would never love anything the way Aboriginal people loved and knew their country—that their sense of connection and belonging would forever allude a person like me, trapped as I was between Aboriginal, Asian and European cultures. I'd felt a profound sense of loss that I was a perpetual foreigner, a person of no place, cut adrift. But the Lurujarri Trail had shown me that even if I could never be as intimate with the land as Aboriginal people, I could still learn from those who'd come before me, or whose ancestors had come to this continent long before mine. And with every lesson I learnt and step I took, I was being nourished and loved, completely, by the land.

PART FIVE
Top End

27 AUGUST
Day 83

I was fascinated to see my Chinese stepmother on Aboriginal-controlled land. She and my father had flown to Darwin, the Northern Territory's capital, from Sydney for a long weekend over the final days of August. I had taken a circuitous route from Broome that included a detour to Derby and through breathtakingly beautiful parts of the Kimberley, then east back into the Territory. We met at a hotel deep in the savanna woodlands of Kakadu National Park, with its cork-screw pandanus and thousands of termite mounds.

My stepmother, Mary, was fifteen years younger than my 62-year-old dad, a classic Chinese beauty with very smooth, straight hair one imagined she had brushed carefully every evening since she was a child. A decade had passed since she moved from Beijing to Sydney. Aside from a trip to Uluru, she had barely interacted with Indigenous Australia. She'd come into this trip neither callused with racism nor teary-eyed from colonialist angst, unlike so many Australians who interact with Indigenous Australia.

Kakadu is roughly the size of Israel, and the traditional owners are the Bininj people in the north of the park and Mungguy people in the south. At a gunbim (rock art) site we joined a tour led by an interpretive park ranger. The gunbim was painted in red, white and yellow ochre, mainly in the X-ray art style that sees figures depicted with anatomically accurate skeletal features. According to the Bininj and Mungguy peoples, many of the older paintings—up to twenty thousand years old—were created by mystical, long-limbed Mimi spirits. It was from these spirits their ancestors learnt to paint. What they depicted were more than stories: they were Law. Among depictions of turtle, fish and wallaby species is a thylacine, while the 1880s arrival of hat-wearing, pale-skinned buffalo hunters is depicted with them standing stiffly, hands in pockets.

Despite the thirty-degree weather, Mary was dressed in long pants and a cream Burberry-style trenchcoat to protect her pale skin from the sun and mosquitos. She listened to the ranger with interest as he spoke about the twelve languages formerly spoken in the park, and the traditional owners' complex kinship system dividing all people, plants, animals, songs, dances, ceremonies and the land into two moieties: duwa and yirridja. I picked up a tourist guide from the park that had said the calendar was divided into six distinct seasons: gudjewg/monsoon, banggerreng/knock 'em down storm, yegge/cooler but still humid, wurrgeng/cold weather, gurrung/hot dry, and gunumeleng/pre-monsoon storm.

Mary was less fascinated by a sample of basket-weaving displayed in the park museum. 'I can do that,' she said, with a little shrug of her trenchcoat-draped shoulders, after I'd pointed it out. 'When I was a little girl I used to have to weave many hats and shoe soles out of wheat.'

Like so many Mainland Chinese people she was middle class now, sure, but in Mao-era China everyone had been dirt poor. Mary's father was the first in his village to own a bicycle in the 1960s; wherever he rode kids chased after him, delighted by the sight of this novel contraption, and shouted, 'Foreign donkey! Foreign donkey!'

She told me about a property developer she and my dad knew, Mr Zhang. A real Mr Moneybags. During China's Great Famine of 1959–61, he remembered eating nothing but sweet potato. During the winter, when there was nothing to harvest, his family would add water to dehydrated potato. Potato, potato, potato. Now, he hated them—couldn't even bear being in the same room as one.

As I was primarily raised in air-conditioned shopping centres, the idea of living off the land had some novelty to it. I was prone to adopt a romantic view of the ingenuity Bininj and Mungguy people displayed, and their mastery of bush tucker and bush medicine: a view propped up by a complete lack of firsthand experience with the tiring and tedious work of traditional life.

But just two generations back, my own relatives had been in China—foraging, fishing, building, farming, weaving, carving out an existence from the landscape—as they had for thousands of years. In Kakadu, Mary was just a woman from one ancient culture coming to another. Because of that, she was able to cast a more discerning eye than me.

At Cahills Crossing we saw saltwater crocodiles. They were known to congregate there, so infrastructure had been built to allow visitors to view them safely. The crocs drifted lazily about in the water reminding me of overweight tourists in a hotel swimming pool, occasionally propelling themselves with their tail by swishing it back and forth.

Crocodiles exercise a sit-and-wait approach to hunting. Through routine lassitude they conserve energy and go months without food. Their agility and speed are only on display when they have the opportunity to strike, which makes them all the more unnerving. It's easy to anthropomorphise the crocodile as a slick Sicilian mobster who spends most of his time sitting nonchalantly at a diner table, puffing on a cigar, but who at any moment can have those who dared cross him beaten to a bloody pulp and chucked into a shallow grave.

The stories I'd heard about croc deaths were gruesome. One doctor in Darwin had told me about a father out fishing in Kakadu with his wife, son and daughter-in-law on a relaxing Saturday afternoon. He was alone on a boat, washing or emptying a bucket, when a 4.7-metre saltie jumped up, nabbed him by the arm and dragged him into the water.

Crocs' victims aren't executed with a snap of the jaws but are instead drowned or crushed to death. The body is then jerked or spun in a death roll so that croc-bite-sized pieces twist off and can be swallowed whole. As the crocodile only has a stomach the size of a basketball, unfinished chunks of meat might be stored in mangroves and are sometimes used as bait to attract fresh meat like turtles and mud crabs. It's discomforting to think of a human rendered into something as lowly as fishing bait.

We went for a sunrise boat tour of the river, its water splotched with round, green lilies and filled with birds. I spotted comb-crested jacanas, whose exceptionally long toes allow them to tread evenly across lily pads, and elegant pygmy geese dressed in dark iridescent green. Rainbow bee-eaters provided fluttering splashes of colour. But my favourite birds here were the softly honking magpie geese. As their name suggests, they look like geese that have borrowed the smart piebald plumage of magpies. That morning they floated on the water and tipped like jugs being poured until their feathered tushies and orange legs were the only parts sticking out.

Later Mary and I were in the park museum, where we learnt that Kakadu was one of few UNESCO World Heritage sites listed for both its natural and cultural wonders. In a not-so-distant life Mary had worked as a local guide in China. As she was well versed in traditional Chinese culture I asked her if the Chinese imbue the landscape with spiritual meaning, in a similar way to what the Bininj and Mungguy do. She told me there are many sacred mountains in China—some connected to Buddhism, others to Taoism and still more to ancient animistic Chinese religions—that for thousands of years have drawn pilgrims and powerful emperors for worship. We spoke of the parallels between Bininj and Mungguy ontology and that gentle, ironic, nature-loving Chinese philosophy of Taoism, with its emphasis on balance, intuition and adherence to natural cycles.

Whereas what do most non-Aboriginal Australians see when we stand before a mountain? Maybe a photo-op, an athletic hike or, for the more industrious, a new mining site to blast the hell out of. The colony was born from a British culture that understood sacred churches better than sacred earth. For us non-Aboriginal Australians to feel that a rock escarpment or waterhole can be imbued with the spirits of ancestors and ancient creators requires a certain imaginative leap not all of us are able or willing to make.

I told Mary that for all the diversity of the Aboriginal nations I had travelled through, from Wiradjuri to Warlpiri, what remained universal and constant was this deep love of their land. They loved the land as though it was family and seemed to know every rock, tree and cloud.

She said before the great bulldozers of urbanisation tore entire villages down, Chinese people also had a deep kinship with the land. 'When Chinese people moved overseas, such as the miners who went to America or Australia during the gold rush, they'd always bring a jar of soil from their home village.'

How wonderful was that? And back then you had to be extra judicious about what you packed. You were about to embark on a dangerous journey overland and over sea for months on end to a strange new place. You had no idea when or if you would ever return to your village, and there wasn't an overnight FedEx service for your relatives back home to post you anything you missed. Yet a coolie would find room to pack a glass jar containing the earth that had sustained him—for they were almost always male—since he was a child: the same earth that had sustained his father, his father's father, his father's father's father, and maybe a hundred fathers prior.

*

On the morning that I watched my dad and Mary's rental car drive away, destined for Darwin airport, I headed to the Chung Wah museum downtown. It was adjacent to a small Chinese temple that in various incarnations had stood on the site since 1887. Inside the temple were pillars and beams painted red and decorated with gold-embroidered silk banners, and several shrines with Taoist, Buddhist and Confucian statues shrouded in clouds of incense. It reminded me of temples in Hong Kong, Singapore and Taiwan: places where the Chinese diaspora lived and hadn't seen the Cultural Revolution sweep through, and therefore retained more vestiges of traditional beliefs.

The museum—like many regional, volunteer-run efforts—was a cheerful assortment of bits and bobs. There was a yellowing mahjong set from the 1920s, pewter vessels from the temple, wooden mooncake moulds, a wide-brimmed woven hat worn by a Chinese market gardener in the 1940s, and displays printed and hand glued onto colourful construction paper.

I was struck by a photo taken in 1893 during a local Chinese New Year procession. The Chinese participants were dressed in ankle-length fine robes. Carrying parasols and silk banners, they marched down a dirt road past a corrugated iron shack instantly recognisable as Australian. Another photo featuring a sixteen-year-old Chinese Australian girl called Dolly Ng Yuen, wearing a beautiful headdress with tassels and pompoms, had been taken on Cavenagh Street, Darwin's Chinatown, in 1930.

I was enthralled by the world conjured up in this museum. In late 1800s Darwin, Chinese people outnumbered Europeans at least four to one—it was known as 'The Orient in the Outback'. They first arrived in 1874 to work the goldfields south of the town, but after the gold rush they took up all the other jobs involved in keeping a colony alive and running. The Chinese residents grew the town's rice, fruit and vegetables, and raised pigs. Darwin's earliest buildings were the fruits of Chinese labourers who were skilled carpenters, stonemasons, cabinet-makers and boilermakers, while the Overland Telegraph Line and Darwin Port had been built, in part, by the Chinese. I was moved to see how difficult life had been for my people, but also by their resilience, indefatigable persistence, instinct for survival and propensity for hard yakka.

I wondered what Australia today might look like had Federation in 1901 merely united the colonies under the banner of the Australian Commonwealth, without enacting the *Immigration Restriction Act* later that year. Implemented through a discriminatory dictation test applied to non-British immigrants, it had swiftly curtailed the steady stream of Chinese people settling in Australia.

This was the first Chinese Australian museum I'd been to. And in this room, all the clichés of Australia's past split apart: the blue-eyed Digger, fair-haired children in a schoolhouse of corrugated iron, European Australian men in dark woollen suits with starched white collars. Suddenly they were confused with images of my own people: silk-robe wearing, black-haired, yellow-skinned, pig-tailed men, women and children, in a dusty, dry Australian landscape.

I was amused to read, on one museum display, that so established was the Chinese community in Darwin, many Chinese Territorians reported their first taste of alienation or racism only after going to other parts of Australia. Take the story of Tanya Fong Lim, who moved to Sydney after Cyclone Tracy devastated Darwin in 1974. Being labelled 'the Chinese girl' in her new school was a new experience for her. She said, 'People kept asking me where I came from. And when I said "Darwin", they'd say, 'Yes, but where did you come from originally?' It came as a bit of a shock to them that I was actually born in Darwin, and so were my parents and so were my grandparents.'

I wandered over to a row of dancing lion heads hanging from a ledge, their flap mouths frozen open like those of hunting trophies. Standing near a replica bridal sedan was an elderly and sweet-looking Chinese Territorian. He must have been pushing eighty and told me he volunteered in the museum. 'My grandparents were the first in our family to come out here from China,' he said, in a broad Australian accent. He was tanned with crinkles around his eyes and sun spots on his balding head.

'No way!'

'Yup. And I married another ABC and her grandparents also come out here from China.' (ABC stands for Australian-Born Chinese.) He told me that many 'old' Chinese families in Darwin traced their origins back to the gold rush and were related through marriage. He took me to a series of laminated yellow paper scrolls, hung on wooden handles and grouped by family dynasties: Chin Toy, Low Dep Chit, Yet Fah.

'What does Chung Wah mean?' I asked. I'd read in the museum that after World War II Chinese families returned to Darwin, only to find the local government had demolished Chinatown. The Chung Wah Society helped unite a community scattered throughout the city.

'Apparently it means "Chinese society"? I don't know, I don't speak Chinese,' he replied, looking faintly embarrassed.

Viewing Australia through a racial prism is often an exercise in cognitive dissonance. From appearances he was little different to the old fellas I'd seen riding rickety bicycles on the streets of Beijing. Except instead of a wrinkled, navy Mao suit, he wore a polo shirt with shorts. Only when he opened his mouth was it evident he was Australian, through and through. It was weird for me to meet a Chinese man so much older than me whose understanding of Chinese culture was just as patchy as mine. In his awkward fumbling in the dark for cultural knowledge, I recognised my own gaps.

He asked about my travels, so I told him about my book and said I was heading south.

'You should meet Eddie Ah Toy in Pine Creek. He might even take you out to the old goldfields where all them Chinese miners worked.'

Just over a week later, on a day bursting with sunshine, I left Darwin and drove two hours south to the historic mining town of Pine Creek. The town lay on a small, two-lane detour off the Stuart Highway lined with gum trees and billboards advertising local businesses lettered in the style of a wanted poster from an old western. When I'd called Eddie that morning, he'd suggested I drive up to his family's now-defunct general store. It was easy to find—Pine Creek was a compact town, made up of squat buildings whose corrugated iron roofs were striped with brown rust. The store occupied a prime spot on the short main street and bore a red-lettered sign: 'Established 1935 Ah Toy's Store'.

There was Eddie, waving me in and opening the wire gate of his driveway. He wore a rabbit-fur Akubra and a maroon shirt tucked neatly into his shorts. We shook hands and he led me into the store. Inside it felt cool with the windows boarded up. The shelves were empty although there remained rows of plastic bags, stuffed round and fat as Chinese steamed buns, sitting on the floor. One wall was decorated with old beer and soft drink stickers.

Eddie offered me a glass of water and pulled up two stools by a countertop. He looked around the store and apologised for the mess. 'I'm a bit of a hoarder.'

Some Chinese traits never die. While living in China I'd discovered a generation of old people in dire need of Marie Kondo's *The Life-Changing Magic of Tidying Up*. I'd presumed this a side effect from surviving the lean times of recent Chinese history. But now, meeting a third-generation, removed-from-the-Motherland self-confessed Chinese hoarder, perhaps a longer view was required. Five thousand cyclical years of floods, famines, warring kingdoms and the occasional despotic ruler had perhaps embedded hoarding into our DNA.

I told Eddie I had driven over a conspicuously named 'Chinaman Creek' near Manbulloo Station earlier that morning. I'd startled— wasn't it a racist term? I had gone online and learnt that Chinaman creeks were all over the country. In colonial times, these were places Chinese people likely lived or ran market gardens. Along with broken pieces of soy bottles and Qing dynasty coins that occasionally turned up in building sites or were excavated by metal detector-wielding grey nomads, they were signs of Chinese occupation of the land—if you only knew to look for them.

'Is that rude?' I asked Eddie. Did I feel offended? I wasn't sure.

He didn't understand my question. 'Manbulloo?'

'No, "Chinaman". Is that a not-nice term? Is that a racist term?'

He ruminated on this. 'I suppose I'm a Chinaman.'

'So am I, then!' I said triumphantly.

'No, you're a—'

'Chinawoman!' I said, laughing.

'Or Chinalady.'

We settled on 'Chinaperson'.

Eddie was a small guy, fit and mobile for his seventy-eight years, with a shrewdness camouflaged by a blurring, friendly stutter. He was well known in town. For decades he had run the general store and owned several properties in Pine Creek. During the heady gold-rush era, the town had over two thousand Chinese miners. Today just three Chinese people remained in this half-white, half-Aboriginal town: Eddie, his daughter and grandson.

Eddie said in 1890s Brocks Creek, NT, his maternal grandmother Linoy Wong was the first in his family tree to be born in this country. I was boggled by the mere existence of an ABC during that period. For me, an ABC was someone from my generation, whose childhood had passed in neon prints, bowl cuts and hi-tops—the 1990s, not 1890s Victorian-era Australia swathed in folds of stiff silk and satin.

'She didn't speak English. She could understand—' said Eddie.

My jaw dropped a little. 'Whoa, wait. She didn't speak English? Even though she was born here?'

'Yeah.' Eddie had a thoughtful look. 'It's funny how she kept that all that time.'

Trying to imagine Eddie's grandmother—an ABC who was born, lived and died on these soils without so much as a 'g'day' having dropped from her lips—seemed to break my brain. It indicated how insular those Chinese communities must have been, plonked at the arse end of nowhere.

During that period, the immigration process became so established a Chinese man could walk off a boat, be received by a Chinese labour agent and directed to Chinese lodgings, load up on equipment at Chinese-run shops and be ready to make his fortune within days. Communities were so large that workers could associate with other Chinese from their own district or village: thus, the Sze Yap men lived, worked and played with other Sze Yap men, just as the Sam Yap men did with other Sam Yap men. Each 'village' could operate independently, with its own general store, inn, doctor, cook, carpenter, shoemaker, fishmonger, baker and butcher, as well as internal systems of governance, arbitration and punishment outside the domain of colonial courts.

As the supply of British convicts slowed to a trickle throughout the nineteenth century, a demand for cheap labour remained. Boatloads of mainly southern Chinese, indentured labourers, were lured to Australia by exaggerated tales of excellent work conditions and mounds of money to be made. They were known as coolies, or kuli 苦力 in Chinese, and as I had learned with the pearlers in Broome, usually spent their first year just paying off the price of passage—there was good reason the word meant 'bitter work'.

Eddie's paternal grandfather wound up in Pine Creek as one of three thousand Chinese employed to construct a railway line linking the town to Palmerston. Those old folks were tough. With no forklifts to do the heavy lifting, the foundations of pioneer-era towns were forged in back-breaking fashion: lift this, grind that, plant here, hammer there.

I asked Eddie, 'Do you feel Chinese, Australian or a mixture of the two?'

'I feel more Australian.'

I cocked my head. 'You never had a sense of a mixed identity? You never felt any kind of confusion about that?'

'No, no.'

It seemed all Chinese Australians I met from these 'old families' in the Top End said something of the sort and shrugged, noncommittal, when I asked them if they'd ever felt like a banana—'yellow on the outside, white on the inside' (okay, so just me then).

'The Territory is a very cosmopolitan place,' Eddie said. Then he changed his mind. 'No, no, it's very multicultural.'

There was safety in numbers. Here, the story of Chinese Australia was both long and healthy. It had never withered on the vine as it had elsewhere.

Eddie's father was called Jimmy. During his time, Chinese people weren't allowed to work for the government, join a union or be a member of social and sporting groups like the Buffalo Club, and were often turned away from the main hospitals. They could, however, own businesses and buy property; Jimmy opened the Ah Toy store when he was just twenty years of age. Throughout his life Jimmy was loved by the town, remembered for giving store credit to families in need regardless of colour or creed, and even learnt to speak some of the local language, Wagaman. He was eventually awarded a Member of the British Empire ('a great honour', emphasised Eddie) for his services to Pine Creek and the broader Australian community.

'And I'm very proud too,' Eddie told me. 'You know, I was in local government for a long time, fifty-five years, and on school committees and the national trust. I was awarded Territorian of the Year in 2005.'

'Congratulations.'

'So it's in our genes. Dad's philosophy is if you live in a place you should do your best.'

By the time Eddie was born, Chinese businesses in Darwin had begun to move outside of their ethnic ghetto and into the 'white' areas of town. First- and second-born generations of Chinese Australians were more assimilated. Not only did they swap pigtails for short back and sides, eschewing traditional Chinese dress for local singlets and bushman shorts, but in time they also began to forget their 'native' tongue.

Darwin's lord mayor, Katrina Fong Lim, is fifth-generation Chinese Australian—an affirmation of our people's incredible trajectory in Australia. And plenty of streets in Darwin are named after prominent Chinese Australian figures: Lorna Lim Terrace, Yuen Place,

Cheong Street (named after Ah Toy's grandfather Cheong Ah Yu) and Alec Fong Lim Drive (after Katrina's father, who had also served as mayor of Darwin).

Eddie could speak a bit of the Chinese language Hakka, which he'd picked up while living with his grandmother during high school in Darwin. But he seemed wistful at how that language was fading out of his family.

'Your kids don't speak Chinese, ay?' I asked.

'No, it's a shame. I say ho man to them or jo shin—good morning and good night. I try to.' He crossed his arms and sighed. 'That's something Mum and Dad said: "We mustn't speak Chinese in front of the customers, they might think we're talking about them." I regret that now, because we lost it.'

His dad was a 'stickler' for celebrating Chinese New Year, though, and his annual dinner would draw back all the family from across the Top End to their home town.

'He was pretty old-fashioned in his way and a very hard taskmaster. He taught me some bad habits as far as "work, work, work" goes.'

'You think that's a bad habit?' I asked.

'Well, really, in a way it's one of the reasons why my wife left me, I think. Which is sad, after thirty years of marriage.'

'Sorry to hear that.'

'That was the hardest thing of my life. I should have moved on, which I haven't done. That was 1998. Terrible, anyway.'

✻

Pine Creek was named for the area's termite-resistant cypress pines; few remained, for they had proved popular as a building material. Over the past century, the town's population fluctuated depending on local mining activity—in addition to gold, there had been uranium, galena, copper and iron ore mines. At the moment the town was home to just 328 Territorians, barely enough to fill a Sydney commuter train.

Eddie had some errands to run but promised to reconvene with me later. In the meantime I decided to check out the town.

I walked over to the local museum. Hanging on the wall was a black-and-white school photo of nine-year-old Eddie in 1947, a little Chinese Australian boy with his hair just as neatly trimmed and combed over as it was today. He was born in this very building back when it was a hospital, and brought into the world by the Northern Territory's first flying doctor, Clyde Fenton. The corrugated iron building had had at least seven previous lives, including in the 1930s as staff quarters for what Eddie had told me was a nearby 'half-caste home'—a term, he added, not used anymore because 'that's racial'.

Ever since the Ah Toy store shuttered its doors in 2015, locals shopped in the Lazy Lizard opposite the town park. The Lazy Lizard also served as the local tavern, caravan park and two-pump petrol station. It was a typical outback supermarket, selling limited fresh food at exorbitant prices. I picked up a shrivelled cucumber sitting alone in a plastic tub, and dropped it after seeing the mental price tag of seven dollars. The nearest big-brand supermarket was a one-hour drive away in Katherine.

Next door in the tavern section of the Lazy Lizard, the afternoon heat was setting in and drinkers were gathering like flies. I headed for the attached swimming pool, and as I crossed the floor two men leered at me. I tried to look, without looking like I was looking. They were around my age, sweat-slicked and sunburnt, and stared at me as if faintly aware they had outgrown the loutishness of their youth but didn't know what to do with their half-lit desires. Boredom caused them to smoulder.

The pool was barely long enough for three strokes. I was beginning to suspect that between the croc-infested waters of the north and the waterless red centre, nobody in the Northern Territory really knew how to swim. Pools were just there to dunk your body in: escape pods from the blistering heat and humidity. I slipped into the water and drifted about with my arms spread along the curve of a pool noodle. Mosquitos skated on the surface of the water, which wasn't really cold enough to be refreshing. Nobody else was in the pool area, and I felt strangely exposed.

I thought about Eddie being a workaholic—a trait he not only shared with his father but also mine—and of something the owner of a caravan park I'd stayed at a few days prior had said to me. I'd mentioned how surprisingly multicultural Darwin was; the man had cheerfully agreed but added a caveat that newer immigrants weren't 'as good' as those of the past. 'The Chinese and Greeks came here to work. But people like the Sudanese? They came to collect welfare cheques.'

Disinterested in putting my spoon into that can of worms, I had kept my mouth shut. Plus, I had no knowledge with which to contradict him. But his comment made me think, *god, Australians are so obsessed with how hard people work!* Look at the way we lump ethnic groups into 'good migrant' and 'bad migrant' piles based on willingness and aptitude for hard yakka. Not that Indigenous people and 'white trash' are excused from such condemnation. 'Dole bludgers' are a go-to punching bag for Australian tabloids. This contradicts our supposedly lackadaisical national character. Perhaps it's a hangover from our pioneer days in which the settlers either worked till their fingers bled, eking out something that barely resembled a life on this unfamiliar and dry continent—or they perished. It was and still is the fire in our bellies: a terrible, existential dread that unless everyone held up their end of the bargain, 'project Australia' would collapse into a heap. And, with one spirited gust of wind, it would simply disappear into the red and menacing soil that always and forever threatened to engulf every township.

I wasn't entirely exempt from this national obsession. What pride I'd felt in the Chung Wah museum as I read of Chinese immigrants distinguishing themselves as hard workers—in the past, as now. Boy, if there is anything we Chinese have been good at in Australia, it is working hard. Mining, labouring, market gardening, tailoring, fishing, construction work: you name it, we could do it, and in half the time a white man would take and for half the cost he would charge you. The problem, though, is that while this garnered us respect from some sections of Australian society, it attracted resentment and feelings of insecurity from the rest. Damned if you did, damned if you didn't. How quickly you could get kicked back into the 'bad migrant' pile, with Australia's first attorney general and future prime minister, Alfred Deakin, saying in 1901 of the Japanese and Chinese nationals living in Australia:

> It is not the bad qualities, but the good qualities of these alien races that make them so dangerous to us . . . It is their inexhaustible energy, their power of applying themselves to new tasks, their endurance, and low standard of living that make them such competitors.

In the pool I leant back and sunk my head into the water, feeling my long hair grow heavy and wet. *Fuck work*, I thought, as I swam in lazy circles. *Fuck playing the good migrant.* I had worked crazy hard at *The Guardian* and made myself miserable in the process. So many of my selfies from this trip seemed to capture a change I hadn't been conscious of till now: an open expression with a breezy smile, a brightness to my eyes—I was happy. All my former colleagues were right now in the office, typing, tweeting, making and taking calls, writing important stories to be read by important people, while I was here, doing nothing. Just counting all the mosquitos dancing half drunk in a wordless blue sky. *You fucking spoilt, lazy, immature, irresponsibly childless, disgrace to the nation.*

When I went back through the pub, the men were still there. 'Hiiiii,' the taller one called out to me. He was tapping the side of his beer glass, his face red with drink. I grunted something back.

✱

I met Eddie's spirited daughter, Amanda, where she worked behind the cash register at the Lazy Lizard, and she offered to let me camp out in her front yard. It grew long with yellow grass and had a rusted playground set. She told me she was inclined to let people stay there and all sorts had passed through her hallowed ground—bike-riding French backpackers, an English couple whose car had broken down. I was grateful for her offer and struck again by the generosity total strangers had shown me on this trip.

As I set up my tent I could see through Amanda's chain-link fence. Across the road, the local alcoholics had gathered in the public park. No problem there, turning up for their shift. All the middle-aged women looked big and soft as clouds, and the men's shirts were stained and incorrectly buttoned up. Everyone squinted and had missing teeth. They sloped around, aimless, although every now and then their energy perked up when a fight broke out. Some of them spoke in a local language, although they mainly spoke English.

I had erected my tent and was sitting in my camp chair, writing in a journal, when I heard screaming. I looked up and saw, on the edge of the park, a middle-aged man yelling with an unhinged fury at a large woman—his woman, presumably—some distance away. 'Come over here!' he screamed, his tall frame rigid with anger.

Pillowy and conspicuous in her bright red T-shirt, she was sitting at a concrete picnic table with another man. She spoke in a low voice, her hands loose in her lap, calm but overtly so—a well-practised stillness with a frisson of fear. She seemed aware of the cyclone on the horizon, and silently hoping that it might simply go away.

No chance. 'Come over here! Come over here! Come over here!' He screamed the words with arms hanging stiff as rods by his sides. He seemed to be staring down a tunnel with nothing but her in it.

She, on the other hand, avoided his gaze. 'What do you want?' she shouted back, clearly trying to sound nonchalant.

'Just fucking come over here!' he screamed.

She glanced at him but quickly turned back away, as if his look had been corrosive as acid. 'Why? Why do I got to go over there? I'm talking to my uncle here.'

The man screamed again but this time strode over with long, fast steps until suddenly he was almost in striking distance. In a panic she got up and moved away, just in time, so that the table stood between them. He screamed yet again, and something cold and bitter slithered in the pit of my stomach.

The uncle said something I couldn't hear.

The man seemed to cool down and said, 'I'm okay, I'm okay.'

More words were spoken. Eventually the woman relented and followed the angry man out of the park, her tender shoulders hunched over—a woman who walked everywhere, yet went nowhere.

Eddie had told me that when Australia's policy of forced child removals was in full swing, Aboriginal families around here would smear charcoal on their light-skinned children in the hopes this might be enough to prevent them from being taken away. In many cases, it wasn't.

In a 1997 national inquiry into the Stolen Generation, survivors often refuted suggestions they had been neglected by their biological parents. They contrasted familial love with the horrors of foster care: canings, beltings, solitary confinement, endless church services, a lack of clothing, a lack of food, and many reports of sexual abuse. Girls were taught to scrub, launder and cook, in preparation for a life of domestic servitude. Boys were trained as agricultural workers, with one survivor removed in the 1930s reporting, 'When anybody come to pick up a worker they used to line us up and they'd make you flex your muscles. If you were big and strong they'd pick you—like a slave market. I was sent out at eleven. I worked there for seven and a half years, never got paid anything, all that time.'

As Stolen Generation survivors emerged from institutionalised care, traumatised and cut off from their families, they would often engage in self-destructive and addictive behaviours, suffer in their mental and physical health, and find themselves in and out of prison. Having been deprived of a stable, loving family home, they often were unable to develop stable, loving family homes for their own children. And so the perpetrators of the Stolen Generation created a heartbreaking chain of intergenerational trauma.

I couldn't forget one submission I had read from the inquiry, by a woman placed in the Parramatta Girls' Home in the 1960s when she was thirteen:

> That's another thing that we find hard is giving our children love. Because we never had it. So we don't know how to tell our kids that we love them. All we do is protect them. I can't even cuddle my kids 'cause I never ever got cuddled. The only time was when I was getting raped and that's not what you'd call a cuddle, is it?

A deep melancholy came over me as I sat opposite the park and watched those damaged people drink in a dedicated day-by-day, bottle-by-bottle effort to muffle their pain.

Of course, intergenerational trauma isn't a problem unique to Indigenous Australia, even if the ongoing impacts of colonialism increase the acuteness and pervasiveness of their suffering. My mind swirled with the many dysfunctional families I knew—black, white and Asian, in the country and in the cities, my own family—scarred by some combination of divorce, domestic violence, sexual abuse, alcoholism and mental illness.

We were so alone in this world.

*

That evening I went to a local pub for dinner with Eddie, Amanda and her teenage son, Blaise. I assumed the bartender was Aboriginal, but her accent revealed her to be Maori. She knew the family's drink orders off the top of her head. 'Yeah, well, there's only seven people in this town and three of them are here,' she said, when I expressed my surprise. Her cheerful sarcasm seemed quintessentially New Zealander.

'The three most important people in town,' corrected Amanda.

We took our drinks to a laminate table with four chairs, then ordered from a window looking into the kitchen. We were chatting when our food came out. I had ordered for myself the country pub classic, chicken parmy, and to share there was a plate of oysters topped with chilli mayo.

Blaise was in his final year of school. He was fine-featured like an Asian pop idol and seemed good-natured and well spoken—not glued to the phone like most teens. Every morning he took an hour-long bus ride, one way, to reach school in Katherine. Next year he wanted to work in the fitness industry and planned to move to Brisbane where his adult siblings lived. The family doubted he would ever return to live in Pine Creek. So there you had it, the end of the line for Pine Creek's illustrious Chinese Australian heritage.

'Can you believe you're this family's fifth generation Chinese Australian?' I asked him.

'I'm only half,' he said, with a small smile.

'We'll still claim you,' I said firmly.

Amanda looked at me. 'You know when I see an Asian person I have these stereotypes in my mind—you know, that they'll speak with an accent or what have you—because I assume they're not Australian.' She was talking about her impressions of me when we first met. I liked how she was straight-shooting.

But I was baffled by her comment. Here, of all places? 'But there's such a long history of Chinese Australians in the Top End. I assumed you'd be more used to ABCs.'

'But I know all the ABCs up here,' she said, sipping on her soda water. 'I'm *related* to most of them. So if I see an Asian I don't know I assume they're not Aussie.'

I mulled on that as I chewed a mouthful of chicken. It was strange realising our concepts of an ABC were so different.

In Sydney, the ABCs of my generation were so numerous it was impossible to know them all, let alone be related to them. We were all born to a second wave of Chinese immigrants who had migrated post–White Australia Policy from the 1970s onwards. Our parents didn't wear Akubras and drive Toyota HiLuxes: they spoke English with thick Chinese accents, their fridges were full of pickled vegetables in jars, and their plastic-lined drawers permanently smelt of Tiger Balm. Of course, as children we never saw our place in history. And even now, in Sydney, any trace of our gold-rush forebears was so faint, so forgotten and disconnected from direct ancestry, that it was hard to feel like anything but pioneers in Australia's Chinese story.

But the earliest chapters of that story remained visible in regional historical towns like Pine Creek, whose golden years had come and gone. Those chapters hadn't been buried beneath layers of more recent history as they had in the cities.

Throughout my childhood, meeting an ABC significantly older than me had been so unusual that I still remembered the first time it happened, when I was seven. He was a postal worker, and I already recognised—with a sense of impending doom—the irony of being weirded out by a man in his forties who looked Chinese yet spoke in an entirely Australian accent. To this day, I remain unsettled by a vision of myself in the future as a Chinese amah, cracking open a cold stubby, with a three-tonne LandCruiser parked in the driveway.

That said, meeting Eddie had helped on that front. Maybe it wasn't so weird after all.

Eddie spoke about how his father had gone back to China at least five times and visited their ancestral village. 'I remember it was called You Gum Boo, near Hong Kong, but a bit north on the Mainland. He met about nine cousins, and it made him really happy to have found his roots.'

'Have you ever been?'

'I've been to China but I've never been to the village.'

I took out my phone, offering to look it up on a map. As a former journalist, I liked solving mysteries; plus, I could read and type some Chinese. Unfortunately the family didn't know how it was written in

Chinese, and the internet didn't offer much on any place called 'You Gum Boo' spelt in English, so eventually I gave up.

Afterwards, Eddie and Blaise headed home while Amanda invited me to a leaving do for her colleague at the Lazy Lizard. As we crossed the park, Amanda bristled at the sight of some young people drinking. She called out one of them by name. 'You're not supposed to be drinking there.'

'Yeah, yeah, we're going home,' the young fella said.

'You'd better clean up after yourself.' She turned back to me. 'Otherwise they just leave all their cans about. I know all of them because I went to school with their parents, so they're like my nephews.'

As we approached the pub we saw an older, petite man with a salt-and-pepper beard talking to a tall and dashing white couple—tourists, I assumed. Something about their shining teeth and the way their clothes, casual yet fashionable, hung so attractively off their trim figures signposted they weren't from this one-horse town.

Again, Amanda addressed the diminutive local by name. 'You know you're not meant to do that!'

He looked up at her, then abruptly scampered off. I was amazed at how quickly he had departed—all we could see of him was his backside fleeing into the night.

Amanda frowned and motioned for me to keep walking. 'He was trying to get them to buy him beer.' Pine Creek had strict purchasing limits on takeaway alcohol, enacted through the NT Liquor Commission but Amanda said it was the Aboriginal community who had called for it.

Inside the pub, the alcohol was flowing. Amanda introduced me to her workmates, a mixture of locals and young European back-packer-types. Everyone was busy drinking hard liquor and beer, flirting with one another and playing pool. I wondered what was so different about this drinking session compared to the one I'd seen in the park earlier that day. Was it that most of these people were white? That they were young? That they were laughing and smiling, not crying and fighting?

A group of us sat around a wooden table in the outdoor section of the pub. I found myself seated next to a plumber in his early twenties who said he worked in a family business. He was from Katherine and only in Pine Creek for one night, having just finished a job in a satellite Aboriginal community.

'What was that like?' I asked.

He arched his eyebrow. 'Have you been to an Aboriginal community?'

'Yeah,' I said, and wondered where this was going.

'So you know how horrible it is, then,' he said, leaning back.

Not wanting to concede, I said, 'They're all different.' And they *were* all different, albeit more in degree than in kind. Different in their degree of isolation. Different in their independence from mainstream Australia. Different in their sense of place, language and cultural practices. Different in the frequency with which chaos erupted and dysfunction ruled.

His white skin was flushed pink from work in the sun. 'We saw two guys, on the street, openly smoking bongs. Everyone is either drunk or stoned and all their yards are filled with rubbish.'

He didn't seem vitriolic against Aboriginal people, just incredibly frustrated. It was an almost textbook response by non-Aboriginal people who interacted with these communities. They were baffled, annoyed, saddened and most of all frustrated by the lives led by some Aboriginal people, which to them seemed illogically self-destructive and without direction, purpose or meaning.

The plumber also hated these remote-area jobs because they usually meant spending an entire day either digging a hole or watching one being dug. Small parts of the job were a two-man operation; otherwise, he and his colleague took turns in the digger and sleeping under a tree.

I let the conversations of the young people wash over me as I slowly sipped my beer—more out of politeness than any real desire.

A fit Aboriginal guy with a squashed boxer nose took a seat opposite me and next to Amanda. He said he was originally from Port Hedland, which was 'shit', and I agreed with him on that point.

'I've been to Roebourne,' I said. 'I know some Ngarluma people there.'

'Oh my god,' he said, then turned to Amanda. 'She's been to where my people are from!'

He said he didn't know Tyson. Now he lived here in Pine Creek with his mother's side of the family.

I nodded. 'So, what do you do for a living?'

I immediately regretted asking.

'Nothing,' he said.

I didn't know why I'd said it—I'd already learnt it wasn't something people out in the country ever asked. Whenever I did happen to mention I was a journalist, country people just nodded blankly and had no follow-up questions. Out here, most people had jobs, not professions. Nobody found discussions about how you earned your dough interesting. But it was a difficult habit for me to break—in the city I'd found, at least among white-collar professionals, your career defined you and shaped your interactions with strangers.

I noticed, though, he hadn't said it in a way that was ashamed, but with a small smile acknowledging that not working was considered socially unacceptable.

'How do you like that?' I asked, not knowing what else to say.

He looked down at his glass. 'It's great. I get to spend time with my family, with my nan.'

'I'm kind of doing nothing right now and you're right, it's great.'

He looked back at me. 'I mean, I am a worker. I'm just not working right now.'

'What do you do for money?'

'You don't need money here. I just live with my mum and nan.'

'Do you look after your nan?'

'Sure do. I'm very close to my family.' He asked me, 'What do you like doing in Sydney? Are you into club music or what?'

I almost laughed because it seemed like such a stilted way to start a conversation. But of course, it wasn't. Out here it was standard stuff for party conversations. I almost didn't know what to say; I mumbled something about listening to a lot of hip-hop lately.

'That's cool, I like all kinds of music,' he said, nodding slowly. He changed tack. 'You're cool, Monica, you're smart. Earlier today when a bunch of us saw you in the pub, we thought you were a Chinese girl, you know,' he mimed looking tiny and meek, 'that you couldn't speak English. But listen to you? You sound just as Aussie as us!'

I was a bit stunned by that but recovered enough to say, jovially, 'With Amanda here, I would have thought you'd be used to ABCs.'

A sentimental look came over his face. 'The Ah Toys are a really good family. Growing up I was always at their store, and they always treated me right.'

The relationship the Ah Toys had with their blackfella neighbours resembled nothing like the awkward dynamic between Aboriginal locals and fly-in, fly-out whitefella workers residing in remote Aboriginal communities, which was often rife with resentment and uneasy formalities.

The Ah Toys had history in this community—not sixty thousand years of history, but history nonetheless. With one Aboriginal family in Pine Creek, the Ah Toys could trace four generations of friendship, spanning a century. It began with Eddie's father, Jimmy, and a Wagaman man called Don. Every day after school Eddie would play cricket, barefoot, with Don's son Lennie Liddy, on what used to be a dirt track just in front of the family store. Then Jimmy and Don's grandkids and even their great-grandkids continued that tradition of friendship. It was one of the charms of small-town life. The Ah Toys were, if not part of the mob, at least part of the furniture of Pine Creek.

'Amanda is like our aunty,' the Ngarluma man said, putting his hand on her shoulder.

'You mean "sister",' she replied, with an arched eyebrow that made me laugh.

✻

I continued to take note of the differences between these bushie ABCs and us concrete jungle ABCs. They drove utes; we drove fuel-efficient smart cars. They knew how to catch a mean barra; we knew where to find a decent Korean barbecue open after midnight. They weren't afraid of snakes; we weren't afraid of Sydney peak-hour traffic. But what we shared—besides an unnatural fearlessness when it came to investing in the Australian property market—were family histories where poverty was always just a blink away.

The next day Eddie took me to the building that housed his family's old bakery, which had stood in the middle of town for over a century. Alongside was the house his father grew up in. Its thin concrete floor had cracked in parts like a slab of chocolate, but the cypress-pine frame held up well to the sheets of grey corrugated iron, streaked with red rust, that had been nailed for walls. The floor and walls were polka-dotted with sunlight escaping through holes. I was surprised to find it was quite cool inside.

Eddie said, 'I think my grandfather was about forty when he got married to my grandmother, who was just a young girl of twenty. They had these ten children and all lived in this place. Imagine that! Only well water, no town power, no TV in those days. There was nothing.'

It had several rooms but provided hardly enough space for twelve people, at least not by today's standards. Eddie pointed out a disin-tegrating wood stove propped up on cinder blocks, and a rusting mint-blue Coolgardie safe where long ago the butter was kept cold. There was an outhouse, and they'd lit their house with hurricane lamps—town power in his grandfather's day was as much a reality as the national broadband network was in Pine Creek today.

Eddie had never lived in this house. By the time he was born, his father had another home in Pine Creek. But he was no stranger to living like sardines in a tin. During World War II, he and his extended family were evacuated to Adelaide and crammed into a four-bedroom house. They shared one toilet between nineteen family members. 'Two of my uncles on my mother's side were in the army, Uncle Herb and Uncle Chew, and then Uncle Shin was in the air force, one of dad's brothers,' Eddie said.

At the Chung Wah museum, I'd flipped through a World War II honour roll of Chinese Australian ex-service personnel, recruited to stave off advancing Japanese forces howling down on Darwin in sixty-four air raids. If there was a rule preventing non-Europeans from serving in the Australian forces, it was patchily applied: some Chinese Australians were fobbed off, others reluctantly accepted, and still others conscripted when recruit numbers became lean. And of course, in Broome I had learned there had been men like Tina's father who had been deliberately conscripted due to their race. Chinese Australian enlistment wasn't without its complications, as I'd learnt from the story of Sapper Albert Que Noy's story in the museum display:

When I served in Borneo my hair was shaved off. One day when I went to get water I took off my hat. Next thing I knew a bullet was fired at me—I had been mistaken for a jap. I then went back to my unit at Labuan Island and refused to go out again.

Included was a black-and-white photo of Albert—a handsome Chinese Australian man dressed in a khaki uniform, wearing that famous slouch hat curled up on one side with the strap at his chin.

Afterwards Eddie took me in his HiLux to the edges of Pine Creek, where the low hills were blemished with rocky piles of upheaved soil, evidence of gold rush-era alluvial mining. We parked by the side of a track, a short walk from what Eddie said was the entrance to an old mine tunnel. 'There are quite a few ghost bats down there,' he warned.

The mine's entrance was covered ankle-deep in leaf litter. I was only wearing thongs on my feet; as I nervously crept up the path, dry leaves crunching underfoot, all I could think about was a local snake I'd seen at the Territory Wildlife Park. The death adder is highly venomous, with a nubby tail and squat body dissected by thick sand-coloured bands. The park's description had read: 'By partially burying themselves in soil, sand or leaf litter Death Adders can conceal themselves perfectly. The end of their tail is used as lure to attract unsuspecting prey to within striking reach.'

'No snakes?' I called out to Eddie, who was several metres ahead of me, already at the mine entrance. Death adders, ghost bats . . . why was everything in the NT so ominously named?

'Snakes?' He looked back at me. 'No, I doubt it.' He had socks and a pair of crocs on his feet, and stood a little bow-legged in his shorts.

The mine tunnel was just high enough for me to stand in, around two by two metres and ten metres deep. Mining in that era had been crude and painstakingly slow, done with heavy picks, a methodical chipping away. The miners would have looked nothing like Eddie today, wearing their hair in the Chinese fashion of the time, the Manchu queue: completely shaved but for a circle on the crown that was kept long and plaited.

When gold was struck, word spread, and Australia developed a reputation in China as the New Gold Mountain—a sequel to the Old Gold Mountain of California. Where the European miners worked on their own or in small groups and concentrated on high-yield gold territory, the Chinese worked in highly organised groups that more methodically covered every inch of goldfield. Their thoroughness and cooperation yielded higher returns than those of the European miners. The Chinese also lived more frugally and, as they worked harder and longer, their success stirred resentment among the other miners.

Eddie beckoned for me to come deeper into the mine for a better look at the pick marks on the hard rock walls.

'What's that?' I said, looking at something coiled like rope in the darkness.

'What?'

I pointed into the mine. 'That over there. Isn't that a snake?'

Eddie lifted up his right leg. 'There's no snake here.'

'No, over there.'

'This? This is a stick.' He kicked at it.

'No, that thing over there that looks just like a snake.'

He finally looked in the right direction. 'Oh that . . . yeah, that's a snake.'

We stared at it, stupidly. It was slender and smooth with glistening limey-yellow scales, unravelling from its coil. Its bluish head slowly rose and jabbed the air. Maybe it was just me, but it seemed to have a cranky expression.

Eddie said of countless visits it was the first time he'd seen a snake in the mine. 'You willed that snake to be there.'

Despite his assurances that the snake would give us no trouble, I strongly objected to his suggestion we tiptoe past it.

We returned to his ute and drove up the old Stuart Highway. It was bitumen but barely two cars wide, no good if you were to face-off the 200-tonne road trains that hurtled down the new Stuart every day. That new highway—much like the rest of the 21st century—had bypassed sleepy Pine Creek.

As we occasionally dipped into small potholes, I asked Eddie if Chinese people up this way ever had relationships with Aboriginal people.

'I can talk about it now,' he said, swerving around one unusually large pothole. 'Before my grandfather was married he had a child with an Aboriginal woman. There was no women around the place. That's the way of the world, isn't it?'

I turned to him. 'And what happened to that child?'

'Apparently he was the spitting image of Dad. Not that many people know about that, but I don't mind talking about it now.'

'I don't think it's anything to be ashamed of,' I said truthfully, looking out at all the dry shrub whizzing past.

'It's a fact. But let me make this comment. In twenty years, might be longer, the Aboriginals have declined.'

'The number of them?'

'No, the standard of what they achieve educationally. It's sad. It's gotten worse.' Eddie pinned it on the drinking. When he was young, Aboriginal people weren't allowed to drink or be supplied alcohol, he said. 'Even giving them a drink, I could be in trouble.'

He felt many Aboriginal people simply couldn't handle their booze. 'They go crazy—they want to fight. That's where the domestic violence comes in.' His words seem to echo those of the horticulturalist I had met in Central Australia.

In Darwin a doctor had told me that compared to non-Indigenous Australians, a higher proportion of Indigenous Australians were teetotallers—that is, they abstained from alcohol. However among the population that drank was a higher prevalence of harmful alcohol use, when compared to the non-Indigenous population.

Eddie was sad to see that. 'It's terrible to say but some of the young people, they'd rather buy a can of beer or bottle of wine than buy a loaf of bread.'

We drove deeper into the bush, past a mountain of garbage with a halo of circling hawks, and pulled a hard right onto a faded track leading into a scrubby bit of bush. We parked at what looked like a random spot at the bottom of a low hill covered in gum trees.

This was 'Chinatown', said Eddie, although a century had passed since it had any residents. A short way up the hill, he pointed at a small square of broken concrete, explaining it was once the base of a small temple or joss house. I stepped around it, imagining it joined to four walls and a roof, with a shrine and burning incense sticks.

Better preserved was a nearby can-shaped pig oven, larger than a washing machine and made of rocks and stones. Eddie explained how a fire would be lit at the bottom while a trussed-up pig, marinated in garlic, ginger and soy sauce, was hung from the top over the fire. The oven was covered with a lid and the pig roasted for hours until oily beads of fat dropped from its crispy skin, and the immigrants would gather for a Chinese New Year or Mid-Autumn Festival feast.

I stuck my head in the oven to examine the cement. Eddie said it was made from crushed-up termite mounds, which I thought was pretty cool. If the Chinese were to be given their own totemic Australian animal, what better than the hardworking, stoic, industrious, family-orientated termite? Every colony is established by a king and queen who, like a six-legged Adam and Eve, give birth to millions of babies over many years. Much like Chinese society, termites contribute to a close-knit society through rigidly defined roles: workers gather food, babysit the young, care for the queen and build or maintain the nest, while soldiers defend the colony. Among a third group, the reproductives, are those destined to one day say goodbye to the colony, fly out into the big bad world and begin their very own colony.

I didn't expect to be so moved by this humble evidence of Chinese life in the early days of Australian settlement. Pioneer heritage sites had always left me cold. Now that I was here, I wondered if I'd never been interested in those crumbling sandstone cottages and lanolin-smelling pastoral stations because I'd never had any personal stake in them—they'd always felt like someone else's story. But today I was face-to-face with the story of my people, on my lands.

This pig oven and that slab of concrete from the joss house were enough to transport me back to 1890 and conjure up an entire scene: the hills cleared of trees and covered in tents or huts made of whatever material could be found—native bamboo, grass, paperbark, corrugated iron, canvas, hessian and timber—and thousands of Chinese men noisily cooking, drinking, praying, chatting, smoking, groaning from the toll being put on their bodies, carefully counting their hard-earned money.

If it weren't for Eddie, I would never have recognised the significance of these ruins. It was one thing to read in a history book that my people had been here since the gold rush, but seeing the physical evidence for myself instantly obliterated any sense that Chinese immigration was a new chapter in the country. This seemed to fortify my place in Australia—if not in the land, then at least in the nation-state.

In her 1996 maiden speech to parliament, One Nation commander-in-chief Pauline Hanson said, 'I believe we are in danger of being swamped by Asians' and that 'they have their own culture and religion, form ghettos and do not assimilate'. She didn't acknowledge that my people had been threatening white Australia in a tradition with an almost 200-year history—'as Australian as vegemite, only older', as David Walker and fellow historian Agnieszka Sobocinska describe it in their book *Australia's Asia: From Yellow Peril to Asian Century*.

An American friend once told me that when he first moved to Sydney, having been under the impression Australians were white, he was amazed by the number of Asian people on the city's streets. He then had an epiphany: why on earth should this continent be populated by white over Asian people? Australia is surrounded by Asia and many, many miles from Europe.

From the very first Macassan fishermen to step foot on this continent over three hundred years ago, the people of Asia have only been kept out of this continent by explicit government policy. We have just as much—or little—right as Europeans to be here.

'It's a pity in time this is all going to erode away, with the rain and that,' Eddie said, looking at the oven.

I found a wire fence in a rusting tangle on the ground and just one small, square sign reading 'Heritage Site No 8' (no explanation beyond that) erected by the National Trust.

'I guess nobody really comes out here?' I asked.

'No, not really.'

I asked if his kids knew about the history.

'They've been out here. I've shown it to them.'

'Do you think after . . . It's a bit morbid to say—'

'After I pass on, are they going to remember where it is? Probably not.'

All the other Chinese families that once lived in Pine Creek, including the rest of the Ah Toy clan—Eddie's nine aunts and uncles, their descendants; Eddie's other children and their grandchildren—had drifted off to greener pastures: those with universities, hospitals, supermarkets, airports, cinemas and furniture stores, and job prospects beyond pulling beers at the local tavern.

After the intensification of anti-Chinese sentiment throughout the late 1800s, the implementation of the White Australia Policy had a devastating impact on Australia's Chinese communities. Times got tough as Chinese workers found their services were no longer wanted at the wharves or on the Overland Telegraph Line, and specific state taxes were levied against them. The *Immigration Restriction Act of 1901* effectively cut off the number of new Chinese immigrants when there remained a shortage of Chinese women, which meant existing communities in Australia were quickly isolated and 'swamped' by continuing waves of British immigrants. Many Chinese, facing discrimination and with no pathway to citizenship, decided to cut their losses and return to China.

This will forever be a dark mark on the history pages of the Labor Party. Having come down with a severe case of Yellow Peril, they advocated unsuccessfully for an immigration bill that explicitly banned people based on race. They complained of the Chinese acceptance of low wages driving down the value of labour, of their disinterest in assimilating and inability to speak English, plus their seemingly inexhaustible energy, frugality, business acumen and habit of sending all that hard-earned money back to China. Labor used the language of eugenics in discussions of the bill—'Let us keep before us the noble ideal of a white Australia, a snow-white Australia if you will. Let us be pure and spotless,' suggested one party member— and fuelled an ugly debate that went beyond maintaining Australian working standards.

Such sentiments weren't quickly forgotten by the Chinese Australian community. 'That's why Dad didn't like them—he never supported Labor,' said Eddie, as we headed back to the car.

'And now, to think that Labor has Chinese people in it!' I said. 'Like Penny Wong.'

'She's quite sensible.'

'Yeah, I like her.'

Eddie pointed to an unmarked patch of bush that he said was once the Chinatown cemetery. I peered about but couldn't see anything except a tall curtain of straw-like grass that had gone silver-blond in the harsh sun. Some eucalypts were spaced out from one another. It hadn't rained in yonks, apparently.

Eddie said there weren't any bones in the cemetery. 'You know how the Chinese would bury the dead there, and they would exhume the bones and take them back to China?'

I said I hadn't known of that tradition, and he seemed surprised. I asked, 'So, back in the day all the old Chinese people wanted to be buried in their homeland?'

'Yeah. All the graves are there but there are no bones.'

Throughout the trip I had visited several heritage cemeteries, and found they were always organised into sections denoted by race and religion. Each group buried their dead differently. The Christians used marble gravestones decorated with cool grey-white doves, conch shells and cherubic angels. Visitors left stacks of pebbles on the headstones of Jewish graves. The most colourful graves were the Aboriginal ones, reminding me of Mexico's Day of the Dead with lots of brightly coloured fake flowers, strings of lights and kitschy candles, tile mosaics of the Aboriginal flag and the Mother Mary, and mother-of-pearl inlays. Sometimes the dearly departed's favourite things were placed around the grave—for example, next to the photo of a young man were his striped tie, baseball cap, old tape player and a bottle of Coke.

In the Chinese sections, gravestones weren't only engraved with the person's name and the year they died, but also the Chinese province and village from which they hailed. Much like in Aboriginal cultures, ancestor worship is an important part of Chinese culture. At one heritage cemetery, over a hundred years old, where more than three hundred Chinese people were buried, an austere grey stone shrine read in Chinese characters: 'Respect the dead as if they are still present'.

With neither bones nor gravestones remaining in the Chinese cemetery of Pine Creek, nature had reclaimed the space. Still, I dedicated a moment to all those old people who'd died in this place. Had they died feeling frightened or homesick? According to historian Glenice Yee, while many Chinese returned to their homelands after their working stint, 'just as many died a lonely death in the new land, often from starvation and sickness, totally disillusioned'. Were they disappointed that visions of fortune to be made had proven nothing but yellow specks of fool's gold in their palms? Surely in their final hours they yearned for the home and family they would never see again. Throughout the passing years in Australia, the memory of autumn leaves yellowing in Zhongshan or water gently lapping on the banks of the Pearl River had probably remained steadfastly bolted to their hearts. As they exhaled their last breath, in a country where they never really belonged, perhaps they found relief knowing at least their bones might one day rest in the lands of their ancestors.

But what about the generations of Chinese Australians that followed? For Pauline Hanson acolytes, patriotism is expressed defensively: *Go back to where you came from!* I could fling the words right back in their faces: *Go back to where YOU came from!* The reality is, most of us simply don't have a place to go back to. Eddie didn't know exactly where his family's village was in China. Ah Toy wasn't even his Chinese family name—for official records, his father's parents had erroneously put their family name, Chong, as Jimmy's given name and his Chinese given name, Ah Toy, as his family name; a clerical error that would inadvertently produce generations of Ah Toys in Australia.

Like for Eddie, for many of us non-Indigenous Australians our ancestral village—whether in Ireland, China, Vanuatu or Germany—has faded from descendant memory. We cannot sing its songs. We cannot cook its foods. If you were to show us a photo of its waters or hills, we'd hold it in our fingers as a light-winged curiosity fluttered across our faces but no great yearning would surge in our hearts.

Yet we live in an Australia alienated from the landscape. We huddle nervously in towns and cities where it's a piece of piss to forget whose land this really is. In this wired-up, globalised economy you really can live without a firm sense of national identity or shared culture. We may pride ourselves on being global citizens, but what does that mean beyond 'global consumers'? The whole notion of Australia fades in vitality when you can use an iPhone designed in America, made with German, Korean and Japanese parts, assembled in China and purchased on a recent holiday to Hong Kong. Australia never had much of a chance to assert itself as distinct before it was happily swallowed up by the crisscrossing lines of globalised travel, trade, pop culture and telecommunications.

Because of this, non-Indigenous Australians have always known or feared that we are nothing but shitty, distorted photocopies of compatriots in our respective motherlands. A strong vein of cultural cringe is threaded through all that we do. We read British novels, watch American films, practise Indian spirituality and eat Southeast Asian food. We love Europe for its history even though we live in a country with the world's oldest living civilisation, and we know more about the Jewish genocide in Poland than we do about those that occurred in our own backyard; we decorate our houses with images of foxes, cats and rabbits—feral animals that have decimated local populations of bilbies, bandicoots and quolls. We face out to sea because our minds are always someplace else.

A very new country occupying the homelands of a civilisation with a 60,000 year history poses a considerable challenge. Australia still has one of the highest immigration rates in the world, and each new wave of immigrants adopts the colonial mindset of the first British invaders: an unease with the Australian landscape and a failure to integrate into Indigenous Australian culture.

Unlike those Chinese immigrants in Australia of the past, the jar in our hands has no soil from the motherland and we have no address to send our bones back to.

'The old people wouldn't have seen this as their home,' I mused to Eddie, feeling vaguely sad as we climbed into his truck.

But his mind was on a different track. 'I think that's probably how they smuggled the gold back—with the bones.'

I laughed. 'Really?' Chinese people! Pragmatic as they were sentimental, to the very end.

'That's what they say.'

PART SIX
Arnhem Land

12 SEPTEMBER
Day 99

On my last trip to Arnhem Land I had flown into its central hub, Nhulunbuy. This time I was staring down the barrel of a lonely 729-kilometre drive up Central Arnhem Road, only a short section of which was sealed. Having now driven many remote Outback roads, I was keenly aware of the difference that quality made over quantity. I'd probably cover the first 150 kilometres of sealed highway in an easy-as forty-five minutes. After that, when the road turned into corrugated dirt, with plenty of bulldust and gravel scattered about like loose marbles, my speed would reduce to a painful sixty to seventy kilometres per hour. All up I was committing myself to at least ten hours of white-knuckle driving.

Having farewelled the Ah Toys in Pine Creek, I had spent a few days camping on my own in nearby Umbrawarra Gorge Nature Park before I set off from Katherine for Nhulunbuy. It was the pointy end of a Tuesday afternoon, and the sun was coming in at an angle. With the road hemmed in on both sides by magical old-growth forest, barely touched by agricultural or industrial development, its surface was puddled with white sunlight and dark shadows. I found it difficult to make out the bumps, rocks and potholes, and the branches that stuck up like spikes in a trap. Enough people were passing by to be hailed for help if I needed it—still, it would be a long and expensive tow-truck ride back to a repair shop.

I was heading into Yolŋu Country in the north-eastern corner of the NT, a region famous for its isolation and as a stronghold of Aboriginality. The Yolŋu are leaders and innovators in self-determination. They have inalienable freehold title over these lands, except for a small section excised for a bauxite mine.

As a tourist it was the most heavily regulated region I'd visited so far. To come here I'd had to submit multiple permit applications with detailed travel plans, and to comply with strict restrictions on which areas could be accessed.

Yolŋu Country is one of those rare places where every square metre of land feels strongly nourished and animated by Aboriginal society. This conveys a sense of what the rest of Australia might have been like before Europeans wrested control of the land and its people. The Yolŋu people's relationship to the land remained mostly intact throughout the turbulence of colonialism. They are reputed in Australia for their rich art, the health of their languages, their pristine land and their contribution to Aboriginal land rights, and for producing the 1990s rock band Yothu Yindi, singer-songwriter Gurrumul, and actor David Gulpilil.

On my trip, Yolŋu Country was one of the few destinations I had been to before. Two years ago I'd come here for work and stayed at a hundred-person 'homeland' called Mäpuru. It was surrounded by miles of misty stringybark and pandanus forest, accessible only by air or a dirt track that was at least a twelve-hour drive from Darwin. Annual wet season floods cut it off from the rest of the world.

Many Yolŋu live in similar tiny settlements dotted throughout the bush: connected to their traditional Country, disconnected from mainstream Australia. That separation provides a relatively high degree of control over their lives and land. They are free to be themselves, practise their culture and manage the influence of mainstream Australia.

It will be a long time before I forget stepping off a light plane that had taken me to Elcho Island, just off the Australian mainland, in 2014. I found it disorientating to be surrounded by Yolŋu men, women and children with very dark skin, speaking a language I didn't understand and for whom English may be their fourth or fifth language. There, I was a balanda or 'non-Yolŋu person'—I felt like a foreigner in my own country.

Or is it my country? Officially, every part of Australia falls under the custodianship of an Aboriginal or Torres Strait Islander group and is therefore someone else's country. Yet it rarely feels that way to me day-to-day on the street, like it did for me in Yolŋu Country. The instant decentring of the European perspective forced me to question long-held assumptions. What language should we be speaking in this country? What does the picture of a 'typical' Australian person look like?

There's a slogan often shouted at rallies for Aboriginal rights: 'Always was, always will be Aboriginal land'—the amazing thing about Yolŋu Country is that it makes this phrase feel less like a prayer and more like reality.

I had returned to Arnhem Land to learn about the Yolŋu people's long trade with the Macassans. The most commonly told story of Australia begins with Captain James Cook planting a Union Jack on the east coast on behalf of the British Empire in 1770. It is a story that, like all national mythologies, has tidied up a messy reality: in fact, the first documented landing by a European was that of Dutch explorer Willem Janszoon on the western side of Cape York Peninsula in 1606. And for many Aboriginal Australians living on the northern coast, encounters with Macassan fishermen—not Europeans—ended their long isolation from the rest of the world.

By at least the 1720s, the Macassans' four-month-long visits had become annual. These trepang-hunting fishermen essentially established a sustaining bilateral trade relationship with northern Aboriginal Australians, connecting these First Australians to the global market's supply chain. Some estimates suggest that a quarter of the Chinese trepang market was supplied by northern Australia during the nineteenth century. The practice went on for at least two hundred years, if not longer—a period that rivals the continent's European colonial history in length.

On the road, there was no way I'd make it to Nhulunbuy—the 3000-person regional hub and largest town of north-east Yolŋu Country—before sunset. Apparently there was a campground called Mainoru a third of the way up the highway. A road sign told me Mainoru Station was seventeen kilometres away while Mainoru Store was nineteen kilometres, with arrows pointing in different directions. I wasn't sure to which I was headed. Some little grub had spray-painted on the sign: 'IS A FAG TAKES UP THE ASS FROM'. The two people's names had been scrubbed away, but no one had bothered removing the rest of the sentence.

The land was swooning in a woozy pink dusk. At this time of day I wanted to have my tent set up and be kicking back in a camp chair, wondering what I'd done so right in my past life that I deserved such a sweet existence. Instead I was muddling my way to this campground, and I'd probably have to drive in the dark.

I heard another car approaching and decided to hail it down for directions. It was a jumbo van with enough nicks and scuffs to prove it had seen plenty of Outback trail action. When it pulled up beside me, the passenger window rolled down. An older woman with a toddler on her lap looked at me with a tranquil smile, a hint of curiosity crinkling her brows as if I were some odd but non-threatening bird—a look I'd grown used to. I asked about camping for the night, and the man in the driver's seat, presumably her husband, replied, 'Follow us.'

With that, the van shot off. They were driving much faster than I had been, although the road seemed to improve in this section. I struggled to keep up while maintaining a gap—the van was blowing parachutes of white bulldust that hung around like smoke and drifted into the forest. The sun was now invisible behind the tree line, and everything was turning purple. As the road became harder to see, I prayed I would avoid a twilight tailspin just metres from the finish line.

We pulled up to a low building with a turning circle and gated fence. The old man stuck his arm out the window and pointed to it.

I waved and said thank you. They looked to be getting on their way, veering back towards the main road, but must have changed their minds. The van was parked, and passengers began to disembark: a young man, an auntie, a little boy, two teenagers—and so it went, on and on, family members piling out as if from one of those absurdly puny circus cars from which a hundred clowns emerge. They stretched their legs and some of them looked at me curiously, including the young boy who was shirtless and barefoot.

'Hello!' he said, giving me a toothy grin and toying with a lock of hair, nervously.

'Hello!' I said back.

'Where you from?' asked the old man. He didn't smile but still seemed friendly.

'Sydney.'

He nodded. 'You here for work?'

I still didn't have a good answer for that. 'Not really. Just travelling.'

'You can stay here tonight.'

'What are you guys planning on doing?'

'We go to Nhulunbuy tonight.'

The town was nearly five hundred kilometres away. I was amazed they were attempting such an epic drive this late.

A middle-aged white man emerged from the store. He wore a polo shirt tucked into a belted pair of khaki shorts, the sort of formal bush-wear a politician might don while touring regional Australia. When he reached the gate he said he was not the owner, rather, just a guest helping out. He seemed to know the place quite well. Inexplicably, he looked annoyed and spoke curtly. 'How many of you? Them too?' He nodded towards the family without looking at them.

'No, just me.'

'Hey,' said the old man, 'can we buy a torchlight?'

'What's wrong with your headlights?' asked the white man.

I was astounded: both at how he implicitly understood why they needed a torchlight, and that the family were going to drive through the night without working headlights.

Strangely, he still hadn't opened the gate so that I could drive in. And then I realised he was deliberately keeping it shut so the family wouldn't enter.

After more back and forth, he relented and opened the gate for all of us. 'Be quick,' he said sharply to the old man.

I got back in my car and drove slowly through the gate, mindful of where some of the Yolŋu family were walking, including the little boy who followed his grandfather in. The kid had picked up a stick and was using it to poke at creepy-crawlies in the dust, oblivious to the tense exchange that had just passed.

I didn't know what to think. As a former serf of the retail industry, I knew what it was like to want to close up shop when you were done for the day. Everyone needed downtime but when you were one of a handful of stores on a remote bush highway, you probably had passers-by banging on your door at all hours. On the other hand, the man's defensiveness seemed positively colonial. I couldn't shake the uncanny sense I'd stepped back to a hundred years ago when the settlement still had a frontier moving into the most remote corners of the country. There, small nervous groups of balandas lived in whimpering outposts on what was still, squarely, blackfella territory. And one of the first things balandas always did was erect a fence and barricade the door.

I spent that night sleeping uncomfortably near a noisy power generator. The next morning I went to take a shower and found myself in a long queue of cane toads. They were phenomenally ugly—covered in warts, utterly humourless, staring at me with an unimpressed expression from the grass, inside the shower cubicles, atop the wash station. They were everywhere.

(*Above*) Zen pelicans paddling on the slow-moving Murrumbidgee River, near Yanga Woolshed, New South Wales. The river converges with the Lachlan, running into the mighty Murray River. These waterways are vital to life in Australia's dry interior.

(*Below*) The sculptural sand monuments that dot Mungo National Park, New South Wales, are shaped by ever-present winds blowing in from the west. The park is home to the oldest human remains on the Australian continent.

David Unaipon: Ngarrindjeri polymath preacher, writer, inventor and musician. Australia's $50 note bears his portrait and depicts his former church, which still stands in the South Australian town of Raukkan.

Move over Barnaby Joyce, I absolutely love my Akubra. Here I am near Redbank Gorge in the West MacDonnell Ranges, Central Australia. Ghost gums grow here at sometimes gravity-defying angles.

(*Above*) The west coast of Australia has bewitching sunsets and I'll never forget this one on Eighty Mile Beach. Although I grew up in a coastal city, being on Australia's east meant I'd never seen the sun set over the ocean.

(*Below*) Here I am with Tyson Mowarin, Ngarluma man, filmmaker and founder of the Roebourne-based digital agency, Weerianna Street Media. Behind us are the great art-bearing boulders of Murujuga in Western Australia.

(*Above*) My Toyota RAV4 seeing some action in Karijini National Park, Western Australia. This region is one of the world's major iron ore sources, which gives the earth there such a distinctly orange-red hue.

(*Below*) By the final, ninth day of the Lurujarri Trail we'd hiked 72 kilometres of Western Australian coastline with Goolarabooloo traditional owners.

'Chinaman Creek' near Manbulloo Station, Northern Territory. This marks a place where Chinese people likely lived or ran market gardens during colonial times. One of many signs of Chinese occupation throughout Australia.

You can see how nervous I was of lurking crocodiles, yet how enticing these mermaid waters were. Rangers at Kakadu National Park tell tourists they swim at their own risk.

Kakadu's traditional owners are the Bininj people in the north of the park and Mungguy people in the south. An interpretive park ranger described this gunbim (rock art) site as a 'menu', of sorts, and somewhere you can also see a hat-wearing, pale-skinned buffalo hunter.

The glorious peak of my fishing prowess. I had the impression catching a barramundi was a rite of passage for all Top End fishers, and after I nabbed this beauty I was satisfied I could leave the NT.

Eddie Ah Toy, 2005's Territorian of the Year, is a third-generation Chinese Australian living in Pine Creek. He stands outside a corrugated-iron building that was once the Ah Toy Bakery. It is not uncommon to meet well-established Chinese Australian families in the NT who can trace their roots back to the gold rush.

(*Above*) I visited half a dozen heritage cemeteries with dedicated Chinese sections—yet more evidence of the strong presence of Chinese people during colonial times. I saw this elaborate Chinese shrine in Cooktown Cemetery, Queensland.

(*Below*) I may not quite deserve the title of 'twitcher' but I most definitely converted into a bird lover on this trip. The fabulously coloured cassowary is among the more flamboyant of avian species.

By the time I reached Ballina in northern New South Wales, the sea well and truly looked and sounded like the ocean of my home town. I loved hearing that roar of bolshy surf again.

My final campground was situated in the densely wooded Kanangra-Boyd National Park, part of the Greater Blue Mountains. Here mist and rain are rarely gone for long. I took a nerve-wracking night of storms as a sign I should finally go home.

I pushed off from the campground and hit the road as birds roused the sun. Two hours passed and the scenery hardly seemed to change: columns of stringybarks and termite mounds set against a blue sky iced with spurts of cloud, and a dirt road with no end zooming like an arrow towards the horizon. There was nothing but bloody bush to look at. My eyes began to go fuzzy. This was worse than watching paint dry—not only was it mind-numbingly monotonous but it also required my unremitting attention. Maybe it was like watching paint dry while balancing a jug of water on your head.

A few animal encounters helped break up the tedium. I stopped when I saw on the side of the road a feral buffalo, or gatapaŋa as they are known here. It was the size of a tractor with a wet, grey nose and a pair of very thick horns that curled at their tips. The first eighty pioneers of this species arrived at these shores in the mid-1800s, imported for meat from Asia to Melville Island and the Cobourg Peninsula. Since then they had gone feral with 150,000 gatapaŋa ravaging the Top End, each weighing up to 1200 kilograms. They cause soil erosion, chew through native vegetation, and pollute critical swamps and springs that out here are like water-system nerve centres.

This gatapaŋa did not seem at all intimidated by me or my car. It stared me down as if contemplating philosophically: *To charge, or not to charge? That is the question.* Then, very much in its own time and with a look that said, *Manymak,* okay, *you lucky this time, missy,* it turned away. Eventually, all I could see was its enormous mud-covered backside receding into the bush, its tail swishing to-and-fro nonchalantly.

I kept driving and saw plenty of feral cows. I'd just spotted a pair jostling aggressively, when I startled—I'd caught sight of my shadow in the car and what appeared to be a gun pointing to my head. I whipped around. Of course, no one was there and certainly no gun.

I thought, *What if I die on this trip?* My final words might be what was written in my journal, and of late that was something about how flatulent I was feeling. And maybe that was *fine*, really, because as my siblings knew all too well, flatulence was one of my defining features.

On and on I drove. I had wild thoughts. I imagined myself as Queen of Australia and how I'd give all the land back. I wouldn't even discuss it with the people first, I'd just hand back every inch of this brown continent. I'd say to all the traditional owners: 'This has been hanging over our heads for over two hundred years, and it's just never felt right.'

I even considered how it could be executed. I could give back all Crown and public land within ten years and put a 99-year expiration limit on all other leases, after which ownership would revert to the traditional owners. Then I'd go about dismantling my own rule. It would be the end of 'Australia'. Every non-Indigenous Australian would immediately become an alien, and we'd have to negotiate our right to remain in the country with individual Aboriginal and Torres Strait Islander nations, and accept living under their rule. We'd have to adapt to their world, rather than the other way around.

Stringybark, stringybark, anthill.

Stringybark, stringybark, anthill.

I thought about that some more. Good for some, but a lot of people would flee. Imagine that—a mass exodus of Australians back to their 'mother countries': pale-faced families standing in long lines at the airport, watery-eyed and dishevelled in shorts and thongs, clutching hastily packed suitcases and their dog looking miserable in a crate. What reception would they receive in the UK, in India, Lebanon and China, when they turned up on those foreign shores without the correct paperwork? Oh, what irony after their decades of treating asylum seekers so poorly.

Stringybark, stringybark, anthill.
Crunch!
Ugh, big stick.
Stringybark, stringybark, anthill.

Then again, before it got to that point there would probably be a military coup. I'd be dethroned, if not killed, and the handback would never happen. Generations later, nothing would have changed, and Australians would remember me as 'the tyrant Queen Monica' who had failed, spectacularly, at doing something utterly unhinged.

That was the thing, I thought—you couldn't rush change. There was a right time for everything. Whenever a defining moment or leader of change appeared to burst onto the horizon, hurtling history into a new epoch, behind it were many years of grinding work to convince people and communities this was the correct course.

I wondered how the different Indigenous nations would respond if wholesale, no-strings-attached land handbacks were offered to them. Back in Sydney I once joked with a Gomeroi friend that when the nouveau riche Chinese had finished buying up all the land in Australia, I could negotiate on their behalf to give it back. He'd said, 'I love this idea, but we aren't greedy so you guys can keep some too.'

In Nyunggai Warren Mundine's book *In Black + White: Race, Politics and Changing Australia*, the Bundjalung provocateur and former Labor Party president wrote of attending the 2012 UN Permanent Forum on Indigenous issues in New York, and feeling frustrated at discussions of sovereignty he called 'highly theoretical'. In one, delegates argued that the foundation upon which Europe made land claims during colonisation was built on a Christian edict that, in a single stroke, the contemporary Catholic Church could overturn and send former colonies crumbling. 'What then?' Mundine asked. 'Are you going to expel millions of Australians and Americans who don't have indigenous ancestors from their countries? Where will they go? And how will these new sovereign nations function? How will their economy work after they've expelled ninety-seven per cent or more of the population? How will they defend themselves, provide essential services?'

Throughout his career, Mundine has advocated for adapting Indigenous Australian life to a postcolonial reality, often in a manner that rubs leftie-activist types up the wrong way. In his book, he emphasises the way his ancestors not only used the land for ceremony and sacred tradition but also as an economic asset: to hunt or harvest food; build shelters, boats and tools; and source goods to trade with neighbouring groups. Mundine argues that under current circumstances, a true expression of the Indigenous Australian value system—in spirit rather than a slavish adherence to the letter to their law—incorporates multibillion-dollar resources projects on Indigenous Australian land, and unleashes through business ventures the ingenuity, creativity and power of Indigenous people.

I was beginning to wonder if my fantasy of handing back the land didn't come from a place of respect and integrity, but rather from a pervasive feeling of frustration. Reconciliation felt too hard and too messy. Indigenous Australians suffered too much in our world, and their numbers were too small for there to be hope that non-Indigenous Australia might change and incorporate their worldview into our own. Some Indigenous activists feared that reconciliation was nothing but a Trojan Horse designed to sabotage their resistance to absorption into the mainstream.

Ours was an abusive marriage marked by incarceration and power inequality. We had no common goals, and we didn't share the same values. It was simpler, better, for both parties to get a divorce. But if Indigenous people got to keep the house, where did that leave the rest of us but kicked to the kerb with no place to go?

Stringybark, stringybark, anthill.

Trying to keep my mind from slipping into a stupor, I played Yothu Yindi's album *Tribal Voice* on my car speakers. The band's biggest hit was 1991's 'Treaty', sung in both English and Yolŋu, and accompanied by both traditional rock instruments and Yolŋu instruments such as the yidaki (didgeridoo). The song was composed by Yothu Yindi in collaboration with balanda musicians Paul Kelly and Midnight Oil's Peter Garrett. It's more than a clarion call for Aboriginal self-determination: it proposes that great meaning emerges from the meeting of

Western and Aboriginal worldviews, like two long-separated rivers joining and running as one.

The idea that both parties could be better together still seemed radical to me. History seemed to show us otherwise—Indigenous people had suffered so much since colonisation, and non-Indigenous people rarely saw value in integrating their concepts into our worldview. But perhaps there was another way to be, over the horizon.

The road changed colour. Sometimes it was chalk-white, then yellow and sandy or pink as salmon. In areas rich with bauxite, it took on an almost Agent Orange hue. The bush continued to stutter out lean stringybarks like bars keeping me prisoner. (And as I was planning to drive back out on this road, I knew I would curse every pothole and stray rock again in a week's time.) At least I knew that beyond the haunted forests visible from the road, this land was fringed by mangrove-covered tidal flats and plenty of clean white sand beaches that, like the edges of a bathtub, sloped gently up from turquoise waters.

My mind was muddy with delirium when a horse bolted in front of me.

I swerved and my car slipped. For a second the universe lurched to the right. I regained control of the car and squeezed the brake, coming to a stop several metres ahead.

The young horse had been nothing but a blur of chestnut, ribbons of blond mane streaming behind it. I stared into the bush, but there was no sign of it.

I had been on autopilot, my eyes so steadfastly glued to the road that I'd failed to take notice of what was happening on either side ('tunnel vision'—I could hear Tyson tsk-tsking me). Spooked, I was sure I'd missed hitting the horse by inches.

Earlier that morning I had hit a medium-sized bird with the hunched shape of an elderly man leaning on a walking stick. I had been driving at the speed limit of 130 kilometres per hour, and the instant I saw the bird I was gripped by dread—I knew I was going too fast to stop in time. From my rear-view mirror I saw the car had clipped it and sent it into a heartbreaking tumble, a stream of tawny-orange feathers flying into the air. I had no intention of hitting anything that large again.

I took a few deep breaths. When I felt calm enough to drive, I restarted my engine.

*

After a pit stop at Nhulunbuy I headed to a remote campground a friend had tipped me off about. 'Paradise on earth,' he'd called it. I veered off the main road onto a dirt track that headed to the sea through dense coastal retja (monsoon vine forest). Bats swooped down from the sky and wallabies tore away in fright.

This was Yirritja land. Of the two moieties Yirritja and Dhuwa, every Yolŋu person belongs to the moiety of their father, and is required to marry someone from the other moiety—that is, their mother's moiety. Kinship law is further complicated by clan groups and three-tiers of generations: grandparents, parents and children.

This Yolŋu system of governance, known as gurruṯu, encompasses not only human beings but the entire Yolŋu universe—including the land, sea, ancestral beings, plants, animals and elements, as well as clan groups—all split into the two moieties. Rights and responsibilities are distributed and a social protocol written along the lines of the gurruṯu's internal structures. In the people's fidelity to the gurruṯu, order is established while ego, greed, pettiness, chaos and individualism brought to heel.

Much of this I had been taught by an impressive, young Yolŋu filmmaker, Ishmael Marika, based at the Buku-Larrnggay Mulka Centre in Yirrkala. We'd met in 2014 during my first trip to Yolŋu Country, and subsequently stayed in contact. At the centre he had shown me a pair of painted panels, twelve-feet tall, lit dramatically in a darkened room. They were created in 1962–63 for a Methodist mission church, with designs sacred to the clans of the Yirrkala region: eight from the Dhuwa moiety and eight from the Yirritja. Ishmael explained to me,

'Church people used to think our culture was evil. But in our view, this is our bible and church—it give us discipline and respect to the other people or to other nations.'

The panels, painted by eight artists from each of the two moieties, including members of Ishmael's family, communicated Yolŋu sacred Law to the broader Australian public. Beyond their artistry, they are a political declaration of sovereignty emphasising the connection of the Yolŋu people to the land. The panels are regarded in mainstream Australian history as the first significant statement of Aboriginal land rights, and came at a critical time. In early 1963, Prime Minister Robert Menzies gave the tick of approval to a bauxite mine in an area excised from the Arnhem Land reserve—without consulting the Yolŋu people.

On the road to the beach, I thought about those panels and how fortunate I'd been on my travels to see so many significant pieces and sites of Australian history, in such remote corners of the country. The pleasure of seeing them was increased by the knowledge of what vast distances they had required me to traverse.

Through the endless hours of driving, I'd been holding my breath, terrified that each time I veered into a dip and the whole car shuddered I had pushed the poor thing one step too far. With every strip of heavily corrugated road I imagined all the teeth-chattering vibrations loosening screws, nuts and bolts. Surely, at some point my abused RAV4 would collapse into a heap of metal with me sitting on top, a useless steering wheel still in my hands.

I almost cried with joy when I reached Ngumuy Beach. I parked in the small turning circle at the end of the track. From out the window I could see it was an incredible beach: a quick breath of sand taken between the stanzas of pronounced burnt-orange rock headland. An ocean accompaniment was playing on an infinite loop—first, the muffled explosion of a well-travelled wave connecting with the land, then the giggling, girlish champagne fizz as it collapsed and spread out on the sandy shore. The other side of the sand was barricaded by sprawling forest that stayed lush and green by sipping at permanent water soaks.

There were only two camp spots in a clearing, just a few metres back from the intimate beach. One was large enough to host two families and set deeper into the retja, while the smaller, nicer spot had ocean views but was occupied by an imposing troopy. Shame—I had hoped to have the beach to myself.

Still, I decided to introduce myself to whoever was driving that monster truck. Not something I usually did, but to access the beach I had to cross through their camp so it seemed rude not to say hello. I just hoped they were the quiet type.

'Hello?' I called out.

A man stepped into view. He wasn't wearing a shirt.

Whoa.

'Hi,' said the handsome man.

Perhaps I'd caught him off guard, for he didn't smile. In fact, he seemed to close his mouth as if he didn't want to interrupt me. I felt as though I should have prepared something to say and had disturbed him for no good reason.

Just say something.

'Just these two spots then, eh?' I asked. He looked around my age or a few years older, well built without being brawny. His ash blond hair had probably seen some sun.

'I think so.'

I nodded. *Shit, I've forgotten how to speak.* Breaking eye contact, I looked to the ground and wondered when I'd last showered.

'Are you driving on your own?' he asked.

'Yup. All on my own.'

I snuck a glance at his set-up. He'd pulled up a camp chair next to a cheap fold-out table and a circle of rocks around some half-burnt logs. A small shovel was standing erect, planted next to the fireplace. No tent, so I guessed he slept in the troopy.

When was the model-like leggy brunette girlfriend going to drop out from the back of the troopy? Handsome men like him always had a model-like leggy brunette girlfriend hovering about somewhere.

'Are you afraid of buffalo?' I asked, grasping at straws for conversation.

He frowned. 'The buffalo?'

He was standing bare-chested with his arms crossed. *He'd make a good television policeman*, I thought.

'All those big-arse buffalo roaming the jungle! I can't stop picturing their pointy horns gouging my tent in the middle of the night. I asked a guy in town about them. He said the Yolŋu believe the danger times are at the beginning of the day and at the end of the day. And if you see one, you're meant to run straight into the ocean.'

He stared at me and didn't say anything.

'Then I said to this guy, "But there are crocs in the ocean!" And he said if you see one of those, you're meant to run up a tree. Also, keep a log burning on the fire between the ocean and your tent, and watch out for snakes.'

God, why isn't he saying something?

'In short, get ready to do a lot of running,' I said.

B-boom, fizz went the ocean. Somewhere, far off, a bird cried out.

'He also said don't worry about them too much, or you're just inviting them to appear—but, ha-ha, too late for that!'

'Right,' he said.

No girlfriend had materialised. I guessed it was just him and me then.

I coughed. 'I probably sound a bit crazy.'

'Well, you've made it this far,' he replied, cool and polite.

He introduced himself as Samuel. He was a remote-area health worker based a few hours out of Darwin. It was common for remote-area contracts to involve rotating shifts: three months on, three months off. Much like with fly-in, fly-out mine workers, the assumption was that your real life was somewhere far, far away, so you could only be convinced to work in Nowheresville with the promise of plenty of time off. He'd spent the past three months travelling through the NT.

The sun had ducked behind a low bank of cloud and would not be seen again today. 'Well,' I said, chewing my lip, 'guess I'd better go and set up before it gets too dark.'

'Come by for a beer later, if you want,' he offered.

Our camp spots were separated by vegetation: a childlike scribble of roots, branches and vines, tendrils thick as skipping rope, growing vertically, diagonally and horizontally. The area had two wooden platforms that looked wide enough for me to put my tent on.

I chastised myself for that mortifying display. And god, how retrograde was my fetish for conventionally good-looking, Anglo, true-bloody-blue Australian alpha males? (And from whom my affection was rarely returned.) For a non-white woman like me, being with a man like that seemed to offer instant membership to Team Australia; a seat next to both the ruling patriarchy and ruling racial majority. Was that attraction an unconscious expression of hatred towards my own culture? I thought it no coincidence that since learning to accept my culture and with exposure to Australia's Indigenous cultures, I'd had a few romantic escapades with Asian and Aboriginal men. But old habits die hard.

By the time I unpacked my gear, the night was sinking like an deep purple balloon deflating over the Earth. By the feeble light of my head torch, I sat cross-legged on the wooden platform and ate forkfuls of undercooked pasta, thinking dumb things like, *If marriage were based on looks alone, I'd marry him tonight.* Perhaps I was on a secret-camera reality show. I could already hear the voiceover: 'Two single people meet on a magical beach in remote Arnhem Land. Will sparks fly? Find out on the season premiere of *Babe Island*.'

I was still feeling stupidly giddy when I heard something. It wasn't the bright swish of wind or a bird launching off a branch, but a rustling that was steady and rhythmic. It could only be a creature moving through the forest towards my campground. I shone my head torch in the direction of the sound and waited for two pointy horns to slide out from the wall of vegetation. What was I meant to do again when I saw a buffalo? Run into the ocean? Stand still like a tree? *Ack!* I couldn't remember.

But I was wrong. No swaggering buffalo appeared. A very long snake slithered from the thick carpet of leaf litter. It was far bigger than the one I'd seen at Pine Creek—at least two metres in length, so probably a python and likely non-venomous, although I had no desire to test that assumption. In the dark it looked olive or grey, with stripes.

I thought of how the Maḍarrpa clan in the homeland of Bäniyala have a Dreaming story about a lightning snake called Burruṭtji. I'd seen depictions of this story at the Buku-Larrnggay Mulka Centre. He is found in the continuously shifting sandbar of Baralatj, an area of floodplains, south from here, that drains into the northern section of Blue Mud Bay. Come the beginning of the wet season, the rains flush out the stagnant dry season waters of Baralatj and push them over the sandbar towards the ocean. As Burruṭtji tastes the fresh water, he rises up on his tail and spits lightning towards the cloud-filled sky. Fresh water mixes with sea water, and the lands of the Dhuwa and Yirritja moieties are submerged as one. All manner of life is revived in a time of turbulence, energy and fertility.

I fumbled for my phone to take a photo of the snake. When the flash went off, the creature froze and its rustling stopped. It raised its nose ever so slightly, as if to say, *How bloody rude of you.*

Neither of us moved. A tense Mexican stand-off.

Eventually, convinced I was nothing but a nuisance, the snake continued on its way. It was swallowed up by jungle on the other side of the campsite.

I hopped down from the platform and returned to my neighbour's camp spot. Somehow I had the sensation that snake was slithering under my clothes, on my skin. The man (whose name I'd forgotten) had a fire going and was leaning back in his camp chair, one foot casually resting atop the planted shovel. He now wore a fitted T-shirt and a pair of glasses. He was only visible as a well-drawn silhouette, cast by the half-light of the fire and the polished moon on this clear night.

He looked at me, again without smiling, and asked, 'Would you like a beer, Monica?'

There was something oddly formal about the way he said my name. After all, who else could he be talking to? There was no one but us and the odd python for miles.

'That'd be awesome.'

I put my mug of tea on the ground, and he passed me a cold can of cider from his car fridge. Having convinced myself he was some combination of gay, married or plain not interested, I was feeling calmer and more myself compared to earlier, when I'd been in the grips of lust-induced hysteria.

'I'm sorry, I forgot your name,' I confessed.

'It's Samuel,' he said.

We spoke about his work in remote communities. He'd seen it all: alcohol abuse, unhealthy diets, cigarette addictions, child neglect and domestic abuse—the worst of which was a father who had been raping his daughter. Samuel said the NT had some of the most stringent mandatory reporting requirements in the country, and that was a good thing. He didn't approve of welfare and mining-royalty dependency and said that nobody in these communities ever did anything with their lives, except for a few motivated individuals who did everything.

'I started out wanting to make a difference, but now I'm not so sure what good I'm doing,' he said. 'It would be better if this job was being done by someone in the community. They'd know the culture and language and could integrate the care with local bush medicine.'

I added, 'And they'd actually live there all the time instead of the community bringing in FIFO workers.'

'Yeah, instead of right now: where's Samuel? Sitting on a beach.'

I asked if all the garbage in Aboriginal communities annoyed him. He said he couldn't understand why, if someone loved their country so much, they'd leave all that rubbish everywhere. Once he had asked an Aboriginal guy, who replied dismissively, 'That white man things'—even though he'd been the one to drop it. It really did frustrate Samuel.

I smiled. 'You know, I have a theory. In the end, what gets to burnt-out balandas in Aboriginal communities isn't the domestic violence or the drinking or the depression in the community. It's the rubbish. The rubbish is the straw that breaks the camel's back.'

Personally, I have a high tolerance for rubbish because throughout my childhood my parents regularly took me back to their home town in rural Malaysia. And as an adult, I'd spent four years living in China including visiting many areas which remained impoverished. In those rural areas, rubbish is everywhere. In places where plastic culture remains relatively new, one realises that tidily disposing of trash is a social responsibility that has to be inculcated. Doing so takes time and resources. After all, in the not-so-distant past almost all objects were reusable, organic and sustainable; only with the advent of plastic did such words come into existence. In Australian cities, for decades we've been trained like dogs to 'do the right thing'—altogether unlike the residents of these remote Australian communities. Also, many of these places don't have rubbish collection services.

Samuel's other clientele were the grey nomads. He said a lot of them pushed their no-longer-young bodies too far on the hiking trails. 'I feel sorry for them. They work their whole lives, and now they want to travel and enjoy their retirement, but they're too old to do lots of the walks. That's why I travel now, while I'm still fit enough. Even if lots of people say I should be more serious: get a mortgage, work more, get married—you know, settle down.' Changing topics, he asked, 'What do you like to do for fun in Sydney?'

Dang, people out here love their hobbies. 'I don't know, I worked too much,' I said.

He didn't respond. I was noticing he liked to let my words settle. And he spoke economically as if every word was a small sip of water on a long walk through the desert. I wondered where this was going. He was cordial and not flirty but attentive—gentlemanly, you could say.

It was late and I didn't want to impose. 'Let me know if you want to go to bed.'

'Oh no, that's okay.'

We spoke about fishing, and I said I didn't want to leave the NT until I'd caught a barra. It seemed to almost be a rite of passage for fishermen in the Top End.

Barra-fever has been immortalised in the lyrics of a Slim Dusty song, 'Plains of Peppimenarti', which I'd heard playing in a Katherine supermarket and been written for his Ngangikurrunggurr friends living in Peppimenarti, a small community in the Daly River region of the western Northern Territory.

'We should throw a line in the ocean tomorrow,' Samuel suggested and stood to find a good spot.

Not one puff of cloud blemished the sky. Every inch of beach was highlighted with ice-blue moonlight, and all the edges of the land had sharpened.

Samuel's eyes narrowed—he was inspecting a wing of rock unfolding from the end of the beach. He seemed the sort for whom self-worth rested on getting such practical things done; it probably gave necessary backbone to otherwise shapeless days. The rock ledge looked a precarious place from which to fish, but perhaps with some luck we could scale its rough surface and send our hook over the noisy whitewash.

All of a sudden, he turned to me. 'Shall we go down to the beach?'

'Why not?'

Our feet squeaked on the sand. My mind was clear as the night sky, and the same tides that agitated life under the sea seemed to pulse through my body. I walked a few steps behind Samuel, who was gazing out to the horizon, and heard him say without turning around, 'How can you go back to Sydney after all of this?'

We came to a spot that was roughly the centre of the beach. Without conferring we folded down until we sat side by side on sand that was bright as paper.

Even though I knew here on our little beach we were penned in by an ocean lined with crocodile teeth, and by that steamy jungle infested with pythons, scorpions, spiders and sandflies, I felt perfectly safe. There was no way anything with sharp teeth or horns could attack without first being seen from a million miles away on the moonlit sand.

I could barely make out the dark horizon of water merging into the black night. Here we sat at the edge of Australia, looking out to the rest of the world that in the 1700s came rushing into the Yolŋu universe. A funny thing about the ocean: was it the bottomless ditch that protected us from foreign contact? Or the blue bridge that connected us to it? With Australia's south-east dominating our national story, novelist Arthur Upfield once described this northern region as 'Australia's backside pointing at the Asians'.

Behind me lay a continent that was still mostly silent and sparsely populated. At the time of Federation, those qualities were a sore spot for a young and desperately insecure white Australia. After all, 'if white had replaced black because black was not developing the continent, why should yellow not replace white on precisely the same grounds?' wrote historian David Walker in *Anxious Nation*, wryly using 'the blunt language' of the late nineteenth century in his exploration of colonial Australia's long fear and fascination with a rising Asia.

I looked over at Samuel, who was laid out lengthways on the beach, sipping his beer. His face was turned to the water and bore his usual serious expression.

I had picked up a few small clues he might be interested in me: he was attentive, he had asked how old I was and, the clincher, whether I had a significant other. Sitting on the cool sand with my legs stretched out, I looked up to the night sky and basked in this moment alone in a secluded paradise with an easy-on-the-eyes stranger.

Beaches are, by their very nature, romantic. They are soft, cool and wet. A place for lovers. And at that point, I just thought there was no way I was going to crawl back into my tent frustrated I hadn't tried anything. My mouth felt soft, and I was smiling when I said something of no importance, and my hand reached out to rest on his.

It was as if some spring door had snapped open. I could almost hear the restless rattle of the cage—for although I had still been mid-sentence, he bolted upright.

He put his mouth over mine, and with that two solo travellers discovered sometimes it really is quite nice to have some company, every now and then.

✱

The next day I drove around Yolŋu Country with Samuel in his Troop Carrier. At 2400 kilograms, it was a heavyweight car—a real tank, a bush-bulldozer—that showed me how relatively underprepared I was for danger and disaster in my Toyota RAV4. In suburban Sydney where streets were pinched in by parked cars, and the horizon masked by trees, buildings and hills, the RAV4 had felt like a big car. Upon purchase I had quickly 'blessed' it by scratching it on stone walls as I backed out of my mother's narrow driveway. But out here in open country, the titanic sky seemed to weigh down on my little RAV.

Over these past couple of years of going bush, I'd experienced a few close shaves on the road. The most heart-stopping had been on a very remote dirt track, drowning in puddles the size of swimming pools after some unseasonal rain. I had driven at least three hours from the main road when I got bogged in mud. For twenty minutes I skidded and sweated cold bullets as the wet brown slop came up to the bottom of the car door. Then, by some miracle, I edged onto firmer ground and came unstuck. I was still facing another three hours of similar driving, and from there didn't risk heading straight through the pools and kept at least two wheels on the dry bank— which was studded with thick, sticking-up branches, rocks, termite mounds and small shrubs.

'You could have gotten a flat tyre!' said Samuel, after I told him about this from the passenger seat of his car. He shook his head, his face full of disapproval.

'And yet, I didn't.'

'I hope you've learnt your lesson.'

'The only lesson I've learnt is that no matter what I do, everything turns out great,' I said. I knew my flippant attitude would needle him. He could be a bit uptight. 'I bet if I'd been more prepared, something actually bad would have happened to me.'

'Yeah, and you would have been able to get out of it!'

After four months on the road, I'd become accustomed to sharing it with blustering five-cabin road trains and four-wheel drives hauling caravans the size of a Hong Kong studio apartment. The way Samuel's troopy was able to steamroll through the bush without any care impressed me. Samuel, on the other hand, was amazed— but not impressed—by the fact that not only had I tackled so many rough and remote roads in a humble RAV4, but also done so without a SAT phone, car snorkel, toolkit, air compressor or puncture repair kit, or even a proper spare tyre as my car was designed to only carry a saver tyre; Samuel carried two spares.

I liked other features of his set-up that were less about survival than convenience. What I called 'luxury items' included his axe, car fridge, canvas garbage bag that fitted around one spare tyre, solar panels, LED strip lighting, cast-iron camp oven, and pull-out drawers installed under the mattress in his troopy. He was always considering what upgrades could be made, and next on the list was installing a whirlybird through the roof to suck out heat.

It's customary when a pair of Outback nomads meet and spend time together, for them to eventually give each other long and detailed tours of their set-ups and custom-made fit-outs. I'd seen elaborate tents that unfolded from car roofs and self-assembled with the push of a button, and pull-down flaps revealing fully kitted mini-kitchens. One nomad I'd met had jacked up his ute with $20,000-worth of install-ations, including heated water for showers, a top-of-the-range stereo system, a coffee machine, and a fuel tank big enough to cross two state lines without a pit stop. It was a ritual I took immense pleasure in, though it inevitably highlighted how simply I was travelling ('my car, my tent, my junk').

Samuel and I were exploring the western side of the Arnhem Land peninsula, thick with open eucalyptus forest and laced with rivulets that perpetually split like veins. These forests teem with native frogs, reptiles, birds and mammals. Australia is in the top five nations for its number of flora and fauna extinctions, but north-eastern Yolŋu Country is a happy exception to this decline, with wildlife here rel-atively intact. There are turtle nesting areas and seabird colonies of international significance, and both the endangered northern quoll and gove crow butterfly can be found here.

The area isn't without ecological threats, though, including the inva-sion of the evocatively named yellow crazy ant, the gatapaŋa, the spread of weeds, commercial fishing—and visitors, like Samuel and me, scarring the earth with monster trucks.

'What's that over there?' he said, bringing said truck to a stop and peering through the bush. 'I might have a Captain Cook.'

'Huh?' I asked.

He winked at me. 'Captain Cook, a look.'

'Ha! Teach me to speak Australian.'

'It's 'Strayan,' he said. 'By the time you go back to Sydney you'll meet all your friends in a pub and say, "Man, I'm dry as a dead dingo's donger." And they'll all wonder what the hell you're going on about. Then you'll say, "I need meself a Richard Gere."'

'Richard Gere,' I mused aloud. 'A beer.'

'There ya go.'

Samuel had an impressive bank of colourful Aussie rhyming slang that he dropped regularly in conversation. Later I collected all my favourites on a back page of my journal:

Make like a tree and leave

They'll charge you like a wounded Brahmin

I'm so hungry I could eat a horse and chase the rider

It's windy enough to blow a chain off a dog

Banging like a dunny door

Hard as a cat's head

That last one made me laugh: 'A cat's head *is* hard,' I said.

In the words of Samuel, it was hotter than a flat screen in a pawn shop. Thankfully we'd stumbled upon a tranquil stream to cool off in called Wathawuy. As it was the dry season, the water was barely deep enough to come up to our chests and just wide enough for two, but so clear you could see straight to the bottom. At least there was no danger of a saltwater crocodile launching from the water like a surprise missile attack.

The surrounding walls had a similar crumbly texture and white colour to the ochre I'd seen on the Lurujarri Trail. Every so often the level of the stream bed dropped in a set of tiny waterfalls, over which delicate golden orb-weaving spiders built sticky, intricate webs.

As we waded about in the cold water, Samuel and I pinged softly between the walls of the stream. Together we followed the natural current of water, then were swept into a small eddy that gathered near a submerged rock. Bubbles slid along the edges of our skin. Samuel positioned himself onto the rock, which was flat and smooth as a bench, leaning back against the stream wall and stretching out his legs. He pulled a face and complained about feeling sore from his workout the day before.

'How on earth did you do a workout? I can't imagine we're close to a gym right now,' I said. I held on to one of his brown arms like he was an anchor and let the rest of my body drift about in the wavering water. He had thick shoulders and coarse, tanned skin.

'I just lifted tree logs.'

I found that image profoundly funny.

Remembering how unsatisfactorily I had answered his question about what I liked to do for fun, I asked about his hobbies—besides working out in pre-colonisation jungle gyms.

'Camping, four-wheel driving, fishing and drinking beer.'

'Drinking beer? You can't count that.'

'Why not? I sure practice it a lot and I'm pretty good at it.' He thought for a second. 'Actually, I'm not that good at it,' he said, looking sheepish.

Later, he showed me a photo on his phone of his troopy. His steed made of steel stood proudly in front of an epic Northern Territorian backdrop of craggy mountains and sweeping sky. He was thinking of getting the photo custom-printed on some pillowcases and a duvet cover. 'What do you think of that idea?' he said.

I couldn't tell if he was being ironic. 'I think that's an awesome idea,' I said with a grin.

He nodded, satisfied it was the right way to go.

He was a long-time subscriber to *Australian 4WD Action* magazine and, when it became clear I was uneducated about the finer points of four-wheel driving, asked me with surprise, 'Don't any of your friends have four-wheel drives?'

'No.'

'People in Sydney *do* own four-wheel drives,' he said.

'Not the kind of people I know,' I said. 'They all live in the inner-west where none of the roads are wide enough to own a four-wheel drive. If you tried to drive this troopy down the street I used to live on, you'd take out everyone's side mirrors.' Come to think of it, I knew more people who couldn't drive at all than owned a four-wheel drive.

'Well, there you go,' he said. 'But you like camping.'

'I'm transitioning.'

'Good for you.'

✱

Later that afternoon, we continued our explorations and came across a prime fishing spot. A full-bodied stream funnelled into a gap, tumbled down a staircase of rocks, then abruptly turned left where it widened and the water became flat and calm again. A firm patch of ground jutted into the water like a natural jetty and bore a warrior paperbark with a thick, solid trunk. It stood alone, having stamped out any other saplings, with arms shooting rigidly towards the sky so that its leaves guzzled all the precious sunshine.

Samuel stood under it, sipping a tinnie and looking into the turbulent water. 'I'm going for a swim first,' he said.

'Are you crazy? There could be crocs here.'

Having to maintain constant vigilance to the presence of salties as I travelled the Top End was a real pain-in-the-arse. I'd been warned never to use live bait and always fish at least ten metres from the water's edge or off a bridge out of reach. The most terrifying piece of advice: never return to the same fishing spot twice in a row or at the same time every day, because salties are clever enough to spy on your habits; just as you let your guard down, they snatch their opportunity to turn you into fresh carpaccio.

Despite his threat to jump in, Samuel's feet were still firmly planted on dry land, with his head tilted down staring at the waters. Rather than repeat my warning, I changed tack and said, 'If you really want to do it, do it already.'

'Well, now you got me scared,' he said, looking up at me.

I shook my head, amused. 'If a dude had been here with you rather than me, you'd both be in the water by now.'

One of few people to survive a crocodile wrestling match was Australian environmentalist and philosopher Val Plumwood. In a gripping essay, 'Being Prey', she documented one rainy afternoon in 1985 she spent alone in a red, four-metre, fibreglass canoe exploring the isolated backwaters of Kakadu National Park. Initially, she wasn't perturbed by the sight of a crocodile in the water, believing 'an encounter would add interest to the day'—until the creature began to strike her canoe. On the verge of capsizing, she saw the degree to which she had underestimated the situation. She was shocked to realise she was, quite simply, prey—juicy and nourishing.

She tried to leap into the lower branches of a paperbark, only to be seized at the groin by the 'red-hot pincer grip' of the crocodile. She described the roll as 'a centrifuge of boiling blackness that lasted for an eternity, beyond endurance, but when I seemed all but finished, the rolling suddenly stopped'. She was death-rolled three times before she took advantage of one of the intermittent rests and scrambled away. With fat, tendon and muscle visible in a wound on her left thigh, she knew she was gravely injured. Yet she found the willpower to limp for hours through the bush, drawing on formidable navigation skills, and reached the edge of the swamp where she had the best chance of being found. She was discovered by a ranger who had noticed her absence and gone out to search for her.

Plumwood was an ecofeminist and sophisticated critic of how the human world, through agriculture and industry, had brought the natural world to heel—and how we viewed its existence as solely to maintain the health, safety, longevity and pleasure of our species. Over centuries of perfecting this master–slave dynamic, with few exceptions we live presumptive of our transcendence from the animal realm. Crocodiles joined a short list of animal outliers. That they're still occasionally able to kill a human challenges our place as supreme top predator and our authoritarian control over the natural world. This is what makes them so terrifying and so subversive.

When Plumwood encountered that crocodile and in a split second saw herself through its 'beautiful, flecked golden eyes', her immediate reaction was one of stunning denial: she was a *human being*. In our anthropocentrism, humans are always accorded more dignity than raw meat home-delivered on a canoe-platter. Alas, such 'desperate delusion' split apart as Plumwood hit the water, and she glimpsed the world for the first time as if from the outside looking in: 'an unrecognisable bleak landscape composed of raw necessity, indifferent to my life or death'.

It's unsurprising that fresh reports of croc attacks often renew calls for a cull. When crocs upset the rule 'animals are food for humans, but humans are never food to animals', it triggers in the public a reflexive defensiveness: a sense we've given the animal world too much leeway and should tighten our leash.

Yet following her narrow escape from the jaws of death, Plumwood remained a strong advocate for the integrity of not just crocs but the entire natural world. In later years, as she processed her terrifying experience, she saw that 'not just humans but any creature can make the same claim to be more than just food. We are edible, but we are also much more than edible.' Crocodiles, she wrote, presented an important test for humans.

> An ecosystem's ability to support large predators is a mark of its ecological integrity. Crocodiles and other creatures that can take human life also present a test of our acceptance of our ecological identity. When they're allowed to live freely, these creatures indicate our preparedness to coexist with the otherness of the earth, and to recognise ourselves in mutual, ecological terms, as part of the food chain, eaten as well as eater.

By 1971 crocodiles were teetering on the brink of localised extinction, so hunting them was banned. Since then, numbers have bounced back. An estimated hundred thousand saltwater crocodiles live in the NT wilderness—one croc for every two Territorians. Certain parts of the Top End are certifiably infested, and in the decade before my trip one human on average had died by crocodile in the Territory each year. Hardly numerous, but more so than the single fatal snake bite in the same period.

Samuel abandoned his plans for a swim, having concluded that today wasn't to be the day he sacrificed himself to our saurian neighbours. Instead he gathered his fishing gear from the car. The lover of kitsch in me was enchanted by his tackle box full of lures: pretty plastic fish in every garish colour, some glittery, some iridescent, some attached to miniature metal balls that clattered when shaken, or feathers or long ribbon-like tails.

I watched Samuel string his rod. It was fiddlier than how the Roe family on the Lurujarri Trail fished with simple handlines. He stood up and approached the edge of the water. With a graceful flick of his wrist, the line whipped out, creating a smooth arc and landing with a *splosh* at the centre of the river. He reeled in the lure, wavering the rod so the lure quivered underwater like a real little fish. Within seconds it was wound back to his rod and, with another flick, sent flying back into the water.

After fifteen minutes of watching him, I asked if I could have a go. He showed me how to hold the rod in my left hand so that my right was free to reel in any potential catch, but my left wrist was weak and the rod felt ungainly. My cast had none of the power or grace of Samuel's, and the bait landed at a spot much closer to shore.

I took my time reeling it back in. Because I couldn't manage to flick it about, it feebly skimmed the surface rather than wiggling its artificial tail underwater as it had when Samuel had pulled the puppet strings.

I kept trying, though, and as I did he barked out suggestions to improve my technique:

'You need to flick your wrist more.'

'You should reel it back in immediately.'

'You're not getting it deep enough. Point the rod down more. No DOWN, not up.'

All of his helpful suggestions were making me nervous.

There was a commotion in the water: some sloshing and the briefest flash of dark colour. I yelped. Was it a croc? If it was a fish, it didn't bite—but whatever it was, it had made a big splash.

'Did you see that?' I said to Samuel. 'Something's there.'

He nodded, distracted by his coaching efforts. 'Look, you need to be standing closer to the bank.'

'But I'm scared of crocs,' I said.

'Well, you'll never catch any fish from there,' he said impatiently. 'Also, you better put your pointer finger on that plastic bit, or if you hook a fish it'll just pull the rod out of your hands.'

I could tell he was getting frustrated watching me fish in such a numbskull fashion. He seemed on the verge of going up to the nearest paperbark and banging his head against it. I cast my line again; although it got a little further out, it wasn't enough to satisfy Samuel. For some reason, wavering the lure was beyond me.

'Did you even look at the way I was doing it?' he asked, incredulous.

But there was no opportunity for me to reply, for I felt a massive yank. The entire rod was bent into a curve as the tip was dragged down to the water.

'Oh, crap!' I said.

'Pull!' yelled Samuel.

I grabbed on to the rod with both hands and tried to lift up the fish from the water, but it was too heavy for me. The rod was curving precariously towards the water as the fish strained to swim away.

'Pull harder!' urged Samuel.

'I'm trying,' I cried.

Realising I wasn't too far from the shore, I decided the best course of action was to take a few steps back and simply drag out the fish. With one last pull, it snapped free from the surface. The magnificent silver fish lying on the dirt had a pouty mouth and a low sloping forehead with the widest part set back from its gills. Its colour was brightest at the belly like that of a half-polished jug.

'It's a barra—you caught a barra!' said Samuel.

On the shore it flipped about—every flip a cry for life, for water—but it could only manage bouts of twitching. Between episodes, it lay on the dirt panting painfully with one liquid eye staring up at me, begging me to have mercy and throw it back in.

'I can't believe I caught our dinner!' I said.

'Well, wait up, is it more than fifty-five centimetres?'

'I reckon! Do you have a tape measure?'

It came to just a few centimetres above the legal limit—it was a goer.

Samuel passed me the knife so I could kill it. However, that was yet to be a straightforward task for me. I hesitated as the barra flipped and gasped. But I knew the longer I took, the more it suffered. I plunged in the knife behind its eyes. Its scales were tougher than they looked, and the blade crunched as it didn't fully penetrate. The fish flipped furiously about, in full panic mode. I swooped over it and stabbed it again, forcefully, and brought the knife lengthways to cut vigorously at the neck.

Thank god the flipping stopped. There was blood on my fingers, on the knife and seeping into the sandy bank.

There could be no doubt the fish had passed into the netherworld. I picked its limp body up and moved it further from the water lest the smell attract any crocs.

'You'll be able to leave the NT now!' said Samuel in a tight voice. He was busily restringing his rod.

I put the barra on the lid of our esky. Now that it had stopped jerking, it seemed a lot more like food. I slowly slid the knife lengthways across the belly—as I'd watched Tay do on the Lurujarri Trail—and reached in for the guts. I was amazed at the way they all came out in one contained Rubik's Cube, barely connected to the skeleton. The cavity was empty and all the thick, juicy, delicious flesh was attached to the exterior of the bones. I dragged my knife over the skin from tail to gills in short strokes—stiffly at first, but quicker as I became used to it. Translucent scales thin as fingernails came flying off. Then I flipped it over and did the same, until the flesh was slimy and smooth on both sides. It was finally looking like the slabs of plastic-wrapped fish from the supermarket.

I'd read somewhere that 'barramundi' is a loanword from the Gangulu language of central Queensland. The Yolŋu have several words for the fish, including whether for young or mature barramundi. The distinction is an important one, for the species is sequentially hermaphroditic: it matures as male, and at about five or six years of age becomes female. Mine wasn't large enough to have undergone the change. Many species of fish, gastropods and plants have this feature—conceptually challenging to us humans, and wonderful for its biological illustration of sex and gender fluidity.

The Yolŋu phrase yothu yindi, the same phrase the famed band was named after, translates as 'child mother' and alludes to one of their most profound concepts: every child belongs to their father's moiety, which is always the opposite of their mother's moiety, yet the strength of the child–mother bond illustrates a connection that bridges the split universe of Dhuwa and Yirritja moieties. Their universe isn't populated by warring parties flying different-coloured flags, but rather swirling pairs of dancers in which halves are separate yet unified.

I recognised this as synonymous with the Chinese Yin-Yang symbol, which isn't a circle split in half but two teardrops that swirl around each another. In the belly of the white teardrop is a spot of black, and in the belly of the black teardrop a spot of white. It synthesises the interdependence of seemingly opposing forces, showing that coded into the dichotomy can be a gentler unity.

Dualities are rarely fixed or intrinsic within an individual—they flare up and die away moment to moment. One day a daughter is being cared for by her mother, but eventually she can mother her own daughter. In the same way the barramundi switches sexes, how we relate to the world changes over time and is dependent on context.

Throughout this trip I'd been forced to confront an uncomfortable question: had I been colonised or was I the coloniser? I empathised with those Indigenous Australians who had been stripped of their culture and language and had little choice but to assimilate into a whitefella world. On the other hand, the immigrant story is one of sacrifice by one's own volition, of hard choices but choices nonetheless; ancestrally I belonged to the many waves of people who had come to these shores and benefited from the dispossession of Indigenous land.

In a Darwinian worldview, everything is in competition with one another. The strong outlive the weak, and evolutionary processes funnel the passing of time into one line of progress: everything gets better, faster, bigger and stronger. But in many ancient Indigenous Australian and Chinese philosophies, the passing of time is marked by an organic toing and froing between states of imbalance and balance. Neither Yin nor Yang, Dhuwa nor Yirritja has ever been viewed as intrinsically bad or good, but the domination of one half over the other leads to a state of imbalance. Harmony is achieved when these parts cooperate, acknowledging difference yet acting with reciprocity and mutual understanding, and maintaining a reverence for the integrity of the whole system.

I looked up at Samuel, who had headed back down to the edge of the water and was flicking in his rod. He was so different to me: we were the embodiment of 'opposites attract'. With my fish prepped and sitting in the esky, I wandered over to a high bank and collapsed onto it. I sipped from a can of cider that had turned warm and watched Samuel fish. I felt hot, tired, stinky, but also extremely proud of myself. Ol' Slim was right about the joys of catching barramundi. I was a right proper bushwoman now.

Samuel was shirtless again. From where he stood, all I could see was his back, solid and tense as he held his rod. He reached up and pushed his Barmah Squashy Kangaroo hat further back on his head. His body was so much stronger than mine. How easily and quickly he could, if he wanted to, turn that powerful arm into a weapon and knock his fist right through my face. It was an absolute privilege for men to have that advantage—a superpower one half of the population had over the other.

He began yanking at his line in a frenzy. At first I thought he'd caught something, then realised it must have snagged on a root or rock. I fished around for his pliers in the tackle box, then hovered self-consciously behind him, unsure if I should offer them to him. Ever since I'd caught the barra he'd been tense. It left me nervous of further damaging his pride.

He was still yanking furiously. 'I'm snagged,' he said, hopeless.

'I know.' I offered him the pliers so he could cut himself free.

Looking hangdog, he silently went back to the tackle box to restring. His sullenness was mildly irritating. Lord, talk about sour grapes! He was seriously dampening my post-catch high.

I watched a mottled slick of white foam drift down the broad and calm section of the brown river. The trees on its banks were generally of the swampy kind, with thin trunks and branches that grew diagonally over the water. Leaf debris hung from the uppermost branches like socks on a washing line; they indicated how high water levels rose during the wet seasons. I found it strange to think that all of this, where we stood now, could be several feet underwater with grinning crocodiles drifting lazily downstream.

Here in Yolŋu Country the crocodile is called bäru and is the totemic animal of the Gumatj clan. Gumatj elder Galarrwuy Yunupiŋu once spoke of the animal's significance to ABC television: 'I see a crocodile as an animal that is part of me and I belong to him, he belongs to me.' Through thousands of years of living with crocodiles, his people never considered them dangerous animals. 'We have always lived with them. They lived their own life and we lived our own ways, as long as there is common respect for each other.'

In ceremonies, the bäru is sometimes depicted as a nurturing mother searching for her nest, then laying and burying her eggs until she's sick with exhaustion. Yes, bäru are aggressive, but they're also respected for their intelligence and uncanny memory. Over the tens of thousands of years that the Yolŋu have shared this land with the bäru, the humans learnt to identify its presence by depressions in vegetation, tracks on a stretch of beach, or bubbles popping on the surface of a calm river. On the rare occasion a crocodile strikes a human, this isn't viewed as an individual man-versus-monster struggle. Instead it is located inside a dense web of cultural associations. For example, the death might be attributed as divine retribution with lengthy discussions as to which sacred protocol the departed had broken.

I was afraid of the bäru. Not because it was a monster, but because in this highly regulated world, I was the source of chaos, not the croc. I had no place here; I didn't know the rules. I was neither Dhuwa nor Yirritja and therefore occupied no position in the social grid that otherwise managed a human's relationship to the bäru. Anything could happen, and that meant anything bad could happen. I was inept at detecting the bäru's presence. On the other hand, I was certain—from all the macropods and birds that reacted with pure terror at the sight of me—that I fit in about as much as a croc would in a bowling alley. It was hard for me to shake a constant low-level feeling of terror from being on the bäru's terrain.

'Why don't you have a fish now?' Samuel asked weakly, offering the rod to me.

'I've got one. No need to be greedy.' I tried not to sound smarmy. I didn't dare take the rod in case I accidentally caught another fish and showed him up again.

His face was hard as stone as he turned and threw the line back in. It immediately snagged again and he swore, loudly. After cutting himself free, he stomped back up to the tackle box. I took a swig of cider and asked if I could have a go at restringing the rod—I wanted to be able to do it on my own.

'You'll probably do this better than me too,' he said, thrusting the rod to me.

I knotted the line just as I'd watched Samuel do. I might have been a novice at fishing but I'd done a bit of handicraft in my lifetime, and so my braid was tight and even.

'See?' he exploded. 'That's neater than any I've ever done!'

He walked back down to the water's edge with the rod, the vexation almost visibly coming out of his ears like steam. I took another swig of cider and sighed.

In Samuel's injured manhood lingered evidence of pressure to live up to the ideals of Australia's original jolly swagman. The endurance of the Bushman as our national icon is nothing short of astounding, considering Australia has one of the highest urbanisation rates in the world. Even in 1911, only 15 per cent of Australians lived on rural properties or in small towns, with the rest living in regional cities and towns or capital cities.

I had recently finished reading the excellent rollicking novel *We of the Never Never* by Jeannie Gunn. Through her eyes, and the eyes of other Australian writers such as Henry Lawson and A.B. Banjo Paterson, the Bushman was a tireless, salt-of-the-earth trailblazer, taming the wilderness, overcoming incredible hardship, and bearing fruit from wasted, uncultivated lands—or so they believed. This myth has persisted, as seen in the words of former prime minister Tony Abbott: 'Our country owes its existence to a form of foreign investment by the British government in the then unsettled or, um, scarcely settled, Great South Land.' Non-Indigenous Australians always found it more comfortable not to muddy our portrait of the Bushman with his role as the bringer of brutality, death, sexual violence, environmental destruction and racial persecution. To achieve such a simple and romantic vision of ourselves had required bleaching historical accounts until they were pristinely laundered.

In this, a bias for the countryside was born, peddled as the last bastion of Australian morality and national character. After all, in doing battle with the harsh, dry landscape of this continent, the first generation of white Australians was forged. Out there those pioneers were tested by deadly bushfires, floods, dry spells, snakes and bloodthirsty 'natives', and judged accordingly on their strength of character. Life on this inhospitable land was the ultimate demo-cratiser for a nation of British immigrants, among them the Irish, Scottish, Welsh and English, who didn't all share the same educa-tion, class, religion or sense of history. As David Walker points out in his essay 'Broken Narratives':

> it was not so much their origins that mattered as the shared experi-ence of settling a new continent. The floods, droughts and bushfires that were so important to pioneering histories reinforced the story of Australia's particularity and the special qualities needed to survive or, in the vernacular, to make a go of it.

Mateship, egalitarianism and fortitude were romanticised as qual-ities of the stoic stockmen and larrikin sheepshearers. So even as the country's population steadily gravitated towards cities—true of all the rapidly industrialising countries around the world—we wouldn't let go of our nostalgia for the silent, rugged Bushman.

Samuel turned to me, dejected. 'Shall we call it a day?' The sun was fading, and it was time for him to concede defeat. He picked up the esky while I scooped up the tackle box and we trudged off, word-lessly, back to the car.

He turned down a path too early. 'Hey, I don't think that's the way!' I called out. He ignored me and continued to trudge on. I went the correct way and had to wait for him by the locked car as he bush-bashed through, stomping in irritation. He fished his keys from his pocket and we climbed back into the car, still in silence. I paid no attention to his foul mood; to me it was nothing but the squalling of someone else's baby.

Before starting the engine, Samuel took off his sunnies and put his glasses back on. A change of clothing revived his attractiveness in my eyes.

'You look so good in those glasses,' I said. 'You're like Superman. A *Crocodile Dundee* Superman without your glasses, then you're all sophisticated Clark Kent with them.'

He looked at me suspiciously. 'Why are you buttering me up like this?'

As we drove, the crowds of gum trees and lean cathedral termite mounds dissolved into charcoal night. Samuel switched on the head-lights so that a few metres of dirt track were thrown into white relief. He also had the radio on, which was hissing warmly with the distorted sounds of a footy match. The car rattled as it navigated the corrug-ated track. His car wasn't quiet like mine, and I liked its clanking, metallic groans; strangely, it made me feel like I was in something reliable from the era when machines were built to last.

I still felt annoyed at Samuel for spoiling our afternoon with his peevishness. I was reminded of something a friend once wrote to me: how at the centre of Australia's championing of the Bushman isn't triumph over nature but 'doomed endurance'. 'I've always seen the Bushman as a tragic figure of heroic failure,' she wrote. 'The Swagman committed suicide after a botched robbery ("You'll never catch me alive!"), Ned Kelly was hanged, Burke and Wills starved because they refused Indigenous help, the Diggers were slaughtered at Gallipoli—I guess I've always seen having a stoic attitude in the face of inevitable failure as being at the centre of that version of white masculine Aussie culture.'

But Samuel seemed to undermine that myth with his petulance. Perhaps that myth had always failed to account for male petulance, uncontrolled anger and an ego easily bruised.

It was Samuel who finally said something. 'The way you were fish-ing—I swore you were never going to catch anything!'

I looked out the window. It was pitch black now, and all I could see was my faint reflection.

'You know I snagged two lures in the tree?' he said.

I said, 'It's amazing the way those hooks will catch nothing under-water but they seem to want to hook on to everything when they're on land. I snagged my lure in a tree in Kakadu National Park.'

'Showing me up like that! Why are you even with me? What kind of man can't catch a single fish?' he muttered, more to himself than to me.

'Those fish did not see me coming, ay?' I said. 'They lookin' at me thinkin', *Pfft, this girl don't know what she doin'*. And then, I hook myself a 58-centimetre barr-aaah.'

Samuel laughed at that.

He reached round to the back pocket of his seat. After a rust-ling sound, he pulled out a plastic zip-lock bag holding a half-eaten packet of Sakata seaweed rice crackers. He offered it to me first—a peace offering, I guessed. The crackers were on a plastic tray, which only fit in the bag because Samuel had neatly cut it off where the crackers stopped. For some reason I was moved by this evidence of his fastidiousness.

'Me, eating seaweed—imagine that,' he said and popped a cracker into his mouth.

'You can get this Asian snack that's just sheets of flavoured seaweed,' I said. 'It's very tasty.'

✱

I was locked in a grey room.

On the other side of the door, someone violently turning the handle.

The door was made of metal, and its agitated jangling was extremely loud and a little frightening.

When I came to, with a feeling of disorientation I realised it was nothing but the sound of the ocean. Funny how waves could pound the beach all night but only one wave intercepted my dreams and sucked me out, just as I was on the cliff edge of waking.

I was still at Ngumuy Beach. Several days had passed since Samuel had left for the town of Nhulunbuy, about a 45-minute drive away.

On the morning of our third day together I'd asked about his travel plans and he'd kept his answer vague. When I mentioned it again later that afternoon, he snapped that he didn't like making plans—'so stop asking'—and said he was going to Nhulunbuy for a few days to watch the footy and run some errands. 'And,' he added, 'to be perfectly frank I'm planning to meet a female friend from Darwin this weekend. We've never slept together but I don't know what's going to happen.'

Right, of course. What had I been expecting? He'd already made it clear he wasn't interested in 'settling down'. On the other hand—why not? Why not maintain the hope that someone, someday, might make a grand gesture—or even just a gesture! Of any kind. Not a commitment, just a commitment to the potential of commitment.

But no. How stupid of me. And in the meantime, there was no point in asking why I was always just a bit of fun, on the side; some guy's pit stop to another destination. You could only blame fate for that, and you might as well enjoy the pit stop too.

It felt like a slap in the face, but I'm a cool girl, I don't make a fuss. I'd shrugged and left it alone. Shortly before he drove off, we took a holiday snap of us together on the beach, looking suntanned and happy. We swapped numbers, and he kept the door open to the possibility we might see each other in Nhulunbuy.

I unzipped the flap of my tent and stretched. It was good to sleep on the solid earth again instead of in Samuel's troopy.

I walked down to the beach. It had just struck dawn, and the sun rose above a column of clouds, pouring its light over an eastern section of the water. That bit glowed with a white-gold sheen, while the western part stayed dark and gloomy. This reminded me of a Turner painting in which his depiction of evanescent light pulls the eye to one corner and captures that fleeting moment when the almighty allows itself to be oh-so-briefly seen.

I felt the sunrise in my mind as well as before my eyes. I loved waking with the sun. It made transparent how every day was fresh and unwritten and yet, in its basic form, identical to the day before. It was so quiet I could almost hear the thousand tiny breaths and the thousand tiny heartbeats of all the birds and critters and fish I shared this beach with. They were all stirring, as I was, and the boisterous day was beginning. It made perfectly good sense that we had circadian rhythms tuned to the rising and falling light of the natural world. Wonderful life emerged from those perfect circles.

There is a Taoist phrase, ziran 自然, that refers not only to 'nature' but also to 'letting things take their course'. Taoism believes that all things are mutually interdependent in an unfathomably complex process. As in a kaleidoscope whose bits of coloured glass can produce an infinite number of shapes and colours, there are too many variables and dimensions for our simple brains to grasp. Due to this interdependence, otherwise irreconcilable elements eventually harmonise by their own accord, so long as they are left to their own devices rather than forced into any artificial notion of order.

This is similar to a powerful concept in Yolŋu culture called garma, once defined by a Yothu Yindi Foundation spokesperson as 'saltwater and freshwater mixing together and blending, intermingling and moving onwards'. It isn't difficult to argue that if Australia is in a state of imbalance, this is because Indigenous Australia has been forced to accommodate the Western way of life too much, while not enough accommodation has gone the other way. So what's the best response for a country stuck in a canoe veering too far left and heading for a thicket of mangroves? By taking a hard right, you risk going into a tailspin. The only way Australia would ever achieve garma, I thought, was through gentle course correction—we had to eschew zealotry for subtle thinking, tolerance, boundless patience born out of a willingness to place our faith in the universe's ability to self-regulate.

I dug a hole in the sand and dropped a deuce. There was no toilet in this campground. After covering it with sand, I stuck a cuttlefish upright to mark where the deed had been done. 'Poop with a view,' as Samuel had called it. It joined several cuttlefish stuck into the sand, as if a crew of crabs had left their miniature white surfboards on the beach.

There had been a bit of rain through the night. Upon waking I'd heard the occasional weary plop of a raindrop falling from the trees onto the fly of my tent. I could see droplets dangling like earrings from pine needles, a spot of morning sun in their jiggling bottoms. The rain had turned everything fresh, green and cool, making the air feel less humid. With the sun peeking from behind its doona of cloud, steam was rising from the damp sand. This was just a small taste of the wet season, known simply as 'the wet', which wouldn't begin for two months. During the wet, ninety per cent of the year's rain would fall.

I walked to the water's edge and filled up the container I had brought. I'd been too liberal with my water use and was down to my last half a tank of fresh water. From now I'd have to wash my cutlery and cooking utensils in saltwater.

With Samuel and his monster troopy gone, I had driven my RAV4 into the prime position, backing it up so that its tail tucked into a cleared spot enclosed by retja in an almost perfect dome. On one side of this drippy green dome was a latticed view of the ocean, and on the other a steep hill covered in thick jungle. My tent was next to a small fireplace marked by a ring of stones and my 'cooking station': a water tank propped on a short, pink wooden stool, a pump bottle of hand soap and a discount store fold-out table.

I got a little kick out of modifying my living quarters. I had a 'portable shower', just a fancy term for a PVC bag of water with a hose, strung up high on a sturdy-looking branch. It had been unbearably hot sleeping with my tent closed to keep out the intermittent rain, so I used bungee cords to tie each corner of the tent's fly to some trees and vines: a passable waterproof roof. Something was soothing, therapeutic even, about organising my space for greater convenience. I pictured my set-up growing even more elaborate: I could thicken up the walls; add a bed; that low, thick tree branch there was just begging to be turned into a table and bench; I'd have to think about waterproofing during the wet.

Modification of the landscape is a natural impulse—only, what form it takes depends on culture and individual preferences. Across the Australian continent can be found Aboriginal groups who deliberately light fires on their country to create mosaic patterns of regeneration, others maintain stone traps to catch fish. In Australian cities, we have built sprawling suburbs and skyscrapers made of concrete and glass to keep the bush away.

Since Samuel's departure I hadn't seen another soul, save for wallabies, bats, imperial pigeons and an iridescent spangled drongo, and they generally fled as soon as they saw me. I didn't take it personally and considered it a good indicator of their limited contact with the human world. There was something unsettling about the wallabies I'd seen at Nitmiluk, near Katherine, whose first reaction to the sight of a human being was to hold their little paws out; they snatched food right out of your hand if you weren't quick enough to give it over.

At my campsite I'd also seen the plump orange-footed scrubfowl. It clucked in such an alarmed and fussy manner, I laughed every time I saw one. Its deep chestnut crest seemed gelled back to a jaunty point, while its head was a dusky imperial blue, bobbing comically backwards and forwards like that of a chicken as it scampered away. These noisy birds are active fossickers that maintain mounds of jungle debris up to thirteen metres in diameter. Heated by the decomposition of this organic material, the mound reaches a toasty thirty to thirty-five degrees when the female bird lays her eggs. Throughout their life, no scrubfowl receives parental care: after incubation in the heat of the mound and independently breaking through their eggshell, chicks struggle to the surface. Having emerged into the wider world, they discover they can both fly and feed themselves from day one. I admired such total self-sufficiency—and, at the risk of anthropomorphising, saw my own independent streak in it.

I explored the area a little and took a long, winding track that connected Ngumuy Beach to others equally empty and remote. Cliffs
the reddish colour of roasted coffee beans crumbled into an energetic
ocean ruffled at the seams by white foam. Most of the coastline was
lined with a roughly textured, hole-filled rock called laterite. Much of
the path had no trees or shade, and the sun burnt me as I meandered
on exposed cliff tops. I kicked myself for not bringing a shirt or scarf
and wearing nothing but a skimpy singlet dress. I didn't even have
sunscreen to reapply. Every cell of my skin was toasting to a crisp.

The turquoise waters spanned out to the horizon, uninterrupted
by an island or ship. Every year, for many years, this ocean had carried
at least a thousand seamen to northern Australia from the Indonesian
archipelago.

Debate remained over exactly when these Asian seamen first
arrived at our coastline. One study had dated rock art depicting their
prau—wooden sailboats identifiable by tripod masts and rectangular
sails—at the Djulirri rock shelter in western Arnhem Land to at least
1664; that would make this the country's oldest-dated rock art depiction of contact. The annual visitors were known generically by the
Yolŋu as Maŋgatharra, a localisation of the word 'Mangkasara'—an
ethnic group of Makassar, the capital city of South Sulawesi in present-
day Indonesia. It grouped together the Makassar people with other
Sulawesi-based populations from further afield, who were also homo-
genised in English-language Australian history as the Macassans.

I walked barefoot up Garanhan Beach, a long strip of white sand
bricked in at one end by a shelf of laterite. My wandering took me
beyond an assembly of tall, stately casuarinas, swishing their thick
skirts of needle-like leaves in the wind, to a spot called Wurrwurrwuy.
Here in the late 1800s, the Yolŋu people arranged some inconspicuous
rocks, each not much bigger than my foot, depicting aspects of tre-
pang-collecting Maŋgatharra life: mainly their leaf-shaped prau, but
also fireplaces, storehouse and canoes. The drawings were set on a
wasteland-like bit of windswept pinkish-red, hard, gravelly earth.

I was no stranger to trepang. Once in Beijing at a formal, lavish dinner I was served a course of haishen, as trepang are called in Mandarin. It was spiky and brown, almost translucent, and cylindrical—as if the chef had squatted over my gold-rimmed plate and painfully pooped out a thorny log-shaped turd. It looked soft and squishy, but when I poked it with my fork it was surprisingly firm. Haishen were very expensive and considered a delicacy, so despite my strong aversion to anything worm-related I forced myself to try some. It was tasteless, like gelatinous things often are, and hardly seemed worth the strain of overcoming my vermiphobia.

In Chinese culture, the most disgusting things to eat are inevitably touted as a miracle cures. Haishen is not only regarded a restorative for a number of maladies, it's believed to have aphrodisiac qualities and the effect of lengthening a man's penis—no surprise, considering its phallic shape and habit of stiffening and squirting a jet of water when under attack.

I reached the lip of laterite, pouting over the ocean, and threw in a fishing line. The water clashed with the shore in excitement, shards of white spray leaping acrobatically then streaming like silk off the coarse surfaces. Surely there were plenty of fish about, but the roughly textured rock was particularly sticky for my hook and it snagged immediately. I used a knife to cut my line, and when it happened a second time abandoned my fishing attempt. I sat down, feeling moody, and gazed at the infinite waters. Two snagged lines— if only Samuel could see me now.

I looked out to where sea met sky and imagined sixty approaching praus, powered by north-west monsoon winds the Yolŋu called luŋgurrma. Each year the Macassans journeyed 1600 kilometres on the high seas over two weeks; their safe arrival was no mean feat. In *Macassan History and Heritage: Journeys, Encounters and Influences*, edited by Marshall Clark and Sally K. May, I'd learnt how knowledge of these oceans had been accumulated and passed down orally through the generations. It allowed the Macassans, without sophisticated tools, to navigate hazardous coastlines of rocks sharp as teeth and long sections of open water. The Macassan sailors knew well the winds that set them on course or blew them off it; the precise stars that mapped their locations; the animals and birds whose behaviour sometimes foretold incoming bad weather and the men were ever vigilant to the shifting mood of the oceans.

Much like in other 'first contact' stories, the Yolŋu say the arrival of the Maŋgatharra shocked their ancestors, who presumed the visitors were some sort of spirit. Surprise turned into fascination as the Yolŋu familiarised themselves with the many unusual and useful items the Maŋgatharra brought with them: cloth, glass and ceramics; food such as rice and cocoa; alcohol and drug substances such as betel nut, opium and tobacco; tobacco pipes and fish hooks; and metal tools such as tomahawks, spearheads and knives. These were traded for Yolŋu labour, and fishing and harvesting rights of not only trepang but mother-of-pearl, tortoiseshell and timber. Some Yolŋu words still used today reflect the influence of the Maŋgatharra, such as rupiah (money), while the word balanda was derived from the Maŋgatharra word for the Dutch (Belanda or orang Belanda).

Over the summer, the fishermen moved along the coast collecting trepang that dotted the sea floor and became exposed at low tide. Then the dhimurru—Yolŋu for east winds—picked up and carried them home again in March or April.

The full stop to this centuries-long tradition was the good ship *Bunga Ejaya*, which left Australian shores in 1907 under the command of Using Daeng Rangka. The industry had been in freefall following the introduction of licences and customs taxes by the South Australian government, back then the administrators of the Northern Territory. A fortification of national borders by a federated Australia, combined with a domestically popular suite of anti-immigration policies, was symptomatic of a new, heavily regulated and protectionist modern nation-state. For a long time after, any interactions with our nearest neighbours were first rerouted thousands of kilometres north to Great Britain as an intermediary.

Even though this historical Asian trade was limited to a strip of Aboriginal Australian groups living on the north coast, it fascinated me as a rare example in this country's history of an Asian–Aboriginal interaction neither managed nor mitigated by European control—or at least, not until its end. As well, it represents the first connection between my ancestral people, as Chinese consumers of trepang, to this continent.

While the story of the Maŋgatharra isn't without its own chapters of violence and cultural clashes, the Yolŋu today chiefly characterise that relationship as business-like and cordial. It stands out as a stark example of a people's isolation coming to an end without being forced to endure brutal invasion and colonisation. Perhaps the crucial difference is that at the end of the season the Maŋgatharra always left, but the balanda remained.

*

I had taken Central Arnhem Road a week prior, and would take it again tomorrow on my drive back to Katherine. But first I had to restock and refuel at Nhulunbuy, the region's largest town and a curious dot at the end of that wearisome road cutting Arnhem Land in half like two triangle sandwiches. Curious because I doubted few travellers would expect that at the end of a ten-hour drive deep into virgin bush, could be a town populated enough to support a big-brand supermarket, car dealership, Christian college, thirty-bed hospital and even a country golf club. In the suburban section of town every second house had a fishing boat parked in the driveway—not scrappy dinghies but proper, sleek, double-decker cruisers.

I only had to take a couple of wrong turns to end up on the edge of town and find myself staring down 'Restricted Access' signs. Rio Tinto's bauxite mine, Nhulunbuy's raison d'etre, loomed on the horizon. The mining giant's hefty pay packets had attracted

Australians and non-Australians of every stripe and paid for all those shiny boats sitting in concrete driveways. When I'd been here two years prior, the company had just closed its refinery arm with more than a thousand job losses. I'd expected to return to a ghost town; however, on the surface little appeared to have changed. There were signs of the Yolŋu people's growing business acumen, including a company owned by the Gumatj clan that had opened a small-scale bauxite mine and training centre on their traditional lands.

Samuel was still in town, and we arranged to have dinner at a local tavern. It was dark by the time I arrived. I found him standing at the entrance looking freshly showered, wearing his Clark Kent glasses and a clean shirt. I had showered as well and, as had become customary on this trip, a good scrub down was enough to leave me feeling like a total babe—a squeaky clean, overly pampered princess with shiny hair and golden skin. I had to remind myself that in my former, mostly sedentary life, showers were an everyday occurrence.

'You look hot,' he said, pinching me on the hip.

'Thanks, darl,' I said. 'Not bad yourself.'

The tavern was half-empty. Like so many Outback drinking holes, it was fitted out with tacky plastic furniture. The bar top was lined with damp beer mats, powerfully emitting the ghostly smell of many thousands of drinks past. Samuel ordered a horrible-sounding dish called beef parma-gedden, a Tex-Mex spin on a beef parmy, and I ordered lamb shanks. We took our beers to a free table, sitting on a couple of high chairs opposite each other. I told Samuel about the rock drawings I'd seen, and our food came out not long after. The parmy was the size of Samuel's head: a pig's slop of plastic cheese, chilli beef and tomato sauce. Typical of Aussie pub food, it was high on fat, low on nutrition. I watched him polish it off, leaving cubes of cucumber he had neatly eaten around.

'You don't like cucumber?' I said.

'No, what makes you say that?' he said sarcastically.

My shanks and mash tasted fine. A bit bland.

My eyes widened at the appearance of an Asian woman behind the bar. Her body was half covered in tattoos, and her straw-dry peroxide-blonde hair was swept up in a high ponytail that reached all the way down to her G-stringed arse. As she tossed her chin into the air, her hair flicked about like a horse's tail.

Also, she didn't have a top on. Her tits were huge. I couldn't stop staring at them.

Samuel turned to see what I was looking at. He turned back and rolled his eyes as if to say, *Christ, Monica, you can be such a yokel.* 'They're called skimpies, and you're supposed to slip a note in their G-banger,' he said, with a smug look.

'Did you ever go to the Roey when you lived in Broome?' I asked.

'Yes.'

'On a Thursday night?' I asked, referring to the pub's weekly wet T-shirt competition.

'*Every* Thursday night. Skimpies are real popular in WA. Some even go on tour.' He took a sip of beer and said loftily, 'To be honest, it doesn't really do it for me. If I can't touch it, I'm not interested.'

I was still staring at the woman, although trying my best to appear that I wasn't.

He had another look at her and said, with an arched eyebrow, 'Of course, I might try and get her number later.'

I didn't say anything, but he was looking at me with a barely disguised smirk.

'How would you feel if I did that?' he asked.

I didn't bother saying his attempt to goad me into playing the 'jealous wife' was about as retrograde as a pub with a topless waitress. 'If you did it in front of me I'd think that was pretty rude—but hey, what you do when I'm gone is your business.'

'You're prettier than her,' he said quickly.

I hadn't, in the slightest, needed such an assurance. I was sure there was little overlap between my 'game' and hers; if she and I were athletes we'd be playing different sports, and a cyclist was never in competition with a cricketer.

'The only difference is you don't have any tats,' he said.

'You might need to change one of the vowels there,' I said, and whispered 'tits' just in case he didn't get it.

'Yeah, but they're a bit too fake,' he said.

'Because you only want them a little bit fake, not *too* fake.'

'Yeah, just fake enough to feel like you need to check.'

'Can you tell?'

'Only if you bury your face in them and just—' He mimed two giant boobs with his hands and tipped his head forward, then shook his head to-and-fro. This was called motorboating, apparently.

I laughed. Once again I was struck by how absurdly different Samuel was to all the cardigan-wearing, Twitter-scrolling, super-woke hipsters I knew in Sydney. At times I toss up what plays a more significant role in my alienation from Australia: my Chinese heritage or the fact I am a fast-talking intellectual trendoid?

According to David Walker in *Anxious Nation*, a distrust of city folk is the flipside to our nostalgia for the Bushman. After all, cities are sites of experimentation, commerce, leisure, fashion, migration and trade, where races mix, gender and sexual orthodoxy is challenged, and social stratification becomes infinitely more complex. Cities are breeding grounds for bohemians, merchants, academics, politicians, feminists and immigrant communities. Historically, city slickers were viewed in white Australia culture as decadent and subversive. When push came to shove, and the throngs of faceless Asiatic armies were finally at our doorsteps, were we to believe that soft-palmed, paper-pushing city folk had the mettle to defend the nation? No way.

'Do you have any tats?' I asked Samuel.

'You don't put bumper stickers on a Maserati,' he said, with a wink and a grin.

That said, he was thinking of getting a giant back tattoo to honour his beloved AFL team, the Western Bulldogs. The Doggies were founded in Melbourne's Footscray, traditionally a working-class area and where Samuel proudly traced his roots.

True to their name, the AFL team were known as perennial underdogs. This year, however, they were tracking exceptionally well late in the season. A smile met my lips as I considered just how deep a feeling Samuel could conjure for eighteen men on a footy field wearing blue, white and red. 'It's a sure bet, isn't it, for a tattoo?' I said. 'Your love for the Doggies is a love for life—a surer bet than any wife or girlfriend.'

From the tavern's ceiling hung a green canvas swag: the prize for a raffle you could enter if you played a game of keno.

'Have you ever played keno?' I asked Samuel.

'I'm Australian,' he said.

'I've never played before.'

'Let's play, then.' He pulled a ticket from a stack on the table and a pencil from a holder beside it. He explained keno to me, and we marked how many games and numbers we wanted to play, the numbers we picked to win and how much we wanted to spend per game, before Samuel took our ticket to the bar. Keno principally operated on dumb luck, although every variable affected the amount of risk we were taking, which correlated to the potential size of our winnings.

Later I discovered that keno—apparently the most Aussie of games—is actually a Chinese cultural import brought over by nineteenth-century coolies. Back in Canton the game was called baak-gap-piu 白鴿票 (white dove ticket), because after draws were taken in the city, messenger birds announced the results to outlying districts. In baak-gap-piu, players didn't use numbers but rather picked characters from the well-known rhyming Chinese poem 'The Thousand Character Classic' that contains precisely one thousand characters, each used only once.

No country is truly an island—even the world's largest island nation. Culture, technology and ideas have a habit of slipping through borders. What at first feels alien quickly absorbs local flavour to become something unique and peculiarly native. It sends its roots deep into the landscape and over time becomes old hat. Did Britain become less British when tea was adopted from Asia? Did China become less Chinese when communism was adopted from Europe?

Samuel came back to our table with two fresh beers. He had one eye on the tavern walls—they were installed with sports television screens, and filled the air with the blurred sound of racing commentary.

'What music are you into?' he asked me, half-distracted.

I felt a ping of deja vu—hadn't Amanda's friend asked me the exact same thing, back in Pine Creek? This time I confessed, half-sheepish, that on my drive to Nhulunbuy I'd listened to the *Les Misérables* movie-musical soundtrack.

Samuel liked Red Gum, Paul Kelly, Slim Dusty, Lee Kernaghan and The Waifs—all Australian, mainly Anglo men. He liked reading Australian books about war heroes and watching Australian films about nihilistic lowlifes and criminals like *Chopper* and *Idiot Box*. I wasn't nearly as enthusiastic about domestic pop culture—something I harboured some guilt over. I looked back on my youth and regarded myself the worst manifestation of cut-and-paste globalisation: a jet-setter with a severe case of cultural cringe, mindlessly collecting all the shiny objects from other people's cultures (mainly American). Only since returning from China and working at *The Guardian* had I begun to deliberately seek out Australian books, films and television shows. Then again, perhaps I was being too hard on myself. Maybe I'd be inclined to enjoy Australian stories, if only some of their prot-agonists looked a little more like me rather than always like Samuel.

He could barely contain his derision when I confessed my Yankophilia. He said he hated Americans, then imitated them: 'Oh my gawd, oh my gawd, oh—my—gaaaaawd!'

'They make good films,' I said mildly.

'No, they don't! They're all *boom-boom-boom*.' He mimed explosions.

'Well, they're good at stand-up.'

'Are you joking? The Brits are better at stand-up!'

He was beginning to annoy me.

I deliberately needled him. 'You really are cut from the cloth of the mother country.' I knew he'd find that insulting.

He frowned. 'No, I'm not. Anyway, I like Aussie stand-ups best, like Wil Anderson and Carl Barron. I'm Aussie and,' he paused, and rather haughtily added, 'I'm an individual.'

I laughed at his airs.

He immediately shot back, 'You're mad for those Seppos.'

'Seppos?'

He could see I didn't understand. 'The Yanks? Septic tanks? The Seppos.'

'What rhymes with Chinese?'

He didn't need to think twice. 'Evil.'

I didn't say anything.

He clutched his beer in one hand and looked at me with a nervous smile. 'You're angry at me?'

I looked away, to nothing in particular.

'That doesn't rhyme with Chinese,' I said placidly.

I had to assure him I wasn't upset, which was true enough, but at the same time I was feeling something. We weren't on the same page; it would never work between us.

'Did you vote for Tony Abbott?' I asked, all of a sudden. I knew that to him this probably seemed an abrupt segue. But in my circles, the short-lived former prime minister was a symbol of Australia's worst tendencies. He was a loyal monarchist who notoriously tried to revive the titles of 'knight' and 'dame', a parochial nationalist and political dog-whistler, inclined to invoke the country's deep-seated fear of the Other. If Samuel had voted for Abbott, it would immediately confirm my sinking suspicion of the kind of person he was.

'Yes,' he said.

'Why?' I asked, unable to hide my incredulity.

'Nobody else loves this country like he does, and I love this country.'

'Was he a good prime minister?'

'Shocking, but he did some good things.'

'Like what?'

'Stopped the boats.'

Christ, Samuel was one of those. I had to stop myself from rolling my eyes.

Abbott's pithy and disturbingly catchy political slogan would forever be linked to his two-year prime ministership. However, from the vantage point of history it was just the latest incarnation of more than a century of attempts to 'stop the boats' from Asia—which included halting the trepangers from the Indonesian archipelago, the coolies from China and then, in a less paranoid fashion, the warring Japanese.

In the minds of many Australians, our viability as a young and fragile nation continues to rest on strong borders. And to those Australians, there is no more potent an image than that of a boat full of refugees infiltrating our heavily patrolled maritime border zone. Apparently these asylum seekers have 'flooded' into Australia and left an iron-fisted conservative government with no choice but to 'clean up the illegal immigration mess', as Home Affairs Minister Peter Dutton has said, employing the language of crisis otherwise used during natural disasters. These boats come from Malaysia or Indonesia but aren't anything like the proud, well-maintained praus once sailed by trepangers: they're rusting or rotting fishing boats packed to the brim with half-starved, dark-skinned, paper-less passengers from war-torn parts of the globe, supposedly 'preying' on the sympathy of Australia. As historian Ruth Balint wrote in *Australia's Asia*, boats that sneak in via the country's 'back fence' instantly confirm every worst fear mainstream Australia has about the developing world: a dirty, crowded, poverty-stricken place, where human beings are turned into disposable cargo, their dignity stripped to its bare bones.

And it was never too long before someone, somewhere in Australia—sad, scared and pissed off—cried out it was time to batten down the hatches and pull up the drawbridge.

'All those poor people drowning,' Samuel added.

'Fine, but don't say "stop the boats"—it's an ugly phrase,' I muttered.

A yawning chasm had opened up between me and Samuel. From the faraway place where I viewed him, he sat in his chair hard and cold as stone.

'What else can we disagree on?' I said caustically. 'Do you think we should trash the Great Barrier Reef? Or that we shouldn't let gay people marry?'

'No. I've been to the Great Barrier Reef and I love it and definitely don't want to see it destroyed. And I don't care if gay people marry, they can do what they want—although frankly, I don't see why anyone would want to marry.' He quietly mimicked me, 'What else can we disagree on?'

I felt ashamed that I'd so quickly picked up the battleaxe. I had betrayed my hand—not as a staunch leftie, rather a sucker of the so-called culture wars. In Australia those wars are mainly rooted in the history wars of the 1990s, when conservatives and progressives diverged in their interpretations of colonial history and national identity. In particular, the nature and extent of past violence against Indigenous Australia, and the place British symbols and culture occupy in modern Australian society. The wars had ebbed for a while, then in recent years morphed into the culture wars sweeping the Western world. I often felt as if we were now in the midst of a bitter and rising backlash against an equally powerful tide of activism from traditionally oppressed groups including women, racial minorities and the LGBTQI community.

But how much of the culture wars was trumped-up noise? If you paid attention to all the back-and-forth arguments, you might come to believe that Australia could be neatly halved between progressives, greenies, feminists, human rights activists and unionists on one side, and right-wing conservatives, bankers, farmers, Southern Cross tat-bearers, talkback-radio listeners and the white working class on the other. But that was a distortion and exaggeration of our country through the lens of the cynical mass media, whose bread and butter was manufacturing outrage, and reflected in social media.

Samuel narrowed his eyes. 'Who do you vote for?'

'The Greens.'

He scoffed with disgust. 'Might as well do a donkey vote!'

We were silent as we let the dust settle. I prickled with the thought he might be thinking the same thing I was: *I can't believe I've had sex with this person.*

Over the course of my travels overseas, I'd concluded that few countries genuinely like immigrants. Australia is no exception: we swallow that bitter pill with the caveat that only the *right* sort of person is allowed in. But why should assimilation be the most important obligation of any migrant? What legitimacy does any cultural group have to dictate how others should behave? Those early colonists of Australia and the waves of foreigners that followed have never assimilated into Indigenous society, so legitimacy can't be based on who came here first. Underlying the policy of assimilation, quite simply, is Western supremacy.

I tried to explain this to Samuel, but he firmly disagreed. 'This isn't about race. It's about keeping violent and dangerous people out of this country—no matter what their race.'

I remained sceptical and said so.

The more I'd learnt of Australian history, the more sensitive I had become to this country's long fear of its neighbours to the north and the way the 'Orient' has been used as a foil from which we assert our national identity. We are the light to Asia's ancient shadow; they are savage countries of corrupt autocratic leaders and chaotic military coups; regressive, anti-feminist religious practices; environmental destruction, terrorism and perverted sexuality; and unhygienic, impoverished living conditions in smog-filled cities crammed with people—whereas our country is a young, virile and well-functioning democracy, with opportunity and a fair go equally portioned to every person no matter their sex, colour or creed; we are ruled by blind justice, Western rationality and Christian values, and have plenty of clean, sunlit space that our neighbours look upon covetously.

Watching the slow fade of one's cultural dominance is no easy thing. It's little wonder that change births zealots such as Pauline Hanson, who take up the mantle of moral crusader against a shifting tide.

'The issue is that there are some of you who don't want people like me in this country,' I said to Samuel.

'But you're one of us.'

'It's always that way around. *You* decide if *I* belong.'

'But you decide if I belong too.'

The idea I had any right to qualify the Australianness of the most Australian person I'd ever met was ludicrous. Wasn't it self-evident he was 'more Australian'? He was white, he lived in a country town, he drove a troopy, he listened to Lee Kernaghan, he came from a conservative family, he could only speak English and he loved footy more than life itself.

I shook my head. 'No, I don't.'

'Why not?' he asked.

I struggled to reply. 'Maybe, because, I don't know—I haven't been here as long as you have.'

He knew I meant that in an ancestral way.

'But why does that matter? They,' he pointed to some Aboriginal people in the pub, 'have been here a lot longer than we have.'

'I know! And yet they've been pushed to the fringes too. And the problem is some of *you* don't want *us* here. You know, Pauline Hanson might be putting shit on Muslims now, but twenty years ago she was putting shit on my people.'

'And I find what she says now as repulsive as I did back then,' he said.

'People like her are in the centre and we're on the fringes, looking in.'

'No, they're on the fringes,' he said.

'No, they're in the centre,' I said, but no longer so confidently.

He insisted. 'They're on the fringes, and they don't speak for us, the silent majority.'

'Hmm.' I mulled that over. A little voice inside me began to wonder if he was right.

Keno numbers appeared on the television screen—we didn't have a winning ticket. I was still holding out for that swag, though. 'I'd like to own a swag,' I said.

He shrugged. 'I reckon those prizes are always "won" by some mate of the bar staff.'

Our conversation moved on to more light-hearted matters. Our verbal sparring had just died away, like when the bright flames of a fresh fire settle into a softly radiating heat. If only all the Twitter wars and Facebook blow-ups could find such a peaceful conclusion. On this trip I'd often noticed that while digital environments bred extremism, face-to-face conversations fostered natural empathy.

Samuel wore a suspiciously innocent expression as he drained the remnants of the beer. 'Do you have any Australian in you?' he asked.

My eyes narrowed. I didn't reply.

'Would you like some?' he said, with all the politeness of an English maid offering a tray of biscuits.

I smiled, despite myself.

PART SEVEN
East Coast

14 OCTOBER
Day 131

The Barkly Highway started almost dead centre of the Northern Territory and took me east towards Queensland through open plains. There was no hill, tree or shrub to be seen except in the pale distance, just an ocean of swaying green grass. Red soil turned sandy and yellow the closer I got to state lines.

In the Queensland mining town of Mount Isa, I tried to eat lunch on a windy hill but there were so many bloody pigeons. They shuffled about pecking the ground, puffing out their chests like plump businessmen in grey suits. Every time I tried to take out my bread and cheese, they hopped on the table to humbug me. I hadn't seen these pigeons, so prevalent in the eastern states, in yonks. This was just one of many signals that I was returning to the Australian mainstream, the land of plenty. Bunnings, Coles, Woolies, Shell and Maccas all looked utterly strange to me now. From here on, I'd have no trouble finding fuel stops, phone reception, sealed roads and visitor centres.

My car still carried the soils of the Northern Territory. The doors, bonnet and boot were painted in a terracotta-red mud mask—not only from the week I'd spent in north-east Arnhem Land, but also the three that followed in other remote parts of north-west NT. Even my back window was caked in the stuff, except for a fan-shaped clean spot left by the windscreen wipers. I took my RAV4 to a drive-through car wash and, with a small part of me grieving, let the spinning, soapy brushes clean it all away. I was amazed at just how long I could hold a hose to the crevices around the headlights and watch a thick stream of red dust come pouring out. I didn't recognise my car afterwards—I had forgotten it was white. I drove away feeling like I was in a brand-new vehicle, with a mixture of relief and disappointment that the challenging portion of my trip was complete.

Over the next few days I veered east through Queensland, and as I drove past stretches of plain that dragged on and on, and through former colonial towns that had long ago faded in importance to the rest of the country, I heard the same strange story.

I heard it for the first time two days after passing through Mount Isa. I was in Karumba, a town that bills itself as the 'Outback by the Sea'. It's located on the northern coast at the bottom corner of that missing wedge from the Top End. There, the still waters of the Gulf of Carpentaria teem with barramundi, salmon, grunters, snappers, mackerel and jewfish.

I met Robert, a retired drover, when we happened to fish at the same spot by the end of town, where the buildings petered out and the blue water crept up a shallow bank of wet sand.

Despite an accumulation of failed attempts over the past few weeks, I woke each day and found my determination to catch a fish renewed. Does it still count as fishing if you don't catch any fish? I was impressed by my relentless optimism. My many failures didn't leave a single chink in my shining confidence that today was the day the angel of death had condemned one mackerel or barra to end up on my dinner plate. I think I was hooked on fishing for the same reason so many people love to gamble: it felt like getting something for nothing. Although the rush from catching that barra a month prior had faded, this period of inaction had been broken up by enough tantalising fish flashes—a tug here, a bite there—to whet my appetite for the game. I'd find myself lingering at the end of every empty-handed session unable to call it quits: just another half an hour, just another five minutes.

Robert had rolled up to this spot in a converted golf buggy. When he learnt I'd come with nothing but frozen bait, he immediately offered to share the live bait he was about to catch. I watched him throw a net into the aquamarine waters; it bloomed in the air like a flower.

In thirty-degree weather Robert was dressed in denim jeans, a button-up shirt and riding hat—an outfit I suspected he'd stayed classy in since about 1961. He wasn't tall but was stocky and strong like a miniature Hereford, with small hands and thick fingers. He had rolled up the sleeves of his flannel shirt, wiry white hair poking out from his chest and arms. 'Where you from?' he asked me for a second time.

I'd already told him Sydney. But throughout this trip, I'd been asked this question often enough to understand what he was getting at.

'I'm Chinese Australian,' I said, even though it was the answer to a different question.

'Chinese—I thought so,' he said. 'So, you should be good at fishing.'

Interesting. Chinese people up here know how to fish. In my case, 'should' was the operative word.

Robert said a lot of old Chinese families living up here could trace their ancestry back to the gold rush—and where I was headed next, blackfellas used to give those miners trouble. 'They'd leave us white-fellas alone, but they'd kill the Chinese and eat them.'

My eyebrows lifted in surprise. 'What?'

'It got so out of hand a whole bunch of blackfellas were killed by the police to teach them a lesson that they couldn't keep eating the Chinese,' he said. 'Look it up in the history books.'

The story sounded highly dubious.

Two days later, I heard it again in the former goldmining town of Croydon. During Queensland's gold rush, eighteen thousand Chinese miners worked the Palmer River goldfields. By the end of the nineteenth century, Chinese immigrants made up almost a third of the population of far north Queensland's emerging towns, including Croydon.

The town's visitor centre was manned by a tiny middle-aged lady wearing a polo shirt and a floppy wide-brimmed hat covered in lapel pins. She told me when the war began the town disintegrated, and a lot of the Chinese residents packed up their gear and headed east. She leant in as if to tell me a great secret. 'Some of them were eaten along the way.'

'By Aboriginal people?' I asked.

'Yup,' she said, giving a smile of satisfaction after my look of surprise.

But I was only surprised because back in Karumba I'd assumed the story was nothing but the ramblings of an old codger—evidently it was quite well established.

'They say, "You whitefellas too sinewy, them Chinese taste good. Like pork."' She'd said it, possibly unconsciously, in a blackfella accent. She elaborated further: apparently the cause of the unpleasant texture of the white man's meat was their beef-heavy diet. Because the Chinese ate a lot of rice and vegetables, their flesh was particularly tasty.

I laughed in disbelief. This story just got better and better!

I walked around the centre, which doubled as a museum. I didn't believe the cannibalism story, but there could be no doubt that violence had been inflicted on the Chinese in Queensland, much like in other Australian mining areas. As resentment among European Australians towards Croydon's 'oriental' colony ballooned, anti-Chinese leagues were formed, and occasionally riots and mob violence broke out.

Later I read a verse titled 'Yellow Agony', printed by the *Queensland Figaro* newspaper in 1883. In brilliantly purple prose, it captures the prevailing racist attitudes:

Shoals of pigtails, almond-eyed,
Flooding all the countryside,
Skimmed off as their country's scum,
Odorous of opium.

Yellow rascals, cunning, knavish,
Bowed in foul vice-bondage slavish,
They, with Eastern filth imbedded,
Form one monster hydra-headed.
Orientals, leprous-fitted,
Blood-diseased and smallpox-pitted;
Noxious, maid-devouring dragon he!
That's Sim's loathsome Yellow Agony.

Another museum display explained the Chinese weren't only on the goldfields but the 'chief providers' of the town's fresh fruit and vegetables as well. Chinese people all over Australia, fed up by discrimination at the diggings, were forced to turn to market gardening; they often discovered the work to be more stable and profitable anyway. They transformed scrub into flowering gardens, and were more successful than the Europeans at working with the wet and dry extremes of the tropical north. The Europeans were inclined to 'cultivate a large area and wait for rain', while the secret of Chinese success was captured in a photo on display: a Chinese man stood beside neat rows of tiny flowering plants, with two buckets hanging from a long pole carried on his back. I laughed out loud—this portrait adhered perfectly with my impression of the Chinese during the four years I spent living in China. No other people on the planet so steadfastly embraced the proverb 'when life gives you lemons, make lemonade'.

And how it infuriated those European Australians! They were often forced to swallow their racial prejudices when the larder cupboard turned up empty. According to historian Timothy Kendall, in 1901 a former independent member for Capricornia called Alexander Paterson told Parliament his horror story of coming home to find a Chinaman standing at the back gate with a vegetable cart, apparently the first time 'the magnitude of this Asiatic pestilence' caught his attention. Paterson chastised those responsible in his household, only to hear: 'It is all very well for you to talk in that strain, but we live six miles from town, and how on earth we are to get vegetables from anyone excepting a Chinaman I cannot tell.' Paterson explained to Parliament, 'The result was that the custom of the establishment was transferred to a German, with which arrangement I was perfectly satisfied. But I may tell honourable members that it broke me all up when I afterwards found that the German bought his vegetables from a Chinaman.' One can imagine that at this point all the parliamentarians were laughing helplessly. Poor Paterson continued, 'While this question has its humorous side, it also has a very painful aspect. How is it that we ever allowed Chinamen to interfere so much with our trade as to put them in the position of being able to dictate to us?'

It was mid-October when I left Croydon and kept driving until I landed on the east coast. *My* east coast.

I travelled to Cooktown where in 1877 British official Dundas Crawford noted coolies arriving at the town. His writing reveals how the Chinese were viewed through European eyes:

> They pass through the town in batches of six to ten, in single file but ever singly, each coolie carrying his own bamboo pole brought from China . . . Men walking with apparent nonchalance on the footpath act as guides, and the different files, never expressing surprise or any other emotion, never mixing together, and never stopping, carry their loads straight to the place assigned them; most to the camping ground beyond the town, where the greatest regularity is observed of the tents.

The discomfort reverberating in Crawford's passage was not unfamiliar to me; it was the same displayed by boarders in my high school sneering at the quiet, studious girls from China, Hong Kong and Taiwan. The boarders were strapping, sporty country girls who cracked jokes through class and dominated the culture of my school— all the teachers loved them. I wondered how much of my cultural self-hatred developed then.

The Chinese were single-minded in their attitude: *Keep your head down and nose out of trouble while in these strange, savage lands, and exploit whatever crack or chasm of opportunity presents itself.* This was just as true of the Chinese students at my school as the 1800s-era labourers. But from the perspective of European Australians, the Chinese showed little emotion, which aroused suspicion; they were tirelessly obedient, which garnered them little respect. To those European Australian larrikins, hard-drinkers, surly miners, knockabout jackeroos, devout missionaries, and stout, hearty pioneer women, the sectarian Chinese were unsettling in their uniformity. Sure, as workers they were hardworking, stoic and dependable, worthy of admiration for their industry and ingenuity in business—but they were hardly a race you could truly like or trust.

As I made my way down the eastern coast of Queensland, I heard variations on the cannibal story. A friendly grey nomad from Toowoomba said, 'My brother reckoned it was actually white miners on the verge of starvation who ate the Chinese.' A Guugu Yimidhirr elder said it was something spoken of among their people, as did a Yidinji man who added, 'It might have happened once but that doesn't mean it happened all the time.' Both said their nation wasn't responsible, but rather an Aboriginal group further south.

There's nothing especially freaky or weird about cannibalism in a historical context. Many parts of the world have a history of human flesh consumption, including China and Europe. These examples often incorporate cannibalism in the grieving process of a mortuary ritual: the consumption of a loved one's remains as sacred and ceremonial, considered the most intimate way to honour the deceased.

That said, I found no credible historians willing to back claims that scores of Chinese miners had been hunted by Aboriginal people for their tasty flesh. As historian Christopher Anderson wrote of the Palmer River story in 1981, 'The spectre of indigenous cannibalism has been used all over the world to justify colonial violence.'

Perversely these rumours sit in the cultural landscape like a bare arse wiggling rudely at the concerted white Australian myth that Indigenous Australians were strangely passive as they were colonised.

Much like Australia's long-standing connections and interactions with Asia, the many stories of Aboriginal resistance to colonisation—be it through guerrilla warfare, reprisal attacks, curses (and other forms of magic), petitions, strikes, protests and political or legal manoeuvres—were given no airplay in my high school history class. I wasn't taught about Sydney local Pemulwuy, a Bidjigal warrior of the Eora nation, who from 1792 led a decade-long guerrilla war against the British to defend the very lands upon which we studied. Nobody taught me about the softly spoken Vincent Lingiari, a Gurindji stockman who led one of the longest strikes in Australian history. At the end of their strike, he and his fellow countrymen were finally given back their land, as captured in an iconic photo of sand pouring through the hand of Prime Minister Gough Whitlam into Lingiari's.

The hundred-kilometre road to the Daintree Rainforest became winding and narrow, hugging windswept hills sometimes known to maliciously throws rocks at cars. But perhaps most dangerous of all were the azure waters further out; under the open sky and hot sun, they winked seductively and made it hard for me to keep my eyes on the road. As I lurched around hairpin turns, the bitterness of motion sickness rose from my stomach.

If Mungo Lake is a museum of dead things, Australia's impenetrable tropical rainforest is a living museum of flora and fauna. It houses species that have changed little over hundreds of millions of years, since a much wetter Australia was connected to the supercontinent Gondwana. By the time Australia broke away, drier conditions were producing the eucalypt forests that now cover the continent, and most pockets of tropical rainforest were confined to rain-soaked humid parts of far north Queensland on the east coast. While over millions of years they mixed with plants and animals from Asia, still preserved is some of that ancient stock that can be traced back to Gondwana.

I spent several nights camping where the Daintree meets the sea at Cape Tribulation. The vegetation grew so dense, the road looked like a square slice of cake taken out clean with a knife. Although the wet tropics covers less than one per cent of Australia, it contains almost half of our bird species, a third of our mammal species, more than half of our butterfly species and over seven hundred plant species endemic to the area. The rainforests seemed to inhale and exhale in a sweaty tangle of heaving biomatter.

One afternoon I went for a trail walk deep into the rainforest. As I walked past some fan palms the size of a Hills hoist, I scratched the back of my neck and found a disturbingly large bump. There were so many creepy-crawlies about: green ants, spiders, moths, butterflies, and lots and lots of mosquitos. The night before, I'd cooked dinner at the campground's public barbecue and watched a dragonfly attracted to the fluorescent lights buzz noisily about. When it came to rest on a post a gecko suddenly appeared, its tail flicking back and forth—in one lightning move, the gecko scampered across the wall and seized the dragonfly's head in its mouth. The dragonfly's wings and legs jerked for a moment, but there was no escape. With my mouth full of salad I had the strangest sensation that it wasn't lettuce but the dragonfly's head in my mouth.

In the rainforest it was humid but cool as I climbed the steps onto a raised boardwalk. Soon I came across two tall young women from Europe in T-shirts and hiking shorts that showed off their muscular limbs, hunched over and whispering. I recognised that caution and wondered what animal they had spotted. A tree kangaroo? That would be pretty cool. Or a rare butterfly? I didn't dare hope it might be one of the birds I'd been most excited to spot since buying my bird guide back in Alice.

Then I saw it: Australia's second-largest bird. At up to two metres tall it's second to the emu, and third in the world as the ostrich takes the top spot. It stepped out from behind some palm fronds, at the teasing pace of a burlesque dancer. With that monster shag of black, cobalt neck with sky-blue cap and folds of loose red skin hanging from the neck, I had no need to get out my guidebook—it was the one, the only, the cassowary.

Like the emu, it's a flightless bird whose dads, not mums, hatch and raise their young. It has a mohawk-shaped horn that's spongy, not at all hard as it appears to be, and absorbs the shock of hitting branches. Because of its horn and raptor-like bill, the cassowary could be mistaken for a missing link between dinosaur and bird.

I was glad to be on the boardwalk because with its sturdy legs and claws the bird was hypothetically capable of killing me. Plenty of warning signs were posted about, advising tourists to be 'cass-o-wary'. Upon encountering the bird in the wild: 1) Don't run. 2) Walk back slowly without turning around. 3) Get something long and thick between you and the bird, such as a tree trunk—or, barring that, hold up your jacket or a bag.

The bird displayed an almost haughty lack of fear towards us humans, swaying her thick bustle of black feathers to-and-fro and looking us in the eye as if to say, *That's right, girls, I'm a cassowary and you better be cass-o-wary when I'm in town.*

One of the women had a camera raised like a gun taking rapid-fire shots of the bird; the cassowary equivalent of paparazzi.

The bird bent down and with her beak picked up a shiny, indigo-blue cassowary plum the size and shape of an avocado. She tipped her head up high, gulping it down whole. After bending her head again, she picked up a sliver of orange fruit and also swallowed it whole.

With a slow swivel of the head, the cassowary gave us one last glance, turned and, swaying her bustle, exited behind thick green curtains of rainforest.

I passed the next few days writing, reading, walking the nearby beaches and trying to fish. I began to think of home and feel a sense of restlessness. As if I were just killing time.

The ocean was only divided from the rainforest by a thin strip of sand. Apparently the water was filled with deadly box jellyfish, and I imagined it like an Asian milk tea with floating pearls laced with arsenic. The jellyfish wafted about cube-shaped and transparent as an X-ray, and it was difficult to reconcile their fragile, ghostly appearance with the fact they were among the world's most venomous creatures. Being stung by their ribbon-like tentacles causes agonising pain, and death comes as quickly as two minutes. I spotted bottles of vinegar, a sufficient antidote, stationed about all the beaches with signs that read, 'Pour, do not rub.'

Unsurprisingly, I saw only a few brave souls escaping the heat and humidity in the water. Probably out-of-towners. Like most born and bred Sydneysiders, I had an almost Pavlovian response to the sight of the ocean: it was rarely enough only to see it, I had to swim in it. I had to feel my limbs push through the waves of blue energy. Or at least, that's how I used to be. Three months of travelling croc and jellyfish infested saltwater country had cured me—I didn't feel even the slightest urge to swim. But I delighted in the sight of the ocean, the fizzing sound as it spread across the beach, the slightly salty taste of the air, and cool, wet sand between my toes.

On my final day in the Daintree, I woke soon after 5 a.m. and walked down to the beach. I'd been getting up earlier and earlier on the trip, and I thought incredulously back to my former life when I'd struggled to rise before 8 a.m. The hills were so covered in plant life they looked like the vegetable stand of a supermarket: spinach, kale, broccoli and lettuce all bunched together. The green was so rich in the wet tropics, as if the saturation filter had been turned up. I could almost feel my body drinking in the rainforest's beauty. The soft sand was crawling with hermit crabs that, upon my approach, scuttled in a mad dash to the nearest hidey-hole. I'd taken a seat on some dark rocks when the rising sun burnt a hole through a fleecy bank of mauve and baby-pink clouds. As it lifted like a hot-air balloon, it created a lemon-coloured afterglow on the horizon. The rippling ocean had the shimmer of a finely sequined sheet of metallic blue fabric.

How many sunrises had I seen during the months of my trip? Bursting over so many different horizons, of pandanus forest or pindan cliffs, spinifex hills or glassy lakes—I could recall the most spectacular ones in as much detail as the lyrics to my favourite songs.

✱

It was the end of November and summer was creeping into the southern half of Australia. I said farewell to the ocean in Ballina on the northern coast of New South Wales. I wouldn't see blue water again until I was back in Sydney, a place that with every passing day I was acutely aware I was moving closer towards. Like an infant who is hypervigilant of exactly where her parent is at all times, I found myself calculating the distances to Sydney wherever I went: *721 kilometres, I could drive that in a day; 369 kilometres, I could drive that in half a day.*

I was leaving Ballina having spent four nights at an Airbnb. I'd visited the town before, although in the intervening decade it had completed its transition from beatnik mecca to backpacker paradise/ yuppy vacation village.

I was far enough south that the ocean looked exactly like that of home. The blue waves had a magnificent glossy sheen and more powerful presence, disintegrating into paperwhite wash over pitch-black rocks. I loved hearing that roar of a bolshy surf again. It was deep and cold water, full of turbulent energy. No jellyfish, no crocs— yes, there were sharks but they were mainly a problem for surfers further out.

I stood on a windy spot along that grand coastline, and as I took in the ocean's overwhelming presence, I smiled. Its familiarity was a sign I was getting closer to home, and that filled me with joy.

One afternoon I put to use the foraging skills I'd acquired from the Lurujarri Trail, shucking two dozen dollar-sized oysters off rocks at one end of the beach. *Ha! Look at me now!* City gal gone bush. I was ending my travels with the ability to forage for lunch, build a fire, change a tyre, get bogged and then get unstuck, tell a kite from a kestrel, catch a barra and recognise emu tracks. And sure, I was still dead shit scared of snakes and crocs, my fishing skills felt more hypothetical than real, and I had no idea how to find water in the desert, but I'd come a long way. I hoped this was just the beginning of my new bushie life. I wanted to be the kind of Australian who could fix cars, wield a chainsaw, skin a rabbit, navigate by the stars, man a tinny and carve wood. There was so much left to do and learn.

It was only when my oyster foraging attracted the quizzical stares of some passing locals—a sunbaked, well-heeled young couple; an old man in a polo shirt and shorts—did it occur to me that in this trendy town it was a little strange seeing a thirty-something Chinese woman squatting on the beach with a stone in her hand, smashing oysters and shovelling them into her mouth. I wasn't in the Kimberley anymore. *Shit*, maybe this ocean wasn't clean? This was the east coast, where millions of people had their waste pumped out to sea.

Oh well, too late.

After Ballina I drove south on the quiet back roads that lined the inner side of the Great Dividing Range, stopping at many parks and towns I'd been to before: Moree, Cathedral Rock National Park, the Warrumbungles, Dubbo. I loved the ocean—always would—but in Australia we were so lucky: if you ever felt the desire to just get away from humanity, all you had to do was drive four hours inland and there was plenty of soul-purifying, heart-awakening space and silence to get lost in.

I had wondered whether, after all I'd seen of Australia, I'd still find my home state beautiful. But as I drove through the western plains of New South Wales, dominated by the twinkling golden bells of wheatgrass that grew as tall as an adult and from a distance appeared like angel hair blowing in the wind, I realised it still occupied a special place in my heart. It was genteel like the European countryside, altered by pastoralism. Towering ironbarks and white boxes dotted the land, each a monument to nature in the midst of an empty town square. How strange to be a person of Chinese heritage, growing up on this continent, and have a childhood so influenced by the tiny island nation of Britain thousands of kilometres away that I should hark for its landscape. As a young person, I had loved the BBC adaption of Jane Austen's *Pride and Prejudice* and mourned the fact that due to my skin I could never hope to one day play the role of Elizabeth Bennet.

I thought about my younger years when I was a stranger to the Australian countryside. My main exposure to regional Australia was visiting my best friend at her family farm outside of Bathurst. I remembered finding all this emptiness frightening. How did you know where to orientate yourself? In Sydney you were bordered by mountains to the west and the ocean to the east; you were either north or south of the Bridge. But here? The ocean was so far away. From the top of a high hill, you could spin right around and see only land and sky. The silence truly was deafening—I'd finally understood the meaning of that phrase. It was unnerving to hear the soft bleat of a sheep from a good kilometre away.

But now, as I traversed these rolling hills, I realised the openness of the land had become comfortingly banal. It didn't trigger any physical discomfort. It was ordinary as a spoon and fork.

I camped as I went and most mornings would wake in my tent to the spluttering song of the kookaburra. I realised, with some surprise, it was a sound I hadn't heard for most of my trip. I'd seen kookaburras in the Top End but they were the blue-winged kind, named for the electric splash of blue on their wings. Their squawking call wasn't particularly memorable. Only the laughing kookaburra, found in Australia's eastern states and the southern tip of Western Australia, boasts a call like an exploding star: its cackle beginning low and quiet, then expanding into a full throttle of ear-splitting, heavy-metal raucousness, trilling up and down, before tapering off into a throaty chuckle.

I'd always assumed that the laugh of the kookaburra, together with the mob roar of cicadas in the heat of the day—one of the loudest insects in the world—was the aural signature of the Australian bush. But it was specific to my part of Australia. To me, it sounded like home.

I spent my final week camping in the Kanangra-Boyd National Park just west of Sydney. The park is part of the Greater Blue Mountains, one million hectares of sandstone plateaux, escarpments, gorges and ninety-one kinds of eucalypt. A damp, cloying mist always hung around the mountains, even now in summer. In the past such high ridgelines, deep precipices and dense scrub acted as a buffer between colonial forces and the many Aboriginal nations lying to the west. For three decades it contained the horrors of the colonialism to the Sydney region. By 1815, a road built through the mountains was complete and the rush for land by European settlers was on.

I deliberately set up my tent in a spot plunged deep into the bush, surrounded by thickly growing snow gums that masked the horizon and gave me the sense of being the only person left on the planet. I'd envisioned my time in the mountains as the poetic climax to half a year in the bush—just me and glorious mother nature, sealing our new communion! But soon I discovered I was too homesick to enjoy it.

The days passed at an excruciatingly slow pace. I alternated between reading in my camp chair and, when the flies and heat became too intense, reading in my tent. I wore nothing but my undies, bra and a floppy hat, yet sweated like a pig. I snoozed, ate three meals a day and went for walks.

Every now and then I spotted tribes of black cockatoos. In the air they were shaped like pointe slippers of black satin—the kind ballerinas wore, only with wings. My only other visitors were three kangaroos with light-coloured fur that one day at dawn came bounding through the bush. When one stopped near my camp the other two, like the wheels of an invisible tricycle, stopped as well. They grazed and appeared not to notice me. But when I began to brush my teeth, all three heads popped up one after the other. They were staring at me, so I waved in a neighbourly way that I hoped might say, 'Want to come over for a cuppa?' The kangaroos stared for a moment, then lowered their heads to continue grazing. A firm, 'No thanks.'

Otherwise, I was all alone.

I cast my mind back six months to the version of me who had driven out of Sydney's city limits—flabby, pale and crumpled with accumulated misery. Over the course of the trip I'd lost weight and now had what I'd been referring to as my 'banging bush bod'. Nature was captured on my body like photo paper; all that sun and rain and wind pressing onto my bare skin had left it tanned and scoured. I was fit and energetic. I walked for hours each day and slept very well each night. I had only occasionally touched alcohol or junk food for half a year.

One morning I read a booklet of rhyming verse by Henry Lawson I'd purchased in Gulgong, then penned my own Christmas verse:

What more could a simpleton need
Than this river, this sky and these trees?
Bush life is grand, traversing the land,
Yet my heart, how it yearns for Christmas in Sydney.

These gum trees are beauties—I know,
Tall, ancient and straight, pale as snow,
I agree it's a sin to chuck it all in
For mum's cheap plastic tinsel and bows.

Wind blows and the kookaburras sing,
I hear pat-pat of wallabies jumping,
Music to my ears, yet part of me fears
I'd rather be listening to Mariah Carey carolling.

At the end of each day the sun sets,
Sky awash with pink, orange and red,
Too nice a show for one lonely soul
Who'd rather be buying presents for friends.

Excuse this poem so sentimental and bleak,
Which I confess written quite tongue-in-cheek,
For soon I'll be home, broke, glued to my phone,
Wishing I was out bush within the week!

By the fifth day, I was starting to lose it.

I was damn tired of the flies swarming over my arms, legs, shoulders, neck, ears, and even my lips and up my nostrils. One marched right into my eyeball—I screamed in shock and, using my phone camera as a mirror, tugged at the bottom of my eyelid to see where it had got to. The fly was stuck in the corner of my eye. When I tried to push it out, my clumsy, pudgy finger squashed the unfortunate thing dead. And still I struggled to remove it from my eye, which was stinging. I blinked reflexively, and with every blink the fly corpse slid further down to the crevice of my eye, threatening to slide right into it. What then? I supposed it would be absorbed, digested even, by my body.

Eventually I pushed out the scrunched-up fly carcass using my smallest fingernail.

Even the indecipherable bushland was driving me mad, and I suddenly understood why Lawson described it as 'the everlasting, maddening sameness of the stunted trees—that monotony which makes a man long to break away and travel as far as trains can go, and sail as far as ship can sail—and farther' in *The Drover's Wife*. I had studied the short story in school and been touched by the central character's despair. The passage that had always stayed with me was about her regular Sunday walks up the bush track; without fail, she would diligently make herself and the children look smart, 'as she would if she were going to do the block in the city', even though 'there is nothing to see' and 'not a soul to meet'.

To me, everything was feeling itchy and off, like a jumper you put on backwards and then when you try wearing it the correct way still feels wrong. Why hadn't I chosen a spot that at least offered fishing? Something to do other than walk circles and read my books. I didn't want to trek through the scratchy bush and be bitten by creepy-crawlies any-fucking-more. What the hell was I doing out here alone anyway? I was tired of my own company and finally exhausted by my role as 'the stranger in town'. It had been six months of new acquaintances and fast-expiring friendships. Now I was hungry for that same intimate sense of home I'd seen expressed by the traditional owners I'd met throughout my travels. Their ancestral relationship to the land was forty, fifty, sometimes sixty thousand years long, and that was beyond anything I'd ever witnessed in my overseas travels—let alone, as a first-generation Australian, experienced myself. And while I knew I could never have that same feeling, I craved some sort of facsimile. Being on the move now felt like a hindrance to its development.

That evening, in the early hours after midnight, I woke to the terrifying sounds of an ill wind howling outside. It was pitch-black and the walls of my tent were buffeting like crazy. This park was full of old trees waiting for the right wind to send one hurtling to the ground. I heard the menacing sound of wood cracking but had no idea how far or near it was. *I'll die if a big tree falls on me*, I thought. It felt as if I were in the cabin of a tiny sailboat being tossed around on a vast ocean of wind.

I tried to calm down by reminding myself that soon I would be driving back to Sydney. Soon I would have love and laughter in my life. *And I'll live in a house! I'll be able to charge my phone whenever I want, shower every day, boil water in a kettle, watch YouTube at two in the morning if I so desire, hear the tinkling of ice in my glass, sit in front of a spinning fan, and have a bedroom door I can shut on the world. What utter luxury.*

I played images of my loved ones and our imminent reunions in my mind. There was Mum vacuuming my bedroom and washing my sheets, as she always did when I returned from an extended period away. *Who's that standing at the door?* It always took half a second for my dog to register who I was—followed by the excited wagging of his tail. I'd sit with old friends around a small table crowded with plates of food in a noisy Chinatown restaurant—people who are the keepers of my history, and I of theirs, and with whom I share a secret, familiar language.

For two hours I lay in the dark, terrified. What if the Earth had been destroyed, and all that remained was my tent and a mean-tempered space wind whirling around me? Perhaps if I were to unzip the fly of my tent, outside I'd see nothing but stars and space dust. Well, at least I needn't worry about being crushed to death by a tree.

Another loud and ominous *crack* rang through the air.

I decided to leave the next day. It was one day short of the full week that I'd planned, but I no longer cared. Every cell in my body was crying for home.

One hour until sunrise. If I can just make it through this hour, all will be well.

✳

I woke to the last gasps of a fading wind, whimpering like a child exhausted by its own temper tantrum. Perhaps I had overstayed my welcome. And in making clear my intention to depart, whatever frightened spirits that occupied this bit of country were now at peace.

I flung open the fly of my tent and was greeted by the sight of steam rising off everything—the rocks, the trees, the earth—as the sun dried out the damp.

When I began packing down my things, I was gripped by emotion. This tent had been my home for six months, and I was dismantling it for the last time. Who knew when I would sleep in it again? (A small part of me was tempted to chuck it in the first bin I came across.)

I'd spent so much of this past week homesick, but I knew I would also miss the sunrises and sunsets, sleeping under the stars, the animal encounters, the silence and freedom of nomad life. That blush of peach in the sky just before the sun rises—I wished I could bottle that. It grew more garish, turning orange and gold, but that early shade of soft, delicate peach was the colour of gentle joy.

It took me an hour and several trips to cart all my things to the car. Back and forth I trudged through damp leaf debris, bags and gear loaded on my shoulders. Eventually, the camp spot was free of any trace I had been there. I snapped one last photo for posterity, then walked to the car carrying three empty water tanks.

With my RAV4 packed, I climbed into the driver's seat. I slid my key into the ignition and started the engine. My window was rolled down as I pulled out of the campground, the smell of eucalyptus oil and fallen rain filling my car.

As I drove, memories of my time on the road swam around in my head like happy, fat, silver barramundi: the swirling sands of Mungo Lake, the storm clouds hanging over the moody Coorong, the sun setting fire to the MacDonnell Ranges, my Goolarabooloo friends showing me how to throw a line into the ocean, Samuel looking suntanned on the pristine sands of Yolŋu Country, the bellow of a cassowary in the dripping wet rainforests of far north Queensland. All of it was stored inside me and could never be taken away.

I had left Sydney wearing the haunted look of so many overworked, sun-deprived journalists. And here I was, one giant loop around the nation later, with my soul heavy as a wet sponge with feeling and my spirit rejuvenated.

I left behind muted-grey gum trees shrouded in mist and was soon back on the main road, winding through villages still sleeping in the hills of Katoomba. A song was stuck in my head, or the fragments of a melody I couldn't quite place, like butterflies flitting about that you can't catch. What was that song again?

My car rocked this way and that as I drove the bitumen bends. The sodden white mist was dissipating to reveal familiar train stations, suburban villages and residential streets.

I felt as if I wasn't only driving back to Sydney but also back to my life. Or perhaps, to start a new life. One in which a different relationship with my country had been forged.

How long had I had kept Australia at arm's length because I thought it didn't recognise itself in me? Because I didn't feel Australian. But I had been mistaken—I'd simply never felt like a specific type of Australian. There was no requirement for me to be, or even aspire to be, a Bushie, Drover's Wife, Larrikin, Digger, Surf Bunny or True-Blue Dinky-Di Top Sheila.

I thought back to what Samuel and all the people I'd met over the past half a year had helped show me. Pauline Hanson, draped in the Southern Cross and speaking Strine, was not symbolic of the Australian mainstream. Rather it was I who shared in common with the majority of Australians a pride in our nation's cultural diversity.

For so long I had viewed our cultural cringe as a symptom of the hole in our heart. We had no ancient history, culture and language to call our own, and had not yet earned any right to belong to Indigenous Australia. But now I saw that while this absence cursed us with disorientation, wasn't it also a blessing? Being Australian did not preclude blood or ancestral membership, or even cultural knowledge, the way being Chinese or Yolŋu did. If there was no fixed idea of Australian, there was also no fixed idea of un-Australian. That elasticity defined the nation more than a particular dress, food, language, religion or habit, or even an affiliation with the land.

It meant *we* could be *me*.

I hadn't needed to be with Samuel for a spot in Team Australia—I'd had one all along.

Then I remembered the song in my head—oh yes, 'Under the Milky Way' by The Church. I had an urge to listen to it. After fumbling around for it from my CD case, I hit play.

And with that, I began to cry.

I was struck not only by the physical momentousness of having completed a 30,000-kilometre drive around Australia for six months on my own, but also by all of its emotional highs and lows. I had fallen in love with the dry, spartan, silent beauty of this country and grown comfortable with its ruggedness. I had come face-to-face with some of the darkest chapters of our history, heard stories of murder, slavery, genocide, dispossession, segregation, child abduction and rape, and yet not once felt a compulsion to turn my back on Australia—quite the opposite: I felt closer to the country having faced its past. A past our young nation struggles to speak aloud. I felt a new sense of confidence in my place in Australia and understood I had a role to play in reconciling our country with the land and its First Peoples.

I was even excited about going back to the big smoke, where the buildings cast long shadows on the earth and hid all kinds of surprises. That noisy urban jungle held potential for a different sort of adventure to my road trip. Sydney—a theatre with five million cast members. And I was so excited to see everyone that I knew.

I was going back confident of something deceptively simple: I am Australian. I have a legitimate spot—not in the land, that was a separate issue, but in the 'project Australia' currently occupying this continent. And every single shareholder in project Australia had an equal stake.

Sure it didn't always feel that way, like when someone tweeted at me to 'go back to Vietnam' (wrong country, mate), or when tabloid media portrayed Indigenous Australians as nothing but bums and drunks, and Muslim Australians as nothing but terror-inflicting jihadists, not to mention the obsession with Sudanese-Australian media personality Yassmin Abdel-Magied that bordered on pathological. But in Samuel's combination of patriotism and pride in Australian multiculturalism, in the way that just about everyone I had met on my trip had treated me so decently, not at all like a outsider, I had finally seen that most Australians understood, implicitly, ours was a country uniquely united by its diversity.

I need not keep my head down and play the good immigrant—need not and should not. By slavishly binding myself to precious or popularly held definitions of Australian, I only perpetuated them. I had just as much right to define Australian as any other, and if there remained national associations with whiteness or Britishness, masculinity, conservatism, anti-intellectualism or pastoral life, I instantly redefined what it meant to be Australian merely by being myself.

Australia had grown up enough to accept me as their everyman. I was sure of it. And the more I asserted it, the truer it became.

All of a sudden, something became crystal clear.

'I love Australia.'

I said the words aloud to my empty car as I sped past old colonial homes, second-hand antique stores and the quaint cafes the Blue Mountains is known for, sandwiched by bush.

Saying it so baldly felt transgressive. This was probably the first time in my life I had said it without irony or reserve. And it was true. I was dizzily in love with Australia.

My love was no abstract concept, kept afloat by the helium balloons of 'multiculturalism' and 'democracy'. My love went all the way to the core of my being. It could be expressed with earthly pleasures. It was the same longing an overseas Chinese person had for the spicy chilli broth of Sichuan cooking, or a British expat for the smell of rain on the heath. It was the love Dorothea Mackellar felt for her sunburnt country. It was a love inspired by the Warumungu people who were so attached to their land that once, when an enormous boulder of the sacred site Kunjarra was removed, their elders became sick. Now that I had tasted Australia, smelt it, walked it, seen the lay of its land and read the story of its life, my love for it was visceral and spiritual.

I came off the last Blue Mountain and, with that, the sloping road tipped me into the western edge of Sydney somewhere near Penrith. The greenery and villages gave way to a walled motorway that I knew shot straight into the concrete heart of western Sydney, dense with factory outlets, fast food joints and industrial parks. In less than an hour I would be back at my mum's two-storey brick home in the quiet, leafy suburbs of north-west Sydney.

It was in this city that the story of 'project Australia' began. Having travelled the country, I returned knowing that being exposed to its strange, wonderful and heartbreaking history had engendered in me a fresh feeling of intimacy.

Through all the pain, anger and frustration, I accepted Australia for who it was. My sense of patriotic duty and care was as solid as the ancient rock lining this continent.

Australia was my family, and our futures would forever be entwined.

Waves of relief, of elation, moved through my body. Somehow, I'd made it. Through my tears, I began to smile.

Afterword

Just over a year after returning from my trip, I landed a dream job: I began teaching Australian Studies at The College at Western Sydney University. At the time, most of my book was written and my money had run out. I have an enthusiasm for Australian history and culture that I'm eager to share with young people, and enthusiasm is an excellent base upon which to build an engaging classroom environment.

The campus is based in Bankstown, an ethnically and culturally diverse part of Sydney. Most of my students have a non-English speaking background: Lebanese, Pacific Islander, Italian, Russian, Chilean, Iraqi and Afghan. I consider it a privilege to show them that even though the Australia of our popular imagination has so often failed to demonstrate its cultural diversity, in fact it has been a defining characteristic almost from the beginning of colonial Australia.

My classroom presentations are peppered with photos and anecdotes from my trip. For many of my students, who are mainly in their late teens, this is the first time that stories of Australia have resonated with them. Over the course of a semester I facilitate their journey of discovering that so much about their country is fascinating: Indigenous Australia's bewilderingly long occupation of the land, the surprising story of two radically different cultures coming into contact for the first time, the unfolding tragedy as one of these cultures attempted to subsume the other, the waves of immigrants who have followed the British and the challenge they pose to a cultural monopoly, and ultimately the survival of the First Peoples of this land.

I very quickly realised that I am writing this book for my students. Few of them have the same privileges that I had in life, and instead many more responsibilities and obligations. Who knows how many of them may one day embark on a similar trip around Australia, but that's the beauty of teaching and of writing this book—the revelations that came to me on my trip need not be mine alone.

My students leave my classroom with more knowledge, insights and opinions about Australian national identity and race relations than when they entered. They are empowered to be both sceptical and hopeful, to make connections between the past, present and future— and, most importantly, to strive for reconciliation with Indigenous Australia and have a voice in this country about where it is headed.

When looking back on my trip there are things that, with hindsight, I view differently. It has become clear that, for whatever reason, throughout my travels I met more men than women. The book I have written reflects that disparity and may unintentionally continue a historical bias that favours the male perspective, including in colonial depictions of Indigenous Australia.

Reconciliation is a painful process of healing, rife with awkwardness and difficult truths. Take one conversation I had with an older white woman in the Kimberley. She was wearing a 'Close the Gap' baseball cap and said it made her very sad to think about Aboriginal people's life expectancy: ten years younger than the national average.

She asked me about my heritage.

'I'm Chinese,' I said to her. 'What's your heritage?'

The question seemed to catch her off guard as if she were rarely asked such a thing. And perhaps it was contrarian of me. If I couldn't feel good and settled on these lands, then neither could she. I wouldn't allow her to take for granted she was the 'default' Australian.

'Oh, you know, British—boring!' she replied. She said she'd done an ancestry site DNA test hoping something interesting might turn up in the family tree. 'I thought, *Wouldn't it be wonderful if I had some French aristocracy or Aboriginal heritage?* But sadly, no. The results were very dull.'

At the time I prickled with irritation. These leftie-types were desperate for some long-lost great-great-great-Aboriginal grandmother to show up in the family tree, when just one generation ago their families probably would have covered it up. This woman wanted to be Aboriginal when it came to culture and connection to Country, or even flying the banner of a persecuted minority. But did she also want to be Aboriginal if it meant being the target of racial abuse on the streets, inheriting the psychological burden of colonialism or, as she had just pointed out, facing a life expectancy so much lower than that of the non-Aboriginal Australian population? Aboriginal identity wasn't parts sold separately—you either ran the full gamut or you didn't.

But later I began asking myself if my attitude had been all that different. After all, I hadn't just embarked on this trip to learn about Aboriginal Australia: I had gone into it as a *Chinese* Australian. I had so badly wanted my relationship with Aboriginal Australia to be different from that of a European Australian. I thought if I could just discover where our cultures overlapped—Aboriginal and Chinese— we would find those commonalities liberating. We needed a story of Australia, I believed, that wasn't so oppressively strangled by the native–invader dynamic and mired in constant tragedy. It would be a story of friendship in adversity, of two ancient cultures actively resisting Western imperialism. One that could give our nation hope and show us another way to live together.

When I thought back on my trip—of my new friends in Arrernte Country, Ngarluma Country, Yawuru Country, to that cinema in Broome segregated by skin tone, a 'Yapa from China'—I knew this had been proven true . . . but only to a point. My trip had also thrown up another, more confronting and equally important truth. One that until now I had been unwilling to face.

The Top End had shown me the extent to which the Chinese played a role in fortifying the hold that white Australia had over this continent. No, we didn't come out on the First Fleet, but the first Chinese settler in Australia is believed to have been a Guangzhou man: Mak Sai Ying (also known as John Shying) in 1818, just thirty years later. Chinese men supplied pioneer towns with fruit and vegetables; helped build the Overland Telegraph Line and the Ghan Railway Line and other essential infrastructure; traded goods, ran general stores, cooked on stations, purchased real estate and dug for gold. We've been here from nearly the beginning of project Australia, and if you were to sketch a portrait of the stereotypical Australian Pioneer it would just as likely be a Chinese man in a straw coolie hat as it would be a European man in an Akubra slouch hat.

We weren't the ones to kick down the doors, but we walked in after the British had done so. If we're going to take credit for contributing to the formation of the colony, we also have to take responsibility for the impact this had on Indigenous Australia. As part of immigrant Australia, how can I ever come close to understanding the pain and suffering Indigenous Australians have undergone in the forced dispossession of their lands, peoples and cultures? I'd been searching for absolution from the devastation that colonisation has caused to Indigenous Australia, and instead been shown the stark truth: we Chinese Australians played a role in it.

These are the complex notions I bring to my classroom. Accepting the ambiguities inherent to life in multicultural Australia, and taking responsibility for making our country a more honest, mature and compassionate place is a considerable thing to ask of my young students. They are barely out of high school, and so much lies ahead of them. Yet time and time again, these young people show me their willingness and enthusiasm to do better than the generations that came before them.

Having a front-row seat to their growth fills me with optimism.

Birdspotting

These are the bird species I saw on my trip, listed region-by-region (repeat sightings removed).

Central Australia

Spinifex pigeon
Crested pigeon
Egret
White-faced heron
Cormorant
Wedge-tailed eagle
Grey-crowned babbler
Black-faced cuckoo-shrike
Australian ringneck
Singing honeyeater
Splendid fairy-wren
Rufous whistler
Red-capped robin
Black-faced woodswallow
Budgerigar
Mulga parrot
Painted finch
Western bowerbird
Inland thornbill
Brown falcon
Pied butcherbird
Zebra finch
Major Mitchell's cockatoo
Grey-headed honeyeater
Magpie lark

The Kimberley & The Pilbara

Brolga
Galah
Red-winged parrot
Yellow-throated miner
Little corella
Willie wagtail
White-necked heron
Straw-necked ibis
Red-eared firetail
Whistling kite
Little egret
Australian white ibis
Black kite
Double-barred finch

Rainbow bee-eater
Masked lapwing
Sooty oystercatcher
Silver gull
Eastern reef egret
Peaceful dove
White-plumed honeyeater
Nankeen kestrel

Lurujarri Trail

Red-backed fairy-wren
Australian pelican
Osprey
White-bellied sea eagle
Jabiru (black-necked stork)

Top End

Blue-faced honeyeater
Silver-crowned friarbird
Rainbow lorikeet
Red-tailed black cockatoo
Little pied cormorant
Pied imperial pigeon
Great bowerbird
Bush stone-curlew
Magpie goose
Radjah shelduck
Cattle egret
Wandering whistling duck
Nankeen night heron
Comb-crested jacana
Whiskered tern

Azure kingfisher
Swamphen
Red-collared lorikeet
Grey butcherbird

Arnhem Land

Bar-shouldered dove
Great egret
Whimbrel
Spangled drongo
White-breasted woodswallow
Blue-winged kookaburra

East Coast

Pacific black duck
Australian brush turkey
Black butcherbird
Australian bustard
Australasian figbird
Olive-backed sunbird
Orange-footed scrubfowl
Emerald dove
Cassowary
Australian darter
Crimson rosella
Eastern rosella
Yellow-tailed black cockatoo
Australian king parrot
Lyrebird
Red-rumped parrot
Laughing kookaburra

Acknowledgements

This book would not have been possible without the many generous Australians who, throughout my six months on the road, opened their doors to me—be it the door of their home, tent, caravan, 4WD or troopy—or simply shared their life with me. In particular, I would like to thank those who feature in this book. In order to maintain their privacy it is impossible to name them individually, but I will never forget what they have done for me and will remain forever grateful.

A special thanks must be extended to the traditional owners whose land I travelled through. Considering the history of this country, it often feels as if all we non-Indigenous Australians do is take from Indigenous Australia—take their land, take their culture, take their stories. In writing this story, I was mindful of the preciousness of what was given to me, and the responsibility to treat that knowledge and those stories with reverence and respect.

This is my first book, and so often as I was writing I felt as if I were flailing on an impossibly difficult endurance course: pain and sheer, brutal hard work. Luckily, throughout that journey I had many teachers, elders, mentors and cheerleaders. Thank you to Janine, Elle, Tom, Michael, Daniel, Rhiannon, Tim, Nicole, Erin and Kylie, and in particular my writing group partners Catherine and Jake to whom I would regularly send ten thousand fresh, unhewn words, and not once did I hear a complaint. I am so lucky to have such exceptionally talented writers in my life, and receiving their feedback on early drafts was a master course in writing.

Thank you to my parents and the rest of my family for their financial support, unconditional love and unwavering confidence in me, including my brother Winston for his meticulous assistance in the fact-checking of this book. Thank you to those friends who continually deepen my understanding of Indigenous Australia, including Tyson, Peta-Joy, Murrumu and Warren. Thank you to the many academics who read early drafts, in particular David Walker. Thank you to the many current and former Guardianistas who provided me with opportunities to understand Indigenous Australia better through my journalism. Thank you to my agent Grace Heifetz, publisher Jane Palfreyman and editors Kate Goldsworthy and Tom Bailey-Smith. Without their faith in this project, artistic sensitivity and cool professionalism, I'm sure this book could have wound up on the rubbish heap of my broken dreams. Thank you to Macchina, the cafe where much of this book was rewritten, for their excellent coffee.

Selected bibliography

Adrian Malone Productions et al. 1992, *Millennium Ep.8: Inventing Reality*, Special
    Broadcasting Service, Sydney
Anderson, Christopher & Mitchell, Norman 1981, 'Kubara: a Kuku Yalanji view of
    the Chinese in North Queensland' *Aboriginal History*, vol. 5, June/Dec 1981,
    pp. 20–37
Bailey, John 2001, *The White Divers of Broome: The true story of a fatal experiment*, Pan
    Macmillan, Sydney
Bednarik, Robert G. 2002, 'The Murujuga Campaign of 1868', *Rock Art Research*, vol.
    19, no. 2
Behrendt, Larissa 2012, *Indigenous Australia for dummies*, John Wiley & Sons,
    Melbourne
Bird, Caroline & Hallam, Sylvia J. & National Trust of Australia (WA) 2006, *A review
    archaeology and rock art in the Dampier Archipelago: a report prepared for the
    National Trust of Australia (WA)*
Broome Movies 2018, Broomemovies.com.au
Chatwin, Bruce 2012, *The Songlines*, Penguin, New York
Chinese Museum 2008, *Queensland Dragon: Chinese in the North*
Clark, Marshall Alexander & May, Sally K 2013, *Macassan History and Heritage:
    Journeys, encounters and influences*, Australian National University, Canberra
Cousins, S., 2005, *Contemporary Australia*, National Centre for Australian Studies,
    Monash University, Melbourne, http://www.abc.net.au/ra/australia/pdf/
    national_id.pdf
Cronin, Kathryn 1973, 'The Chinese community in Queensland, 1874–1900'
    Queensland Heritage, vol. 2, no. 8, pp. 3–13
Culnane, J. (ed), 1988, *Australia–China Friendship Society, Harvest of Endurance,
    A History of Chinese in Australia 1788-1988*, ID Studio, Sydney
Davidson, Robyn 2011, 'Into the Beehive: The Destruction of Burrup Rock Art', *The
    Monthly*, February 2011, pp. 22–29
Davidson, Robyn 1980, *Tracks*, Bloomsbury, London
Dhimurru Aboriginal Corporation 2018, Dhimurru.com.au
Djambawa Marawili, 2005, *Baraltja*, National Gallery of Australia, Canberra

Fijn, Natasha 2013, 'Living with Crocodiles: Engagement with a Powerful Reptilian Being', *Animal Studies Journal*, vol. 2, no. 2

Flannery, Tim F. 2003, *Beautiful Lies: Population and environment in Australia*, Black Inc, Melbourne

Ganter, Regina 2013, *Histories with Traction: Macassan contact in the framework of Muslim Australian history*, Australian National University, Canberra

Goolarabooloo 2018, *Goolarabooloo: The coast where the sun goes down*, http://www.goolarabooloo.org.au

Goolarri Media Enterprises & Broome Historical Society 2006, *Old Broome*, Broome

Hagan, Susanne & Thompson, Gordon 2008, *Whitefella Culture*, Australian Society for Indigenous Languages, Alice Springs

Heap, E.G. 1967, *Some Notes on Cannibalism among Queensland Aborigines, 1824–1900*, Oxley Memorial Library Advisory Committee for the Library Board of Queensland

Horne, Donald 1964, *The Lucky Country: Australia in the sixties*, Penguin, Melbourne

Hughes, Ian 2000, *Ganma Indigenous Knowledge for Reconciliation and Community Action*, University of Sydney

Indigenous Australia, 'McAdam, Charlie', National Centre of Biography, Australian National University, http://ia.anu.edu.au/biography/mcadam-charlie-17808/text29392

Kelly, Damian F. 2016, *James Price Point: The story of a movement*, Broome

Kendall, Timothy David & Australia, Department of Parliamentary Services 2008, *Within China's Orbit? China through the eyes of the Australian Parliament*, Commonwealth of Australia, Canberra

Land, Clare 2015, *Decolonizing solidarity: Dilemmas and directions for supporters of indigenous struggles*, Zed Books, London

Laurie, Victoria 2010, 'Dividing the Territory', *The Monthly*, October 2010, pp. 32–38

Lawson, Henry & Graham, Michelle 1992, *Henry Lawson: Selected works*, Angus & Robertson, Sydney

Le Feuvre, Matthew C. et al. 2016, 'Macroecological relationships reveal conservation hotspots and extinction-prone species in Australia's freshwater fishes' *Global Ecology and Biogeography*, vol. 25, no. 2, pp. 176 (11)

Mahood, Kim 2012, 'Kartiya are like Toyotas: White workers on Australia's cultural frontier' *Griffith REVIEW*, no. 36, pp. 43–59.

Marika, Banduk, & West, Margie K. C., & Museums and Art Galleries of the Northern Territory 2008, *Yalangbara: Art of the Djang'kawu*, Charles Darwin University Press, Darwin

Marks, Kathy 2010, 'Tears of the Sun' *Griffith REVIEW*, no. 28, pp. 6–28.

Martínez, Julia et al. 2015, *The Pearl Frontier: Indonesian labor and indigenous encounters in Australia's northern trading network*, Honolulu University of Hawai'i Press

Martínez, Julia 2005, 'The End of Indenture? Asian workers in the Australian Pearling Industry, 1901–1972', *International Labour and Working-Class History*, vol. 61, April 2005

McDonald, Josephine & Veth, Peter Marius 2009, 'Dampier Archipelago Petroglyphs: archaeological, scientific values and National Heritage Listing', *Archeology in Oceania*, 44–69, pp. 49–69

McIntosh, Ian S. 1996, 'Allah and the Spirit of the Dead: The hidden legacy of pre-colonial Indonesian/Aboriginal contact in north-east Arnhem Land', *Australian Folklore*, vol. 11, pp. 131–8

Mitchell, Thomas 1839, *Three Expeditions into the Interior of Eastern Australia: With descriptions of the recently explored region of Australia Felix and of the present colony of New South Wales*, T. & W. Boone, London

Morcombe, Michael 2004, *Field Guide to Australian Birds*, Steve Parish Publishing, Brisbane

Mowarin, Tyson et al. 2017, *Connection to Country*, Weerianna Street Media, Roebourne

Mulvaney, D.J. 'Willshire, William Henry (1852–1925)', *Australian Dictionary of Biography*, National Centre of Biography, Australian National University, http://adb.anu.edu.au/biography/willshire-william-henry-9128/text16101

Mulvaney, Ken 2015, 'Ancient treasures: Past and present on the Dampier Archipelago' *Griffith REVIEW*, no. 47, pp. 233–241.

Mundine, Warren & Grant, Stan, 2017, *Warren Mundine in Black + White*, Pantera Press, Sydney

Murujuga Corporation 2018, Murujuga.org.au

National Indigenous Television 2016, *Songlines on Screen*, NSW Screen Australia Indigenous Department, Sydney

National Inquiry into the Separation of Aboriginal and Torres Strait Islander Children from their Families (Australia) & Wilson, Ronald 1997, *Bringing Them Home: Report of the National Inquiry into the Separation of Aboriginal and Torres Strait Islander Children from their Families*, Human Rights and Equal Opportunity Commission, Commonwealth of Australia, Sydney

Norris, Ray & Harney, Bill, Jnr 2014, 'Songlines and navigation in Wardaman and other Australian Aboriginal cultures', *Journal of Astronomical History and Heritage*, vol. 17, no. 2, July/August 2014

Parliament of Western Australia 1905, *Aborigines Act 1905*, http://nla.gov.au/nla.obj-55208686

Perkins, Rachel et al. 2008, *First Australians*, Victoria Miegunyah Press, Melbourne

Philip Jones 1990, 'Unaipon, David', *Australian Dictionary of Biography*, National Centre of Biography, Australian National University, http://adb.anu.edu.au/biography/unaipon-david-8898/text15631

Phillips, A.A. 2006, *AA Phillips on the Cultural Cringe*, Melbourne University Press

Pike, Andrew, et al. 2014, *Message from Mungo*, Ronin Films, Canberra

Plumwood, Val 2000, 'Being prey' *Utne*, no. 100, July–August 2000

Queensland Figaro 1883, 19 May, p. 1, http://nla.gov.au/nla.news-article83677319

Ramsay, G.M. 2001, *Contentious Connections: Removals, legislation and Indigenous-Chinese contacts*, University of Queensland, Brisbane

Reynolds, Henry & Rowley, Charles Dunford 1982, *The Other Side of the Frontier: Aboriginal resistance to the European invasion of Australia*, Penguin, Melbourne

Robert Lindsay 1986, 'Nanya (1835–1895)', *Australian Dictionary of Biography*, National Centre of Biography, Australian National University, http://adb.anu. edu.au/biography/nanya-7725/text13533

Rose, Deborah Bird 2004, *Reports from a Wild Country: Ethics for decolonisation*, UNSW Press, Sydney

Sinatra, Jim & Murphy, Phin, 1999, *Listen to the People, Listen to the Land*, Melbourne University Press

Soutphommasane, Tim 2009, *Reclaiming Patriotism: Nation-building for Australian progressives*, Monash University, National Centre for Australian Studies, Cambridge University Press, Melbourne

Spencer, Baldwin & Gillen, Francis James 1938, *The Native Tribes of Central Australia*, Macmillan, London

Stephenson, Peta 2003, *Beyond Black and White: Aborigines, Asian-Australians and the national imaginary* (PhD thesis), The Australian Centre, University of Melbourne

Stephenson, Peta 2009, 'Keeping It in the Family: Partnerships between Indigenous and Muslim Communities in Australia' *Aboriginal History*, vol. 33, pp. 97–116

Tacon, Paul et al. 2010, 'A Minimum Age for Early Depictions of Southeast Asian Praus in the Rock Art of Arnhem Land, Northern Territory', *Australian Archaeology*, vol. 71, December 2010

Tacon, Paul 2005, 'Chains of Connection' *Griffith REVIEW*, no. 9, pp. 70–76

Tobler, Ray et al. 2017, 'Aboriginal mitogenomes reveal 50,000 years of regionalism in Australia', *Nature*, vol. 544, no. 7649, pp. 180–184

Walker, David 2009, *Anxious Nation: Australia and the rise of Asia, 1850–1939*, SSS Publications, New Delhi

Walker, David 2013, *Broken Narratives: Reflections on the history of Australia's Asian connections, 1880s to the present*, Center for Australian Studies, Otemon Gakuin University, Osaka

Walker, David, & Sobocinska, Agnieszka 2012, *Australia's Asia: From yellow peril to Asian century*, UWA Publishing, Perth

Walker, Richard 1986, *Living with Crocodiles*, Australian Broadcasting Corporation

Watson, Helen & Chambers, David Wade 1989, *Singing the Land, Signing the Land: A portfolio of exhibits*, Deakin University Press, Geelong

Western Australian Museum 2015, *Lustre: Pearling & Australia: Uncover Saltwater Country's natural treasures, objects of great beauty, power and desire*, Perth

Wilkins, Robert 2014, *Australia's Secret Heroes: The WWII exploits of Australia's first covert force*, Special Broadcasting Service, Sydney

Willandra Lakes Traditional Tribal Groups Elders Council and New South Wales National Parks and Wildlife Service 2018, *Visit Mungo National Park*, http://www.visitmungo.com.au

Willshire, William Henry 1888, *The Aborigines of Central Australia: With a vocabulary of the dialect of the Alice Springs natives*

Yee, Glenice 2006, *Through Chinese Eyes: The Chinese experience in the Northern Territory 1874–2004*, Darwin

Yu, Sarah & Pigram, Bart & Shioji, Maya 2015, 'Lustre: Reflections on pearling' *Griffith REVIEW*, no. 47, pp. 251–261

Monica Tan is an Australian writer of Chinese heritage, born and raised on Eora and Dharug country. When she is not writing she is teaching Australian Studies and working in politics. Prior to that she worked as a journalist at *The Guardian* in Sydney and spent her late twenties living in China studying Mandarin and working for Greenpeace. *Stranger Country* is her first book.